D1765735

University of Edinburgh

30150   027367652

Raging Against the Machine

Modern Intellectual and Political History of the Middle East
Mehrzad Boroujerdi, *Series Editor*

Other titles in Modern Intellectual and Political History of the Middle East

*Britain and the Iranian Constitutional Revolution
of 1906–1911: Foreign Policy, Imperialism, and Dissent*
Mansour Bonakdarian

Class and Labor in Iran: Did the Revolution Matter?
Farhad Nomani and Sohrab Behdad

*Democracy and Civil Society in Arab Political
Thought: Transcultural Possibilities*
Michaelle L. Browers

The Essentials of Ibadı Islam
Valerie J. Hoffman

Globalization and the Muslim World: Culture, Religion, and Modernity
Birgit Schaebler and Leif Stenberg, eds.

God and Juggernaut: Iran's Intellectual Encounter with Modernity
Farzin Vahdat

*A Guerrilla Odyssey: Modernization, Secularism, Democracy,
and the Fadai Period of National Liberation in Iran, 1971–1979*
Peyman Vahabzadeh

The International Politics of the Persian Gulf
Mehran Kamrava, ed.

The Kurdish Quasi-State: Development and Dependency in Post–Gulf War Iraq
Denise Natali

The Urban Social History of the Middle East, 1750–1950
Peter Sluglett, ed.

Raging Against the Machine

Political Opposition under Authoritarianism in Egypt

Holger Albrecht

Syracuse University Press

ISBN: 978-0-8156-3320-4

Library of Congress Cataloging-in-Publication Data
Albrecht, Holger, 1972–
Raging against the machine : political opposition under authoritarianism in Egypt /
Holger Albrecht. — First edition.
pages cm. — (Modern intellectual and political history of the Middle East)
Includes bibliographical references and index.
ISBN 978-0-8156-3320-4 (cloth : alkaline paper) 1. Egypt—Politics and government—1981–
2. Egypt—Politics and government—1970–1981. 3. Authoritarianism—Egypt. 4. Opposition
(Political science)—Egypt. 5. Political parties—Egypt. 6. Political culture—Egypt. I. Title.
DT107.87.A4225 2013
322.40962'09045—dc23   2013011607

Manufactured in the United States of America

For Peter Pawelka

Holger Albrecht is an assistant professor of Political Science at the American University in Cairo (AUC). Prior to joining AUC, he was a lecturer in the Political Science Department of Tübingen University, Germany, and held a postdoctoral research position at the Center for the Study of Democracy at Leuphana University, Lüneburg, Germany. He was also a visiting researcher at the Center for Contemporary Arab Studies at Georgetown University and a Jennings Randolph senior fellow at the United States Institute of Peace, Washington, DC. Holger's main focus is on the relationship between authoritarian regimes in the Middle East and North Africa. He has published numerous articles on authoritarianism and regime change, state-society relations, political opposition, Islamist movements, and the role of the military in politics. He is also the editor of *Contentious Politics in the Middle East* (University Press of Florida, 2010) and five other collective volumes on authoritarian regimes, Middle East politics, Islamist movements, and political opposition in the Middle East and North Africa (MENA) region.

Contents

Acknowledgments

This book is a substantially revised version of my doctoral dissertation on politics and opposition in Egypt. What first comes to my mind is the place where I have lived for almost fifteen years and where the idea to write this book has materialized. After having worked in the Middle East Section at Tübingen's Political Science Department in several positions during my graduate and postgraduate studies, my first thoughts go to the guidance, trust, and patience that I was fortunate to receive from my dissertation supervisor, Peter Pawelka, to whom I dedicate this book. I am deeply indebted to him for giving me ample freedoms to develop my ideas, as bizarre as they may have sounded once in a while.

As to the Tübingen people who could, owing to their constructive comments, critique, and encouragement, claim a major stake in this study, the collaboration with Markus Loewe and Oliver Schlumberger was particularly fruitful. Other colleagues and students in the Tübingen research seminar Forschungsforum Moderner Orient and the Political Science Department include André Bank, Rolf Frankenberger, Patricia Graf, Roy Karadag, Kelly Neudorfer, Debby Rice, Thomas Richter, Rolf Schwarz, Irmtraud Seebold, and Thomas Stehnken. Some students who I had the pleasure to teach deserve credit for having challenged me to the extent that I was forced to think over some of my arguments; I will keep in mind, representing many others, Julius Kirchenbauer, Kevin Köhler, Fritz Matthäus, Marion Siebold, and Jana Warkotsch, who joined me on a two-month research mission to Cairo in 2005.

While Tübingen and the above people, who I will always associate with this small town in southern Germany, own by far the greatest share in the genesis of this book, I am grateful for ample opportunities to travel. Traveling had two main purposes: acquiring empirical knowledge about my topic, and discussing some preliminary ideas and hypotheses that came to mind with the aim of receiving input from the "academic community." As to the first purpose, several research missions led me to Cairo, where I conducted numerous interviews with opposition figures and other researchers between 2003 and 2006. Some of the people I met during these research missions are referenced in this book. I am greatly indebted to them for their patience and enthusiasm in sharing their knowledge about Egyptian politics. Among my "Cairo connections," who made traveling to Egypt feel like homecoming, I am especially grateful to Alexander Haridi, Mohammed Farid Hassanein, Andreas Jakobs, Maye Kassem, Florian Kohstall, Emil Lieser, Ivesa Lübben, Iman Mandour, Vicky Reichl, Ahmed Saif al-Islam, Emad Shahin, Sabri Abdel-Mordy Zaki, and Walid Tal'at.

Some trips led me to Cairo to learn, whereas other journeys allowed me to attend a number of conferences, where I presented results of my work while the project was still in the making. During several meetings at the European University Institute in Florence, Italy, the European Consortium for Political Research, the German Middle East Studies Association, the World Congress on Middle Eastern Studies, and on other occasions, I selfishly stole the time of a myriad of people—mostly political scientists and experts on the Middle East and North Africa—to have my ideas discussed. While I will always have to bear responsibility for the shortcomings of my efforts, here is a list of people who tried their best to put me on the right track: Paul Aarts, Lahouari Addi, Amin Allal, Michaelle Browers, Jason Brownlee, Peter Burnell, Delphine Cavallo, Francesco Cavatorta, Virginie Collombier, Katarina Dalacoura, Vincent Durac, Farid El-Khazen, Jörn Grävingholt, Steven Heydemann, Maye Kassem, Eberhard Kienle, Florian Kohstall, Hendrik Kraetzschmar, Mirjam Künkler, Kay Lawson, Timothy Lynch, Wolfgang Merkel, Beverley Milton-Edwards, Mehdi Mozzafari, Pete Moore, Katja Niethammer, Agnieszka Paczynska, Chris Parker, Nicola Pratt, Carola Richter, Friedbert Rüb, Bassel Salloukh, Mustapha K. Sayyid, Philippe Schmitter, Jillian Schwedler, Samer Shehata, Peter Sluglett, Josh Stacher, Murat

Teczur, Frédéric Vairel, Frédéric Volpi, Douglas Webber, Mohamed Zahid, and Saloua Zerhouni. The greatest debt that I accumulated in the international academic community goes to Fred Lawson and Ellen Lust-Okar. With Dina Bishara, my most critical reader, I share more than my interest in Egyptian politics.

This book would not have come into being without the financial assistance from various sources. In the initial years of my studies, the state of Baden-Württemberg provided me with a fellowship from the Landesstiftung Baden-Württemberg. The German Academic Exchange Service financed three research missions to Egypt that enabled me to live in Cairo and conduct research for nine months. Several conference trips were supported by grants from the Hugo-Rupf Foundation and resources from Tübingen's Faculty of Social Sciences. The German Middle East Studies Association awarded the results of my efforts with its Dissertation Prize 2008.

Much of the work associated with turning a doctoral thesis into a book was done during my stay as a postdoctoral research fellow, in the first half of 2008, at the Center for the Study of Democracy, Leuphana University, Lüneburg, Germany. For further revisions in summer 2009, I came "home" to Tübingen to escape the summer months in Cairo, where I had accepted, in September 2008, a position in the Political Science Department of the American University in Cairo (AUC). The fall of Mubarak in February 2011 encouraged me to dedicate some additional effort into a manuscript that was initially meant to be a book on contemporary Egyptian politics, but turned out to be of interest mainly in historical perspective. By granting me release time from teaching in the first half of 2012, AUC allowed me to join the Center for Contemporary Arab Studies at Georgetown University, where I found space and calmness to finalize this manuscript.

At AUC, I have come to enjoy friendship, critique, and advice during challenging times, in particular with Lisa Anderson, Sheila Carapico, Eric Goodfield, Clement Henry, Maye Kassem, Ann Lesch, and Javed Maswood. At Georgetown, I owe thanks to Osama Abi-Mershed, Liliane Salimi, and Samer Shehata. Finally, at Syracuse University Press, I owe an immense debt to three anonymous readers; to Deanna McCay, Mary Selden Evans, Kelly Balenske, Marcia Hough, Lisa Kuerbis, and Mary Petrusewicz, who guided me through the publication process with great patience and dedication; and to Mehrzad Boroujerdi, who kept faith in this book despite the time it needed to see the light of day.

Washington, DC, May 2012

Note on Transliteration

To make this book more accessible to the non-Arabic reader, I have used, throughout the text, the spelling of Arabic names (of persons, geographic locations, organizations, such as, for example, Tagammu, Nasser) and terms (e.g., *ulema, sunni*) as they are found in the English-speaking media and publications.

Abbreviations

ACPSS	Al-Ahram Center for Political and Strategic Studies
ADNP	Arab Democratic Nasserist Party
APEO	Anti-Political Establishment Opposition
APHRA	Arab Program for Human Rights Activists
ASU	Arab Socialist Union
CC	Court of Cassation
CCR	Coordinating Committee for the Rights and Freedoms of the Syndicates and Labor
CEDEJ	Centre d'Études et de Documentation Économiques, Juridiques et Sociales
CIJLP	Center for the Independence of the Judiciary and Legal Profession
CLAC	Constitutional and Legislative Affairs Committee
CSPI	Committee in Solidarity with the Palestinian Intifada
CSS	Center for Socialist Studies
CTUWS	Center for Trade Union and Worker Studies
CSF	Central Security Forces
EOHR	Egyptian Organization for Human Rights
FJP	Freedom and Justice Party
FSCP	Free Social Constitutional Party
GDP	Gross Domestic Product
GFTU	General Federation of Trade Unions

HMLC	Hisham Mubarak Law Center
IKC	Ibn Khaldoun Center
LCAC	Legislative and Constitutional Affairs Committee
LCHR	Land Center for Human Rights
LP	Liberal Party
MB	Muslim Brotherhood
MENA	Middle East and North Africa
MP	Member of Parliament
NCDWR	National Committee for the Defense of Workers Rights
NCHR	National Council on Human Rights
NCW	National Council for Women
NFC	National Front for Change
NGO	Non-Governmental Organization
NDP	National Democratic Party
NPUP	National Progressive Unionist Party
PA	People's Assembly
PEC	Presidential Election Commission
PPC	Political Parties Committee
PVA	Private Voluntary Association
SAC	Supreme Administrative Court
SCAF	Supreme Council of the Armed Forces
SCC	Supreme Constitutional Court
SLP	Socialist Labor Party
SJC	Supreme Judicial Council

Introduction

February 11, 2011, marked a decisive moment in Egypt's modern history, witnessing the fall of the "Pharaoh" Hosni Mubarak after eighteen days of a popular mass uprising. The January 25 uprising marked the fall of one of the longest-serving autocrats in the Middle East and North Africa (MENA) and triggered a sea change in Egypt's political life. The events in January and February 2011 also had an immediate effect on the marketing of this book. Initially designed to offer insights into the working mechanisms and persistence of authoritarian rule under Mubarak, this study was to contribute to our understanding of contemporary politics in the Middle East. The reader may now look at the following pages as a history book; admittedly contemporary history but, nevertheless, analyzing a bygone era. I contend, however, that an autopsy on Mubarakism remains valuable for an understanding of the future of Egyptian politics and the presence of authoritarian politics elsewhere.

The Puzzle

Why does political opposition—in different forms of organizations and exhibiting different levels of organizational coherence and popular support—exist over a protracted period of time in an authoritarian regime? And why does the opposition not necessarily contribute to the fall of an authoritarian regime? Applying these questions to Egyptian politics might sound idiosyncratic at a moment in history when a popular mass movement had just brought down the Mubarakist political order. A study that looks at political opposition *under* authoritarianism does not, on first look, seem to be very timely when we just witnessed a spectacular and successful example of opposition *against* authoritarianism. I contend, however, that the topic remains intriguing. We shall not ignore that those eighteen days of mass uprisings between January 25 and February 11, 2011, which came to be known as the "January 25 Revolution," were preceded by over thirty years of opposition politics in the Mubarak era. It is striking that the established opposition, consisting of political parties and parliamentarians, human rights NGOs, a powerful Islamic movement, and a cohort of independent intellectuals who were inimical to both the Mubarak regime and formal opposition groups, where not to be found among those societal forces that brought about the president's fall; some of the groups and actors analyzed in this book were even initially reluctant to participate in the "revolution," a term they quickly came to adopt in their own political vocabulary upon the demise of the regime.

The fall of Mubarak was the result of a revolutionary mass uprising rather than of an intended strategy by the established opposition actors. Whereas the opposition between October 14, 1981 (Mubarak's presidential inauguration) and January 25, 2011, sometimes dubbed the "old opposition," did not engineer the president's fall, let alone the regime's demise, it has been present as an integral part of politics in the pre–January 25 period. Hence, there is an empirical puzzle about the opposition's role when it comes to fully understanding authoritarianism under Mubarak. But we should also learn about these actors because some of the "old opposition" groups were among the immediate beneficiaries of the "revolution" and continue to engage in Egypt's political establishment. And finally, the phenomenon merits further attention for theoretical purposes: Egypt serves as an exemplary case for the relationship between an authoritarian government and its opposition.

The persistence of political opposition in different organizational forms, their strategies to challenge authoritarian incumbents, rules, and outcomes of competitive processes, and the authoritarian management strategies all defy the widely held notion that the Mubarakist era witnessed a hermetically closed and immobile political order, a notion that gained even more momentum after the autocrat's fall. Quite to the contrary, opposition actors in Egypt were the initiators and sometimes the targets— and certainly the indicators—of dynamic processes of change. The term "change" here refers to a sub-systemic transformation of sorts rather than a systemic transition, that is, change not *of* an authoritarian regime but *within* it. Hence, *Raging Against the Machine* will not only be instructive for those interested in contemporary Egyptian history. The book also addresses a larger body of literature in comparative politics that tends to look at authoritarian regimes as a subject of inquiry for which terms such as "change," "transformation," and "dynamics" only apply to instances of regime *breakdown* and *transition*.

This book engages in the study of political change under authoritarianism, but not into questions as to how, why, and why not opposition would contribute to democratization. Hence, I somewhat depart from the viewpoint that has inspired the majority of works on state-society relations under authoritarianism. Most scholars have been looking at political opposition under authoritarian realms driven by two distinct, though interrelated angles. In studies on transition from authoritarianism to democracy, actor-oriented and Przeworski-type approaches have been analyzing the potential of opposition to become a counterpart in "pacted transitions" (see, apart from a myriad of cases studies, Przeworski 1993; Pridham 1995; Linz and Stepan 1996; Bermeo 1997; Stepan 1997; on the MENA region see Blaydes and Lo 2012). This perspective was paramount in comparative and single-case studies focusing on those world regions that did experience democratization processes, particularly in Latin America and Eastern Europe. When the democratizing potential of opposition seemed low—or when an opposition was under suspicion of not favoring democracy at all (such as Islamist movements)—scholars often lost interest in the phenomenon, ignoring that the opposition was still there.

Robert Dahl said that "the two processes—democratization and the development of public opposition—are not . . . identical" (Dahl 1971, 1). In this light, a slightly different perspective was introduced more recently by scholars who looked at opposition in regions where democratic transitions remained exceptional. In the "resilience-of-authoritarianism" literature, studies of opposition have been largely taken as an *indicator* of the regimes' potential and readiness to control society—using repression and cooptation mechanisms—and to keep their hold on the power to rule firm. The question here, if implicitly assumed or explicitly formulated, is essentially an inverse reiteration of the "pacted-transition paradigm"; one would then come to ask: why does opposition fail to force authoritarian incumbents to accept democratization? I depart from the democratization perspective primarily for its teleological bias. The when-will-democracy-arrive puzzle seems inapt to analyze a political reality, that is, regime-opposition relations under authoritarianism enduring for more than three decades. Moreover, while Mubarakism is history, the lessons learned from this experience still remain valuable: with the military taking over in the immediate post–January 25 period, the rise of liberal democracy remains highly uncertain as of the completion of this book.

Whereas assumptions on democratic transitions have highlighted works in a comparative perspective, a second set of questions has become increasingly prominent in studies of regime-opposition relations among Arab countries. With a focus on Islamist movements, scholars on the MENA region concentrated on the effects that an opposition's participation had on the group itself. This debate focused on the impact of the "inclusion" or "exclusion" of opposition groups in formal political institutions, mainly parliamentary elections (see Schwedler 2006; Tezcur 2010; Wegner 2011; Brown 2012). The debate is important because it sheds light on the internal mechanisms and strategic calculations of the concerned opposition groups. Scholars depicted opposition movements—including Islamists—as rational political actors who make their decisions on the basis of perceived opportunities and constraints in the political arena, rather than on their ideological foundations. But the debate remains limited in scope because it reduces the phenomenon of political opposition to Islamist movements (presumably because they were the strongest opposition forces), and the political playing field to electoral politics (probably because empirical research on political inclusion seemed most feasible).

Toward an Authoritarian Opposition

Raging Against the Regime will look at political opposition in an authoritarian regime as a more complex phenomenon. Apart from Islamist movements—by far the strongest opposition groups in Egypt and the entire Arab world—we find other forms of organizations in Egypt, such as political parties, human rights groups, smaller protest movements, organizations representing workers' interests, and informal pressure groups. These different forms of organization and leadership have introduced—usually very selectively and eclectically—different ideological and programmatic perspectives, such as Islamism, nationalism, liberalism, and socialism. Different groups have employed different strategies of contention toward authoritarian incumbents; and the latter have responded with different activities of containment or accommodation. Egypt has become, since the early years of the Mubarak era, a dynamic playground for contentious politics, that is, political activities beyond, and in opposition to, the regime. And the politics of participation—or institutional "inclusion" as from a top-down regime perspective—extend beyond the electoral realm into civil society, social movement activism, and the media, both in print and electronically.

My core interest is to learn what this political opposition does under authoritarianism, irrespective of whether the regime itself might change or not. A first caveat is that this is not merely to explain the very existence of opposition in an authoritarian regime. It would indeed be naïve to assume that political opposition could be generally avoided by autocrats through repression or co-optation; therefore, political opposition as an observed phenomenon at a specific point in time is not a very puzzling facet of politics. However, it is striking to observe political opposition to be *sustained* over a protracted period of time—thirty years under Mubarak—without either changing the fundamental rules of the political game or disappearing as a consequence of the regime's containment strategies. This phenomenon is intriguing because (like democratic governments) autocrats do not like their opposition; but (unlike democrats) authoritarian incumbents have the coercive means and readiness to eliminate their opponents, if they ever wish to do so. Like other authoritarian regimes in the Arab world, the Egyptian regime had abundant coercive capacities at its disposal to crush its opposition, but it made only limited use of them and abstained from destroying the oppositions' organizational capacities. This holds true even for the regime's strongest challengers, the Islamist movement.

This raises questions about the very nature of the regime itself. As Lisa Anderson put it, an "examination of political opposition reveals a great deal not only about the society in which it develops but about the nature of the political authority it confronts" (Anderson 1987, 219). Hence, *Raging Against the Regime* proposes an analysis of authoritarianism as much as of political opposition. Egypt under Mubarak is discovered here as a liberalized authoritarian regime that provides limited—because entirely controlled from above—though surprisingly substantial degrees of pluralism. Changes in the degree of granted liberties depend on time and context. The Egyptian regime under Mubarak was not static and closed, but rather a dynamic, adaptable, and permeable political entity that embraced opportunities for intra-elitist dissent and competition as much as for the establishment of political opposition and organized contentious activism.

A number of imminent questions read: how can an opposition rage against a ready-to-suppress, authoritarian government and, at the same time, secure its sustained existence? And what is the subject of contestation between government and opposition in an authoritarian political framework? The most important single difference between democracies and autocracies is that democracy is about regular, fair, and open contestation for political power, for which the existence of opposition is a necessary precondition. Under authoritarianism, the power to rule is not a subject in the competition between governments and oppositions. Fair and institutionalized contestation was never a trait of the modern Egyptian political system since its inception in 1952 and until Mubarak's ousting on February 11, 2011.

While not necessarily well institutionalized, power *is* at stake in meaningful competitive processes since the January 25 uprising, which ultimately indicates a regime breakdown and the beginning of a transition period, despite the fact that "remnants of the old regime"—as they were called by revolutionary forces—have continued to participate in politics. Where this will lead remains uncertain, and uncertainty is likely to prevail in the near future. Democracy is a possibility and so is a return to authoritarian procedures of rule; and it is not very promising that actors who have been politically socialized as an "authoritarian opposition" came to dominate the political process. Looking back at the Mubarak era, another set of crucial questions has to be asked: what did the opposition do if not challenge those in power and seek office? And what was the rationale for the regime to accept opposition actors at all?

This study supports a functionalist perspective because it is necessary to inquire into the *role* of political opposition in an authoritarian political system. My core argument is that political opposition under authoritarianism represents a schizophrenic personality of sorts. On the one hand, opposition groups perform contentious politics, including the contestation of incumbents, singular policies, and even the basic traits of the body politic. In Egypt, political opposition parties have defied economic policy programs and emergency laws; Islamist groups have constantly advocated for an Islamicization of society; human rights organizations and advocacy groups have used the courts for a legal battle against the regime; and smaller protest movements have targeted the core of the polity, that is, the president and his family.

A different perspective depicts the very existence of political opposition as a necessary precondition of a specific type of authoritarianism—in its more liberal guise. In this light, opposition contributes positively to that type of authoritarianism, most important in that its existence offers a higher degree of legitimacy to the polity compared to hegemonic, mainly coercive forms of dictatorship. Political opposition in Egypt has therefore emerged in "regime-loyal" and "tolerated" forms, prevalent in political parties, human rights groups, and smaller protest movements; and even the "anti-system" opposition—represented by the Muslim Brotherhood as the strongest opposition force—has never attempted to make use of its mobilizing capacities to overthrow the political order.

Raging Against the Machine merges these two perspectives on political opposition to provide a concise study of social contestation under authoritarianism. Accounting for both the challenging side and the regime-supportive side of opposition avoids the temptation of romanticizing the dictators' opponents as an intrinsically democratic force. But it also avoids the "functionalist trap" embedded in a sometimes overemphasized reference to incumbents' capacities to control and manipulate political opponents for the purpose of power maintenance. Third, a conducive analysis of the Egyptian opposition reaches beyond parsimonious approaches based on Robert Dahl's dictum that political opposition "is likely to be permitted in a political system if (1) the government believes that an attempt to coerce the opposition is likely to fail, or (2) even if the attempt were to succeed, the costs of coercion would exceed the gains" (Dahl 1966, xii).

Raging Against the Machine provides an in-depth analysis of this idiosyncratic relationship of opposition and ruler, between contestation and complicity. It builds on previous research on Egypt that provides us with a deep understanding of the control mechanisms of the authoritarian state—and thus the limits, institutionalized and informal, posed to the engagement of opposition actors (see Pawelka 1985; Springborg 1989; Bianchi 1989; Kassem 1999 and 2004; Kienle 2001; Fahmy 2002; Rutherford 2008; Blaydes 2011; Soliman 2011). Yet only a limited number of studies have attempted to offer in-depth analyses of regime-opposition constellations in the authoritarian regimes of the MENA region; and a concise study of Egypt will serve as a comparative and theoretical impulse (see Anderson 1987a; Zartman 1988; Albrecht 2010a). Ellen Lust-Okar has analyzed relations between Arab regimes and their oppositions, as well as among opposition actors, to form specific "structures of contestation" (Lust-Okar 2005). Marion Wille searched for the potential of the political opposition to contribute to a democratic transition (Wille 1993); and Carrie Wickham provided the most sophisticated study of the Islamist movement in Egypt (Wickham 2002).

The theoretical aim of this study is to have the concept of political opposition traveled from its "intrinsic" grounds (democracy) to the "alien" world of authoritarianism. The term "political opposition," in an understanding of the classical conceptual readings of Robert Dahl and others, has been almost exclusively applied to denote a phenomenon in democracies or democratic transitions, but not an integral part of an authoritarian regime. This book contributes thus to the conceptual body of literature on political opposition and contentious state-society relations arguing that political opposition is an inherent part of politics irrespective of any specific political regime type.

Organization of the Book

Egypt serves as an intriguing case study to construct a conceptual framework of opposition activism under authoritarianism. It is shown in this book that several forms of opposition activism have developed and persisted over time: *regime-loyal, tolerated,* and *anti-system* opposition. Despite the authoritarian character of the Egyptian regime, it has granted enough space—both in terms of a physical organizational realm and discourses—in order for opposition forces to develop a political institution that became an integral part of liberalized authoritarianism in Egypt.

The first chapter of this book offers a theoretical perspective on the fabrics, mechanisms, and rationales of contestation between incumbents in a liberalized authoritarian regime and their opposition. It is argued that the struggle between authoritarian incumbents and their oppositions mirrors an intimate relationship between two deeply idiosyncratic personalities. Whereas Egypt, as a liberalized authoritarian regime, witnessed political incumbents to shift between coercive control and pluralist opening, the opposition has concurrently challenged the regime's incumbents, policies, and procedures while contributing to the persistence of the political order. Both these actors have influenced and shaped each other; and, at the same time, regime and opposition have played on the ambiguities of the other to exert themselves for their goals. As a result, liberalized authoritarian regimes develop dynamic, contentious state-society relations that can persist over time and might even expand beyond revolutionary change, as we have witnessed in the January 25 uprising.

The following chapters 2 to 4 provide empirical evidence for these theoretical claims and present an overview of the rich landscape of political opposition in Egypt under Mubarak. Political opposition has emerged in different organizational modes and in different ideological and organizational expressions: political parties of different ideological colors, human rights organizations, street protest movements, and an Islamist mass movement. Institutionalized political opposition has existed for thirty years without altering the overall political systemic settings, not only because it was subject of an established menu of statist containment, but also because the opposition has adapted as an "authoritarian opposition" to the political environment in which it has operated. In chapter 2, a "regime-loyal" opposition is identified in the legal opposition parties in Egypt that came into being since the late 1970s as a consequence of the establishment of a multiparty system. Electoral politics had their heydays in the 1980s, with opposition party coalitions winning considerable shares of parliamentary seats, and again in 2005, with parliamentary and presidential elections being granted a degree of openness unmatched until the fall of Mubarak.

This also holds true for the activities of the "tolerated" opposition addressed in chapter 3. Tolerated opposition comprised human rights groups as part of a larger landscape of civil society activism that has emerged in the 1990s. A more recent phenomenon included an urban elitist protest movement, called *Kifaya* (Enough!), and an independent movement of workers and employees that have broken with the statist corporatist body in times of neoliberal economic reforms. Chapter 4 focuses on the arguably most important opposition force in the country, the Muslim Brotherhood and other groups in the ambit of political Islam forming the arena of "anti-system" opposition in Egypt.

Whereas chapters 2 to 4 focus on the *agents* of contestation toward the Egyptian regime, chapter 5 examines the *sites* of contestation, that is, the institutionalized channels governing relations between the regime and its oppositions. Some general arguments are recaptured in order to analyze political institutions at the intersection between state and society. These institutions have usually been established from above with the aim of controlling society, but emerged into channels of societal political participation. Focusing on the electoral regime and parliaments, civil society organizations, the judiciary, and the religious institution of *al-Azhar*, this chapter reflects on the functions of such institutions between co-optation and control on the one hand, and political contestation performed by the opposition on the other hand. Chapter 6 summarizes the main questions discussed in this book and provides a preliminary understanding of the January 25 uprising as well as on the nature of transitional politics in the post-Mubarak era.

Raging Against the Machine

1

Regime and Opposition

Two Schizophrenic Personalities

Political opposition in an authoritarian regime has a positive reputation among Western media and policymakers: he who opposes the dictator—if not an Islamist—is, at least implicitly, considered a democratic force. This perception includes the notion that the opposition challenges government in its very core, that is, its claim to execute decision making in the polity. Opposition here is "office-seeking" and becomes a force that contains the potential—or, at least, the claim—to replace the authoritarian government (and in this process establish, it is hoped, democratic procedures).

In this view, political opposition is one part of a binary referential system. In the words of Niklas Luhmann, "the term opposition entails its meaning only as a momentum of a differentiation between government and opposition. It does not denote an autonomous phenomenon" (Luhmann 1989, 13). It is this institutionalized opposition—an opposition with a capital "O"—that came to the focus in political science studies. This reaches beyond an everyday meaning of political opposition as a counterposition that a son poses to the words of a father or a defender toward a striker in a football match; moreover, back in the societal and political arena, what James C. Scott described as the "hidden transcripts" of social resistance (Scott 1990)—rumors, gossip, jokes, songs, social rituals, and codes—do not fit into this political science category. Rather, they are part of a potentially ample menu of political action through which an opposition agitates against a government.

The view on political opposition primarily as an institution to control political power and provide an institutionalized alternative to the government in place is rooted in classical theories of democracy (see Potter 1966; Ionescu and Madariaga 1971).[1] Opposition in a democracy has three main functions: the control of the incumbents' power and its execution; the representation of the interests and preferences of political minorities and social actors that are not represented in government; and the identification of an institutionalized alternative in a competitive political system. In turn, "where there is no possibility of alternation in power between governing elements and oppositional elements through a peaceful process of fair and free elections, there is no constitutional opposition, and therefore no genuine democracy" (Lawson 1993, 194). It goes without further reference to democratic theory that the existence of political opposition is a necessary, yet not sufficient, precondition for democracy.

Because of an opposition's inherent democratic substance, contentious activism of an opposition has been viewed primarily as a zero-sum game about political power and the struggle for office, but not as an enterprise to realize relative gains.[2] This renders the study of opposition in authoritarian regimes difficult. Barbara McLennan stated in an early critical assessment that Robert Dahl, and the associated academic tradition, "has avoided the difficulty of comparing competitive systems to noncompetitive ones, where repression is either very real or threatened." McLennan goes on to argue that Robert Dahl's "approach, so dependent on the descriptive analysis of particular Western states, offers no clue as to how to proceed

---

1. Opposition studies had their heydays in the second half of the 1960s and the first half of the 1970s. Robert Dahl developed the early research agenda as the most important single aspect of his larger contribution to theories of democracy (see Dahl 1966, 1971, 1973, and 1975). Other important works of this early period include Kirchheimer (1966); Sartori (1966); Barker (1971). The special importance that political opposition has received in political science studies of this period is reflected in the foundation, by Ghita Ionescu, of the journal *Government and Opposition*, which has quickly developed into one of the leading academic sources in comparative politics.

2. Otto Kirchheimer's classic definition of office-seeking competition says that it is present "if political jobs are filled by selection from candidates whose number is in excess of the places to be filled" (Kirchheimer 1966, 237).

to broaden the realm of comparison" (McLennan 1973, 383).[3] In authoritarian regimes, incumbents do not allow opposition, protest movements, or societal contenders to control their exercise of power and participate in the competition about political office. Democratic *alternance* is not at stake in the polity, and the regimes restrict the equitable representation of society. On the other hand, noncompetitive political regimes are unable (or perhaps unwilling) to prevent the emergence—and the protracted existence—of challengers from society employing different means of contentious political activism.

Patterns of Political Opposition under Authoritarianism

If we accept that regular, institutionalized *alternance* is not at stake in the interactions between authoritarian governments and their oppositions, one question is eminent: what is the nature of contentious interactions between oppositions and authoritarian regime incumbents? A major caveat that will be discussed here describes the relations between autocrats and their oppositions. In authoritarian regimes, there are no clearly delineated *terms of contestation*; that is, the *subject*, *rules*, and *procedures* of contentious politics between incumbents and oppositions remain uncertain.

An opposition movement in an authoritarian regime deals with great insecurity concerning the subject of contention primarily because the individuals in government claim to represent the political regime, but also the state and its dominant ideology. Ever since the regime's inception through a coup d'état executed by the "Free Officers" among Gamal Abdel Nasser, Egyptian incumbents have confused their hold over government procedures with their proclaimed responsibility for the Egyptian state itself. An opposition's challenge of the political incumbency is therefore often subject to the incumbents' framing as an attack on that very

---

3. There are a few prominent exceptions. Studies that highlight political opposition as an analytical category to explain authoritarian regimes include Juan Linz's article "Opposition to and under an Authoritarian Regime" (1973) and, more recently, Franklin (2002) and Gandhi and Przeworski (2006); see also Edward Aspinall's work on Suharto's Indonesia (2005).

state. The Muslim Brotherhood as the most potent opposition force was often accused of threatening national security. Human rights groups have been, and still are, routinely subjected to accusations of imposing "foreign agendas" and attempting to overthrow the state when they accepted foreign funding through Western democracy promotion. Opposition parties were created as "platforms" of a former corporate mass movement or designed to emerge as a "loyal opposition" to the regime party National Democratic Party (NDP); and their participation in electoral politics was seen—by the regime as well as by the majority of opposition party members—as a duty to support the national project rather than an important democratic exercise to control, and possibly replace, the ruling party.

The deliberate confusion of "incumbency" (the policy-implementing authority), "regime" (the pattern of political institutions in a state, and agents operating under the assumption that those patterns persist), and the "state" (the monopolized capacity to execute governance in a given territory) comes as an active strategy of those in power trying to tarnish the opposition's image; but it is also, at least implicitly, accepted by many opposition groups that would refrain from clearly identifying their target. Organized Islamists, when operating under an authoritarian regime, have worked to alter policies mainly in education and social affairs; but they have also repeatedly called for an Islamic state, without stating precisely what they meant by it and how they would implement it in practice. Human rights groups have attempted to change unjust legislatures and coercive state actions; but they have also remained staunch proponents of democratic transition—an intrinsically anti-systemic behavior in an authoritarian regime. Some protest movements might develop petty demands, such as economic aims of a workers' movement, while others communicate fundamental demands, such as the call to bring down the regime voiced—even before the January 25 uprising—by small protest groups such as Kifaya or the "Revolutionary Socialists," loose networks of liberal and leftist intellectuals and activists.

Apart from the subject of contestation, the *rules of contestation* are equally insecure. The Egyptian power brokers have used the law in order to curb contentious activism, but they refrained from accepting universal accountability to the law. Legal restrictions for oppositions included distinctive authoritarian pockets within the 1971 constitution (e.g., the overwhelming executive and legislative powers granted to the president) and the existence of legal pluralism (e.g., the coexistence of a civil judiciary and military courts along with informal mechanisms of legal arbitration). Yet, whereas the law was often employed to contain and discipline opposition activism, the rule of law was constricted or entirely absent. Hence, for the opposition the boundaries of the legality of contentious activism remained unclear. This pertains to the actions of oppositions as well as the organizations themselves. As an observer of Egyptian politics put it quite poignantly, "becoming 'legal' or 'illegal' is not a matter of law" (author's interview with Hazem Mounir).

A *minimum degree of mutual acceptance* defines the relationship between government and opposition and distinguishes the latter from (violent) resistance (Albrecht 2010b, 3). In democracies, legality is a necessary precondition for mutual acceptance; if an actor is found to be illegal, it will be disqualified as an opposition group. Under authoritarianism, the boundaries of judicial legality are fuzzy. Opposition movements may well be illegal in that they are not granted formal judicial authorization but are informally tolerated and recognized. This formally illegal status does not necessarily indicate the regime's readiness to eliminate the relevant opposition group. Rather, it is often an indicator for the regime's selection of one possible strategy of containment from a variety of others, ranging from soft repression to heavy coercion. On the other hand, opposition groups might be legally recognized but face other forms of statist containment, ranging from the limited "freezing" of the respective group to more coercive mechanisms, such as the incarceration of its leaders and confiscation of material and financial assets.

Egyptian authorities have routinely referred to the Muslim Brotherhood as an "illegal group with a terrorist past," a reference to the existence of an armed wing of the group in the 1940s and 1950s. However, the group was allowed to participate in most parliamentary elections since 1984; an office in central Cairo functioned as the Brotherhood's headquarter, and its representatives have been openly active in the media, universities, and professional syndicates. Political parties have also become a target of the inconsistent application of the law; the socialist-turned-Islamist

Socialist Labor Party (SLP) and the Liberal Party (LP) have received "freeze" orders; but the parties were never practically dissolved and their representatives found ways to participate actively in public life. Human rights groups were required to register with state authorities. Some of them refused, others were prevented from registering with the restrictive law no. 84 of 2002 and instead resumed activities as law firms—a trick that was quietly accepted by the security forces; yet it rendered the groups vulnerable to legal action. Public demonstrations and labor strikes were illegal when organizers failed to secure the authorities' consent, which was seldom granted. Even after Mubarak's fall, the new military rulers imposed, on March 23, 2011, a restrictive anti-strike law that rendered this form of collective action virtually illegal. However, the implementation of these laws have remained erratic before and after the January 25 uprising. In general, the opportunities of, and constraints toward, contentious activism on the streets did not ultimately depend on the law, but rather on strategic considerations of the regime to meet social unrest and street politics with blunt repression or concessions.

Apart from the subjects and the rules of contention, a great measure of insecurity also applies to the *procedures of contestation*. Adam Przeworski wrote that democracies comprise a high degree of uncertainty with respect to the outcome of political processes, while relying on significant certainty concerning policymaking rules and procedures. In contrast, an authoritarian system embraces high uncertainty concerning rules and procedures, yet certainty and reliability about the outcomes of political processes (Przeworski 1991, 10–14). In democracies, most competitive interactions between governments and oppositions occur in the "classical" political arena, that is, in elections, the halls and corridors of parliaments, ministries, and bureaucracies, or in firmly established—and legally enforced—modes of contestation, for example, strikes, petitions with ombudsmen, references to constitutional courts, etc. A more nebulous picture is found in authoritarian systems. Here we also find these modern, formalized institutions, but—owing to the lack of the rule of law—oppositions cannot trust the universal application of formally institutionalized procedures.

The Mubarak regime has always secured (by cementing a two-thirds majority for the NDP) its unrestricted capacities to change laws, bylaws, and the constitution itself, which guaranteed the "legal"—and in the eyes of the incumbency, legitimate—adaptation of procedures governing the interactions with the opposition. And the regime has made extensive use of its powers to constantly change the rules of the political game. Maye Kassem identified a "government of men rather than laws" (Kassem 2001, 61). Every round of parliamentary elections since the adoption of multi-party elections in 1977 was preceded by a significant change of the election law. Opposition parties and many human rights groups experienced an uneven implementation of court rulings. With a judiciary system torn between the "regular courts" of civil litigation and "special courts" consisting of state security courts and military courts, it was at the discretion of the state authorities to refer politically sensitive cases to those courts over which they had greater leverage to engineer specific rulings. After all, opposition activists did not even know whether their actions would be judged on the legal framework or would invite a probe by domestic security services triggered by "national security concerns."

One consequence of the insecurity of formal rules and procedures is that informal arrangements play a prominent role in authoritarian politics. Laws and the judiciary will not ultimately judge on the "legality" of contentious activism; and election processes and results do not necessarily reflect on an opposition's strength and the balance of power between authoritarian incumbents and their challengers. Hence, the success of the Muslim Brotherhood in the 2005 parliamentary elections (eighty-eight seats) in comparison with the 2000 elections (seventeen seats) did not necessarily indicate an increasing strength regarding its popular support or mobilization capacities, but rather the regime's significant changes in the management of electoral politics that allowed the group to win a greater share in parliament seats. Neither did the Brotherhood's dismal output in the 2010 parliamentary election indicate in any way its decline in popular support.

When they rage against this authoritarian machine, opposition groups and individuals take into account the fluidity and insecurity of the terms of contestation. In Mubarak's Egypt, the member of an opposition party did not know—for example, upon his or her decision to run for parliament—whether this would result in an effort at electoral campaigning, an exchange of arguments about programmatic issues, a legal case about the party's status and eligibility, a struggle with internal party rivals, or a personal defense from legal prosecution. More often than not, the opposition member would be involved in several of such battles concurrently. A human rights activist would defend the victim of a human rights violation, as much as—as a consequence of his or her engagement—rally to protect himself or herself from coercive countermeasures of the regime. A young member of the Muslim Brotherhood running in elections for his or her university's student board may have as well found himself or herself engaged in a struggle about Egypt's political soul, torn between Islamism and secularism. Opposition activism in an authoritarian regime is usually a multilevel adventure.

Confusion about the subjects, the rules, and the processes of contention does not only pose a challenge toward the actions, organizations, and strategies of the opposition; it also has conceptual repercussions because widely accepted typologies of oppositions, developed in the study of democracy, do not travel easily to the authoritarian world. Typological differentiations between "anti-incumbent," "anti-government," "anti-systemic," or "anti-political establishment" oppositions are often inapplicable to denote the nature of oppositions operating under authoritarianism.[4]

Hence, a categorization of political opposition under authoritarianism is difficult, but not impossible. A good starting point is to recall the decisive trait characterizing the relationship between governments and oppositions: *competition*. In most classical readings, government-opposition struggles are seen as contestation for power in the name of "rule," that is, in the Weberian understanding of *herrschaft* or in the Latin meaning of *imperium*. In this context—based on Montesquieu's dictum of the

---

4. See Schedler (1996) for such a typology of political opposition; Rodney Barker has identified six different modes of oppositions: as (1) total resistance to the state, (2) resistance to the execution of power of a coercive state, (3) resistance to the incumbents of a state and their legitimate occupation of power, (4) loyal opposition, (5) a system of checks and balances, and (6) a description of the mechanisms by which the people check and control the exercise of political power (Barker 1971, introduction). Lisa Anderson has distinguished between opposition against rulers, policies, regimes, and states (Anderson 1987, 223–31).

opposition to be "the power to check power"—it has been widely argued that opposition has the meaning to control and confine the use and magnitude of political power; and the meaning of opposition is one of an institutionalized guarantee of liberties (see Ionescu and Madariaga 1971, 17).

The struggle for power in the meaning of *herrschaft* is foreclosed to an opposition under authoritarianism. If it engages successfully in a struggle about *herrschaft*, the authoritarian regime ceases to exist because it cannot prevent meaningful competition. Authoritarian regime change (in whatever direction) is the result, as witnessed in the uprising of January 25, 2011. The opposition then either goes down with the ancien régime or adapts to the transformation of the political system. Egypt in the post–February 11, 2011 period is a laboratory for such a process and witnesses a transformation of the political opposition described in this book as much as of the regime itself.

Under authoritarianism, opposition engages in struggles with the incumbency about political power in the name of "influence," that is, in the Latin meaning of *potestas*. Oppositions may struggle for opportunities—below the level of policymaking—to influence, for instance, the diffusion of ideological orientations within society, the social implications of certain government policies, or the distribution of financial resources. They can oppose and question three subjects: singular *policies* executed, or planned to be executed, by the incumbency; the basic *rules and procedures* of the regime; and singular members of the political elite, that is, the *incumbency*.

Virtually no opposition actor can be found raging against an authoritarian machine that will be confined to an engagement in either one of these realms. Rather, because of the insecurity and fluidity of the terms of contention, any opposition will find itself engaged, at one point or another, in a struggle about policies, procedures, or against regime representatives. We can nevertheless detect patterns in the landscape of political opposition in Egypt that allows for an ascription of categories relating to the nature of interactions between the opposition and the incumbents of authoritarianism.

Several groups have operated as small opposition parties. They have formed a *loyal opposition* because they largely accepted the legal framework established by the regime to allow for limited pluralism in an electoral arena dominated by its own ruling party NDP. Loyalty of the opposition parties toward regime incumbents is usually addressed at the higher echelons in the polity—that is, the president—rather than the ruling party, which is technically a competitor in the electoral process. This contains the opposition's implicit acceptance of the status quo, whereas opposition activities were largely directed toward specific policies (particularly in economic and social affairs). Only very specific rules and procedures were criticized by this loyal opposition, in particular those regulations that would restrict their own activities, such as electoral laws and the emergency law.

A second category of opposition forces consisted of a small network of human rights activists and a protest movement that took opposition politics to the streets. They performed as a *tolerated opposition*. Toleration by the regime has allowed these groups some space of political maneuvering despite the fact that they have continuously challenged core procedures and rules of the authoritarian state structure. Tolerated opposition has emerged from within society and independently from the state, which, however, has kept it under control through a mixture of cooptation and coercion.

A politicized part of civil society has operated in a number of nongovernmental organizations (NGOs) and loosely knit networks of activists. They have challenged the regime on its repressive mechanisms by questioning the emergency law and regularly reveal human rights abuses of the security forces. By taking politics to the streets, and criticizing the president openly, smaller protest movements under the banner of Kifaya have, since late 2004, overcome previously established red lines of contentious activism. Until the January 25 revolution, however, they were unable to attract significant public support for their causes. By contrast, a workers' movement has proliferated throughout the 1990s into a considerable force and challenged the regime not only on its social and economic policy program, but also on its quest at monopolizing corporatist labor affairs.

Finally, an *anti-system opposition* as an "opposition of principal" (Kirchheimer 1966, 237) was represented by Islamist groups, consisting of the largest and most effective social movement in Egypt, the Muslim

Brotherhood, and smaller groups, some with a moderate, others with a militant, agenda. On the basic character of an anti-system group, Giovanni Capoccia remarks that "the content of its ideology does not render a party anti-system; what matters instead is when such content is considered in relation to the basic values of the regime within which the party operates" (Capoccia 2002, 14). Many modern authoritarian regimes, such as in Egypt under Mubarak, do not possess any substantial value systems, except the maintenance of political power. With respect to the ruling NDP, Virginie Collombier stated that the Egyptian regime consisted more of "a mere grouping of individuals willing to be linked to the state in order to get privileges from it than a group really founded on clear principles and a clearly defined ideology" (Collombier 2007, 97).

Hence, Islamist groups do not qualify as an anti-system opposition simply through its ideological and programmatic foundations.[5] This would be a defining characteristic in Western—secular—societies; but it is not in Egypt, where religion has come to play an increasingly dominant role in society and politics, including the authoritarian regime itself. What rendered Islamists an anti-systemic opposition toward the incumbency was their alternative project to organize society. They provided, in the best senses of the term, a counterhegemonic force to the Mubarakist political order. There is an ironic twist in the fact that the Muslim Brotherhood, a conservative but moderate mass movement, would inevitably be viewed as an anti-system opposition. Whereas their religious foundations would render them anti-systemic in the eyes of liberal democratic societies (but not in an authoritarian regime), their inherent "democratic" property (by offering an alternative to the incumbents in office) made them an anti-systemic political force under authoritarianism.

In the following empirical chapters, I will delve deeper into the every-day struggle of the different oppositions in the Mubarak era after reflecting, more substantially, on the specific characteristics of regime and

---

5. Discussions on the term "anti-system" are often normatively biased in a way that it is equaled with the term "anti-democratic" (see Capoccia 2002, 18), which somewhat confuses our assessment of anti-system opposition in a nondemocratic regime.

opposition in an authoritarian context. A first observation reveals a striking difference to government-opposition relations in a liberal democracy: this concerns the *codes of contestation*. In democracies, political actors differ from one another in historically established ideational and ideological attributes: left vs. right, capital vs. labor, progressive vs. conservative, environmentalists vs. industrialists, etc. Those are firmly associated with parties and movements that cannot easily abandon their programmatic foundations without losing credibility in the eyes of their constituencies. Under authoritarianism, the political activists and parties are often tied to their respective constituencies through bonds of kinship, tribe, neighborhood, and material resources. Ideological incentives are subordinated to economic ones because people in developing societies would expect from their representatives in the political arena the successful distribution of material goods rather than an over-pronunciation of political ideals.

Incumbents and opposition figures alike do not favor firmly emphasizing distinct programs, except under populist experiments. Since they do not exhibit a clear, unmistakable ideological picture, opposition actors develop their own programmatic preferences not essentially in relation to the political incumbents but in a rather eclectic manner, mainly according to the perceived chances to gather public support. As the latter are subject to frequent changes, oppositions under authoritarianism can adapt more easily and even fundamentally change their ideological credentials at relatively short intervals. Often, singular statements of opposition figures in Egypt do not correlate well with their assumed ideological background. One striking indicator of the weakness of the opposition's ideological substance is that many individual figures and even political groups have changed their ideological outlook, that is, from leftist to liberal and even to Islamist ideas, often within relatively short periods of time.

Rather than following the romantic assumption that government and opposition were fundamentally at odds with each other and intransigent opponents, we detect empirically a much greater degree of complicity of, and mutual dependency between, regime and opposition. As Lisa Anderson put it, an "examination of political opposition reveals a great deal not only about the society in which it develops but about the nature of the political authority it confronts" (Anderson 1987a, 219). Naturally, opposition under authoritarianism flourishes best in relatively inclusive regimes, that is, in those permitting a comparatively high degree of access to political institutions. The partial inclusion and co-optation of societal groups, and even contenders, into the political institutions is the nucleus of liberalized authoritarianism; and the more inclusive an authoritarian regime, the more sophisticated the modes of political opposition in it.

The Regime: Between Control and Pluralism

We observe that authoritarian regimes and oppositions themselves—that is, the opponents in contentious relations—remain largely idiosyncratic and inconsistent political actors; and they play on these inconsistencies in their actions against each other. In Egypt, both regime and opposition have incorporated some seemingly contradictory features. The opposition—discussed in further depth below—has challenged the incumbents, but, through its very existence, contributed to the regime's overall legitimacy; the incumbents, in turn, have established a "liberalized authoritarian regime" that has performed contradictory activities: responses toward societal challenges have oscillated between blunt coercion and meaningful concessions; in so doing, the rules, red lines, and rationales for the application of coercive measures or positive responses have remained unclear. Politics in Egypt, before and after the January 25 uprising, swing between pluralism and statist control; between the co-optation of societal groups into the corporate body of the state and the limited acquiescence of autonomy to societal organizations; and between the incumbents' struggle to preserve political stability and their attempts at adapting to changing circumstance.

Egypt under Mubarak has resembled other authoritarian regimes in many ways. In their bid to preserve power, authorities have executed a high degree of unchecked violence, in particular against those parts of society that have organized opposition activities. The regime has maintained a sophisticated security apparatus consisting of the military in the background, the omnipresent state security police (*amn al-dawla*), the intelligence apparatus (*mukhabarat*), and the private security personnel of powerful elite members. Close surveillance of political activities outside of the regime have been part of a routine menu of coercive control as much as direct personal threats, physical abuse, and torture in custody. A significant part of the bureaucratic apparatus formed the organizational backbone of repression and control, most important, the Ministry of Interior and the Ministry of Social Affairs. The Ministry of Information would have been better referred to as the "Ministry of Misinformation," in that it has orchestrated, in cooperation with other statist or state-controlled institutions, the confinement of central freedoms and rights through a well-established system of media censorship and intimidation of the people. Most important for the coercive system in Egypt is that the country has been ruled, since 1981, through an emergency law; the associated security and military courts have imposed significant constraints on the most well-established institutional realm of liberty, that is, the independent judiciary.

This coercive authoritarian structure notwithstanding, the rulers of Egypt have used coercion not arbitrarily, that is, when deemed *possible*, but only whenever judged absolutely *necessary*, that is, primarily as a back-up option when other forms of containment have failed, threatened to fail, or if they have been perceived by the rulers as being in the process of failure.[6] Mubarak's Egypt did not come any closer to a "benevolent dictatorship" of sorts; neither did it qualify for a "hybrid regime" displaying mixed properties of authoritarianism and democracy. It was purely authoritarian; yet, in their bid to stay in power and to control society, incumbents have primarily relied on mechanisms "beyond coercion" (Dawisha and Zartman 1988).

Egypt under Mubarak has come to be seen as a prime example for an authoritarian regime that has embarked on processes of liberalization and deliberalization (see Springborg 1989; Bianchi 1989; Korany 1998; Kienle 1998 and 2001; Kassem 1999; Brownlee 2002; Fahmy 2002). Daniel Brumberg (2002 and 2005) coined the term "liberalized autocracy"

---

6. Examples abound showing that authoritarian incumbents have used whatever means of brutal repression they thought were necessary to curb an imminent crisis; see, on the coercive side of authoritarianism, Brooker (2000); Bellin (2004); Ghalioun (2004); Brownlee (2005).

to denote a specific subtype of authoritarianism that is measured, and where regimes are distinguished from one another, by the degree of pluralism granted toward society (see also Dodge 2002; Lust-Okar and Jamal 2002; Albrecht and Schlumberger 2004; for the Egyptian case, see Paczynska 2010; for a broader theoretical discussion, see Diamond 2002; Levitsky and Way 2002; Ottaway 2003; Schedler 2006; Howard and Roessler 2006). Brumberg observed that liberalizing policies have been institutionalized and maintained over time, though without transforming the polity into a democratic one. Political liberalization comes about as a process initiated and controlled from above. According to Geoffrey Pridham, it is an "opening that results in the broadening of the social base of the regime without changing its structure" (Pridham 1995, 66). In this light, political liberalization has to be distinguished as a process of change *within* a given political regime in contrast to change *of* the regime under consideration. Political liberalization is then an entirely authoritarian package of policies—executed with the aim of crisis management and better regime performance—and has nothing to do, at least not necessarily, with democratization processes. Albrecht and Schlumberger have argued that "(de)liberalization does not render the regime's character 'more authoritarian' or 'less democratic'. . . . The relevant variable for classifying a polity as authoritarian is not its level of pluralism, but whether pluralism is restricted or not" (Albrecht and Schlumberger 2004, 374). Political liberalization comes as a survival strategy in that authoritarian incumbents successfully generate political legitimacy and expand or change the social basis of the political elite and those societal actors co-opted by the elite.

A prominent feature of a "liberalized autocracy" is the regime's preference of co-optation and inclusion over purely coercive mechanisms of societal control. Sabine Carey argued: "Autocratic regimes are inherently less prone to accommodate demands of their citizens since their institutions and procedures are set up to avoid popular accountability and responsiveness" (Carey 2001, 4). Yet, this widely shared assessment underestimates the dual rationale underlying the establishment of most political institutions in authoritarian regimes: to exert control and, at the same time, to govern and accommodate societal demands.

On the early years of Mubarak's Egypt, Robert Springborg said that, "no sector of the population is absolutely and systemically excluded from political participation" (Springborg 2003, 192). The Egyptian incumbents have, since the late 1970s, widened the space for the emergence of civil society. They have also executed judicial and constitutional reforms and economic procedures with the aim of enhancing the opportunities of private capital holders. Reforms within the ambit of electoral politics and multiparty politics have come to be seen as the most important expressions of such liberalization projects. Political liberalization embraces, most important, the abolition of restrictions—though carefully orchestrated from above and persistently subject to potential coercive countermeasures—on individual rights and liberties along with the removal of limitations on the freedom of the press, open speech, and the right to gather in public. Meaningful indicators of the degree of liberty, and thus of the extent of liberalization measures, are institutional reforms, most visible in electoral processes and associated bodies of representation, along with legal and constitutional changes and the proliferation of organizations of societal representation such as political parties, advocacy groups, and nongovernmental organizations.

Political liberalization has never been a consistent development, let alone a stepping-stone for democratization; in fact, the breakdown of the Mubarak regime in 2011 was preceded by a distinct phase of political deliberalization in the years 2006–2010, challenging explanations based on the democratic transition literature (Albrecht 2012, 252). Rather than a linear path of political opening, phases of liberalization and deliberalization have alternated, at times at rather short intervals. A recent example is the year 2005, which witnessed the emergence of the Kifaya movement, the first multicandidate presidential elections in Egypt's history, and parliamentary elections with a strong seat-winning performance of the Muslim Brotherhood. This short period was a remarkably liberal window of opportunity that, however, was quickly closed in the post-election period from early 2006 onward.

Moreover, politics of liberalization and deliberalization are often crafted in a rather exclusive fashion and thus apply to some political institutions, societal groups, and political agents while remaining, at the same time, foreclosed to others. For instance, in the mid-1970s, Anwar Sadat introduced an inclusivist approach toward Islamists, in particular at university campuses, while crushing the leftist followers of his predecessor. During the 1980s, that is, in the honeymoon period of Hosni Mubarak, the emerging opposition parties were on the sunny side of political liberalization. In turn, the 1990s witnessed a severe crackdown on Islamists—and also on other opposition forces—but some scholars continue to refer to this decade as a period of political liberalization, pointing to the emergence of what seemed to be a lively and multifaceted landscape of civil society organizations. Finally, organizations that had come into being during the course of statist-corporatist developments (such as labor unions) lost significant room for maneuver in the dawn of economic reforms.

Whereas political liberalization is designed as a purely authoritarian reform package and adaptation strategy, one cannot exclude that it may lead to the breakdown of authoritarianism and systemic change. The "liberalization trap" poses an imminent question: how do authoritarian incumbents prevent liberalization from turning into democratization? One aspect is paramount: a liberalized authoritarian regime must—in its quest for power maintenance—avoid the emergence of *autonomous* societal agents with a political agenda. Geoffrey Pridham said: "What is threatening to authoritarian regimes is not the breakdown of legitimacy but the organization of counterhegemony: collective projects for an alternative future. Only when collective alternatives are available does political choice become available to isolated individuals" (Pridham 1995, 54–55; see also Przeworski 1986, 51).

An opposition's autonomy is the ultimate challenge for authoritarian control and its well-known working mechanisms: financial autonomy disrupts co-optative and clientelist arrangements, while organizational autonomy on the part of social groups and strata contradicts state corporatism. This aspect is of paramount relevance when analyzing, in the empirical chapters of this book, the differences in state-opposition relations between, on the one hand, the Islamist opposition (in particular the Muslim Brotherhood), which has achieved autonomy from state control, and, on the other hand, the secular opposition organized in political parties and civil society associations, which ultimately failed to reach independence from the regime's interference.

A second danger for "liberalized autocrats" lies in the materialization of "coordination goods" (Bueno de Mesquita and Downs 2005, 84) on the part of opposition groups. Authoritarian rulers have a strong interest to watch over groups in society with notable potential and organizational capacities to form societal dissent beyond their immediate core constituencies. Coalition building, organizational coordination between distinct opposition groups, and the development of a commonly acceptable agenda of change defy the regime's attempts at dividing societal forces by including some and excluding others, and by offering concessions to some and coercion to other societal forces.

For the framing and organization of a common agenda—as it was witnessed in the January 25 uprising's battle cry *ash-sha'b yurid usqat an-nizam* (the people demand the fall of the regime), an opposition's organizational capacities are a necessary prerequisite, but not a sufficient condition. Whereas opposition politics had been organized for decades (in political parties, human rights NGOs, protest movements, and social mass movements), it was the unification of different societal strata—even with partly incompatible aims and grievances—that triggered the mass uprising of early 2011. In sum, the very *existence* of a variety of opposition agents and organizations is not a necessary condition to expect regime breakdown. Rather, contentious societal action must be organized and coordinated; and these organization and voice channels must be autonomous from state control.

Which requirements apply to incumbents who decide to embark on authoritarian liberalization projects? First, a regime must be ready to form formal political institutions within which political liberalization can be organized and channeled. These include parliaments and multiparty electoral politics, legal and informal prerequisites to allow for the emergence of societal interest groups, and, most important, a judiciary that offers at least an illusion of just and lawful oversight of political affairs.

Egypt can be seen as a role model for such a process of authoritarian modernization and institutionalization. Under Gamal Abdel Nasser, the post-1952 period was accompanied by state building and witnessed the formation of large bureaucratic apparatuses, centralized military and security forces, and a corporatist structure for economic development and planning consisting of organizations for workers and entrepreneurs. Anwar Sadat has engineered the breakup of a unitary political mass movement and the establishment of a multiparty system, while Hosni Mubarak invented, in his early years, a system of controlled parliamentary elections and representation, adding "civil society" to Egyptian politics in the 1990s. Both Sadat and Mubarak have strengthened civilian political institutions to the detriment of the military leadership that was virtually sidelined from everyday policymaking since the 1980s.[7]

A second trait of authoritarian regimes of the Egyptian type seemingly contradicts this "modern face" of institutionalized politics; but it is equally important to organize and control a distinct measure of societal pluralism: the concentration of power in a patrimonial ruler. It is he who acts as an arbiter between competing interests of the political elites bound to the power center through co-optation and patronage, but also the interests of those societal agents who have been allowed to operate, or have been incorporated into the regime, as the political opposition. Jay Ulfelder said that "intra-elite bargaining dominates the politics of personalistic regimes" (Ulfelder 2005, 315); and it is this bargaining capacity that qualifies patrimonial rulers well to incorporate political opposition into the political arena. Patrimonial rulers juggle between competing elite agents, play one group off another, and engage in a balancing act among societal forces (see Pawelka 1985; Bianchi 1989; Brumberg 2002). Hosni Mubarak has been a prime example of such a ruler pitting workers against industrialists and property holders, the rich against the poor, Left against Right, and Muslims against Copts. The aim of such a strategy is twofold: first, to generate political legitimacy and public support in order to draw a picture of the president as the "father of the whole nation"; and, second, to control the elite factions

---

7. On the modern institutional infrastructure of authoritarian regimes, sometimes called "hybrid," indicating that they arrange authoritarian and democratic features, see Lai and Slater (2006); Gates et al. (2006); Brownlee (2007).

that represent such conflicting interests by maintaining a counterweight to each one of the factions.

Such a form of leadership necessitates pragmatism at the helm of the hierarchy along with a great degree of flexibility in order to react to the dynamic processes that reflect the conflicting interests in society and in the political elite. Jason Brownlee (2007) has shown that it is decisive for authoritarian rulers to prevent the breakup of elite coalitions that are bound, sometimes quite loosely, within ruling parties. Patrimonial rulers seem to be particularly competent for this task. Contrary to the overwhelming judgment in the Western public of authoritarian politics, and decision-making processes, as rather inconsistent, erratic, and unsound, patrimonial rulers are perfectly rational actors when judged under the assumption that their core aim is the preservation of elite coalitions. The strict adherence to ideas and political programs is inefficient in this system of pragmatic authoritarian rule. Rather, Robert Bianchi maintains that "eclecticism in economy, polity, and culture can serve some very useful purposes and this may be precisely why it is so prevalent and persistent" (Bianchi 1989, 8).

Whereas patrimonial authoritarianism requires pragmatism, political eclecticism, and the readiness for concessions, it also necessitates the monopolization of political power in the hands of the ruler. According to the Egyptian constitution of 1971, the president was the head of state and commander of the armed forces; he would exert executive and legislative rights, had the right to dissolve parliament at his discretion, enjoyed the almost unlimited right to rule by decree; and he would appoint the members of the government, the judges in the highest courts, a considerable proportion of the members of the *shura* council (the second chamber of parliament), and the *shaykh* of *al-Azhar*, the most influential institution of Islamic jurisprudence and higher education in the Muslim world. Apart from the enforcement of legal prerogatives for the regime's power center, informal mechanisms have ruled over formal procedures of policymaking. Elite interactions have been subject to a hierarchical system of personal loyalty; clientelism and patronage politics were the core fabrics of state-society relations. This contradicts, again, the modern illusion of authoritarianism in formal institutions and processes.

In the political arena, prime ministers and ministerial cabinets have formed "the government" only on formal terms, whereas real governance was firmly monopolized by a small group of members of the Mubarak family and close aides. In the last years of his rule, the president's wife, Suzanne Mubarak, and his son Gamal have taken over multiple tasks in day-to-day decision making in domestic affairs, whereas the president himself has focused on external diplomacy. Close advisors and longtime companions of the president, and thus powerful elite members in the background, included Usama al-Baz (advisor), Zakariya Azmi (head of the president's office), Omar Suleiman (chief of the secret security forces), Safwat Sherif, and Kamal el-Shazli. Except for the latter two, who have held ministerial posts and have played key roles in the ruling party, none of these individuals have held a prominent formal political office, but they belonged to the core elite of the country. The same holds true for a number of close cronies of Gamal Mubarak, the president's failed would-be successor—seen as the "doyen of the young generation" (Al-Korachi and Abdel-Hamid 2005).[8] Top "Gamalists" included the steel magnate Ahmed Ezz, Mahmoud Mohyeddin (Minister of Investment), and Hossam Badrawi (the last prime minister before Mubarak stepped down on February 11, 2011)—all members of a large business community—along with the NDP's bigwig and longtime minister of finance Yusuf Boutros Ghali and university professor Muhammad Kamal, another rising star in politics who has gained particular prominence as one of the masterminds behind the presidential election campaign in 2005.

Opposition in Liberalized Authoritarianism:
Between Complicity and Contestation

What does the opposition do in the political environment of liberalized authoritarian regimes? There is no doubt that the form of the governing system designates the form, characteristics, and functions of political

8. For the rise of Gamal Mubarak in Egyptian politics, see Auda (2004); Hassabo (2005); Brownlee (2007, 133–35).

opposition. Jean Blondel said that "the only way to discover the true character of opposition is by examining first government, rule, authority, or state" (Blondel 1997, 463). And in analyzing the *structures of contestation* in authoritarian regimes, Ellen Lust found that "incumbents cannot dictate their opponents' actions, but they can influence them. Through the rules they make and the institutions they establish, governments help determine which opposition groups exist and how these groups interact with each other" (Lust-Okar 2005, 34–35).

In at least one major aspect, an authoritarian opposition, as we find it in Egypt and other liberalized autocracies, resembles the regime against which it agitates: its idiosyncratic character. Political oppositions under liberalized authoritarianism challenge incumbents (or policies, procedures), and at the same time support the persistence of the political system. The intimate dance of two schizophrenic personalities ultimately explains their cohabitation over time. Whereas liberalized authoritarian regimes remain torn between coercive power maintenance and pluralism, political oppositions challenge incumbents while complying with the overall rules of the political game.

The role of political opposition beyond its democratizing potential was not a prominent topic in studies of authoritarianism (for some notable exceptions, see Aspinall 2005 on Indonesia; Lyall 2006 and Robertson 2011 on Putin's Russia; Grodsky 2007 on Uzbekistan; Hagberg 2002 on Burkina Faso). In a 1988 article, William Zartman offered an explanation of the existence of opposition that, back then, did not trigger a broader scholarly debate: Zartman analyzed political opposition, even under Arab authoritarianism, "as support of the state" (Zartman 1988). Zartman argued that the interplay between government and opposition in Arab authoritarian states contributes as much to the stability of the concerned political system as in democracies. He assumed that "government and oppositions have interests to pursue within the political system, and this complementarity of pursuit reinforces the state. Neither uses the other, but each serves the other's interests in performing its own role" (Zartman 1988, 62).

It remains difficult, maybe impossible, to judge the personal motivations of opposition actors, but we have seen Zartman's rationale at work in Egyptian politics. The very existence of an institutionalized political opposition is a necessary precondition for the establishment and reinforcement of liberalized authoritarianism. And apart from the continuing domination of parliament through the ruling party, multiparty politics does not work without the protracted existence of opposition parties and their participation in electoral politics. Whereas the judiciary has played an important part in the regime's aim to imitate the rule of law and seemingly modernized political structures, a societal actor is necessary to operate in the judiciary and endow it with the credibility that it has achieved, both in Egypt and abroad, as a relatively independent institution. Even the Islamist movement, with its potential to develop a counterhegemonic project to the Mubarak regime, has been useful for the incumbents: in the post-9/11 period, the mere hint at an Islamist alternative in power was sufficient to obtain the tacit agreement, and sometimes active support, of Western powers for authoritarian-coercive maintenance of rule.

From a more systematic perspective, the question here is which role a political opposition may adopt in order to facilitate the regime's decision to allow some space for political action, rather than unleashing its full coercive potential. In other words, I am searching here for the *positive incentives* for an authoritarian regime to accept and, to some degree, support the flourishing of political opposition. Some forty years ago, Giovanni Sartori speculated about an authoritarian logic of opposition politics assuming that political opposition may fulfill roles other than those usually ascribed to it, that is, the representation of minorities, balancing power, and controlling the government. According to Sartori, "opposition may also take part in the political communication function, that is, its primary role may be confined to providing a channel of information . . . ; or it may only be a safety valve, a merely verbal outlet, in the sense that opposition is tolerated only to placate opposition." He then infers that "these random observations surely show the need of a more analytical classification of the conceivable roles and functions of opposition" (Sartori 1966, 159). I distinguish between four main dimensions of opposition activism under authoritarianism: (1) the representation dimension, (2) the legitimation dimension, (3) the channeling dimension, and (4) the moderation dimension (see similarly Albrecht 2005, 390–92; Albrecht 2010c).

The Representation Dimension

Irrespective of any discussions of systemic change or authoritarian stability in the Middle East, it is clear that one core function of political opposition here is the same as in democracy: the representation of societal interests that are not represented in government. Simply speaking, there is no government in which all possible interests of the respective society could be represented; thus, if an authoritarian regime allows for the framing and articulation of societal interests—to whatever extent—it subsequently allows for the emergence of opposition. Political opposition is thus the institutionalized channel for the formulation of contentious political participation.

In Egypt under Mubarak, a regime void of any political-ideological substance was merely occupied with the technicalities of power maintenance—quite successful for three decades, yet ultimately failing at the end of Mubarak's tenure. A political establishment that does not leave any room for programmatic and idealistic contributions to policymaking will inevitably see a majority of politicized intellectuals join the opposition. Public space was primarily energized by opposition figures who contributed to discussions on what *should* be done in politics (along their changing programmatic backgrounds); yet decisions were made in closed circles along pragmatic considerations. Apart from the upper-middle class, urban intelligentsia of the country, Islamists (whose leadership was part of that intelligentsia) of all social classes were relegated to the opposition primarily because of the Muslim Brotherhood's potential threat to the regime.

Opposition groups and individual figures were inspired by an often crude mixture of Nasserist ideologies (socialism, nationalism, state-led development, and egalitarianism), Western principles of thought (liberalism in politics, but not in the economy; democracy; secularism), and a conservative-religious background (Islamism).[9] The regime incumbents were clearly not inspired by their own programmatic basis in their decision making. Whereas they have repeatedly adhered to Arab-nationalist resentments, they continued to capitalize on good relations with the United

9. On political thought in modern Egypt, and other Arab states, see Browers (2009).

States and Israel, both heavily criticized in society. Etatist and socialist discourses were a legacy of the regime's fundaments under Gamal Abdel Nasser, but economic policymaking since the second half of the 1990s followed a clear path of neoliberal reform packages in late-developing societies (see Paczynska 2006; Farah 2009; Soliman 2011).

The Legitimacy Dimension

A second dimension of opposition activism concerns the *legitimacy* of the polity. The existence of political opposition is, among other potential traits, an important factor in a regime's bid to increase the legitimacy of the political system. By creating a relatively liberal and inclusive political climate—and the subsequent toleration of political opposition—the search for legitimacy is directly addressed toward the domestic public. Political discourses in the media circulate about political reforms and the quest for "more" democracy; interestingly, the Egyptian regime under Mubarak has repeatedly and actively participated in democracy discourse, the dominant narrative being that Egypt was on a good path but "not yet quite ripe for full democracy." Of course, the materialization of those discourses, that is, the advent of democracy, was not an option. On the other hand, people in such inclusive, liberalized authoritarian regimes will acknowledge a gradual increase in political freedoms compared to what Robert Dahl has called "closed hegemonies" (Dahl 1971). People in Egypt were often fully aware of the authoritarian character of politics, but they also accepted that political life was "better than in Syria and Saudi Arabia."

A second dimension of political legitimacy is external. By tolerating opposition and creating an image as democratizers, authoritarian incumbents respond directly to respective expectations and demands of Western governments and international institutions.[10] True, crucial for the Egyp-

---

10. Whereas the correlation of Western demands with the Egyptian regime's readiness to grant some space to societal opposition seems plausible, the real influence of Western demands and expectations on decision making is unclear. Western foreign policy interests in the MENA region have been inconsistent, and—as the ambivalent signals and maneuvering of the Obama administration throughout the 2011 uprisings has

tian regime in its relations with the West has been the question of whether American strategic interests (Israel, regional stability, containment of political Islamism, security of oil resources) have been supported or not, but not the changing degree of openness of the polity. Therefore, the Egyptian regime had—as long as it did not run counter to such vital US interests—ample room of maneuver for introducing deliberalizing measures. Nevertheless, the very existence of an institutional political opposition and dissent within society was certainly a plus for the image of the Egyptian regime abroad. This helps in two ways. First, the regime felt secure in the face of a possible military intervention in attempts to "export" democracy to the Arab region. This aspect has become particularly eminent following the paradigmatic change of foreign policy rationales in the United States after the suicide attacks on September 11, 2001—and it might well explain the significant political opening in Egypt in 2004 and 2005.

A second aspect of external legitimacy creation is that a mirage of democracy and democratization helps attract political rents, mainly development funds, distributed by the Western states and international organizations not only along strategic or military considerations but also ideational sentiments. According to the latter, opposition parties and especially NGOs fit perfectly into Western expectations and have thus emerged as important societal rent-seeking institutions (see Carapico 2000; Abdelrahman 2004). These "privatized" rents are not directly controlled by the authoritarian state and they cannot be, in classic rentier-state logic, shorthandedly distributed according to political considerations. Rather, such rents accrue to societal actors, sometimes opposition groups. Yet, as mechanisms of coercion and co-optation remain in place and are used whenever necessary, the state has, by tolerating such societal rent-seeking institutions, created a framework for social actors that is highly restricted and controlled from above. Giacomo Luciani highlighted the positive impact of these rents for authoritarian incumbents: "A state that has access to a rent accruing from the rest of the world . . . may experience

---

shown—the real commitment of the US administration toward the establishment of more open and inclusive polities in that region remains questionable.

power struggles and factionalism, but is unlikely to experience a popular demand for democracy. While individuals, groups, and factions, both within and outside the ruling elite, will constantly fight to enlarge their share of the rent, they will seldom advocate the adoption of democratic norms or an enlargement in political participation. In such a state, there is always an opposition, but the opposition will not be any more democratic than the ruler" (Luciani 1994, 132).

The Channeling Dimension

Political opposition organizes contention from society but is not capable of directly influencing policymaking if the authoritarian incumbents do not accept this. However, an opposition is, in turn, useful for the incumbents in that they can assess the degree, form, and intensity of societal anger that is organized through the opposition. To become aware of openly formulated dissent is often better for the regimes than having to cope with subliminal discontent among the populace because this can be very difficult to evaluate and may turn out to become a basis for social unrest, rebellions, and even violent resistance. Political opposition is, then, an organized expression of a comparatively liberal political landscape and, in turn, can be used by the regime to feel the people's pulse. Co-optation as a mechanism of societal control can be easier implemented within a clear, institutionalized framework.

Channeling societal dissent in the form of an institutionalized opposition entails the advantage of being able to observe opponents better than if they were pushed underground. This rationale has applied to the Egyptian opposition parties. It was advantageous for the incumbents to have political activists from the liberal-nationalist-leftist spectrum concentrated in these organizations in order to better assess the changing degree of discontent among the politicized strata of society, the changing subjects of criticism, and the changing readiness to voice this criticism. Such opposition parties—too weak to pose a real threat—turned into a political Geiger counter, used to measure patterns of societal dissent.

In Egypt, opposition parties and NGOs formed the main transmission belt for the co-optation of social groups that were not represented in elitist circles. Yet, the hierarchical, patrimonial organizational structure of most of these organizations was conducive to the aim of statist co-optation: party leaders have been mighty patrons of their organizations and strongmen at the helm of a distinct hierarchy who met in exclusive circles, more often than not attended by incumbent bigwigs as well. Before, but also in the immediate transition period after the January 25 uprising, established political opposition groups feared street politics as much as the Egyptian incumbents did, because social unrest and rebellions defy the strongest asset that an institutionalized opposition has: organizational capacities. Those could only be developed upon the regime's consent—and a necessary precondition for the latter was the opposition's promise not to enhance, or make use of, large-scale mobilization capacities.

The term *channeling* also refers to the task of being a "security valve" that an opposition can play in times of increasing discontent among society. The Kifaya protest movement can be seen as such a security valve in that it has provided, in 2005, the opportunity for the secular opposition to let off steam in times when it became aware of its limited political significance during the showdown between the incumbency and the Muslim Brotherhood. A limited explosion of anger was probably perceived by the incumbency as a preferable option over continuously smoldering societal discontent in the secular camp.

The Moderation Dimension

Space for political opposition usually leads to the moderation of societal groups or the deradicalization of domestic resistance toward authoritarian incumbents. Mohammed Hafez and Quintan Wiktorowicz have argued that "the more accessible the state, even an authoritarian state, the less likely it is to unify opposition behind a violent strategy" (Hafez and Wiktorowicz 2004, 66). Turning resistance into controlled and moderate opposition is the name of this game that has been labeled by Samuel Huntington the "trade-off between participation and moderation" (Huntington 1991, 169). In Egypt, as mentioned above, Marxist, leftist, and nationalist leanings have become the ideological footings for a great part of the intellectual elite and among the politicized urban middle classes. However, except for parts of the Islamist current, no considerable resistance has ever emerged from this direction, an observation that is quite surprising when considering the economic hardship and unjust distribution of capital brought about by projects of neoliberal economic reforms in the last two decades.

One of the most important preliminary lessons that we can draw from the region-wide rebellions in the Arab world concerns the different degrees of violence experienced in the struggles between authoritarian regimes and their societies. Syria and Libya slipped into civil war, with an opposition up in arms against the respective regimes, because there were no institutionalized channels that could engineer negotiations, compromise, and trust among opponents. Algeria looks back at a similar experience when Islamist groups radicalized after the military's intervention in parliamentary elections and a subsequent coup d'état in 1992. While the political future in Egypt remains uncertain—and a radicalization of political groups cannot be ruled out—the opposition has remained remarkably firm in its neglect of violent means of contestation, despite the erratic transition process and around one thousand casualties of political violence during and after the January 25 uprising. Despite unequal rules of the political game and significant frustrations for their hopes and ambitions, oppositions will remain committed to peaceful means of interactions with authoritarian incumbents so long as some political opportunities and a minimum degree of security for their physical well-being is credibly guaranteed by authoritarian incumbents.

This moderation dimension, I contend, pertains not only to opposition *groups* but also to the behavior of *individual activists*. Apart from the recent examples of street politics (materializing in the elitist Kifaya movement in 2005 and in the January 25, 2011 mass uprising), activists in Egypt principally prefer the establishment of organizations, such as political parties and human rights NGOs, over street activism. This can be witnessed in the post-Kifaya period, but also in the immediate transition period following the fall of Mubarak on February 11, 2011. As to the Kifaya movement, most activists have turned away from street politics after 2005. It was obviously perceived as more appealing by the majority of individual opposition figures to found an NGO or participate in electoral politics rather than taking the risk of physical harassment often associated with street activism. The post–January 25 period also shows that revolutionary politics is difficult to sustain with a strong interest among political activists to claim a stake in the ensuing institution building process.

Beyond Functionalism: The Challenging Side of the Opposition

I have discussed above the positive incentives for authoritarian incumbents to accept an institutionalized political opposition. The view on political opposition as a deeply idiosyncratic agent, sometimes supporting authoritarianism as a form of political rule, does not mean, however, to fall into the "functionalist trap" (Brown 2012, 23; for a critique, see also El-Ghobashy 2008, 1604–5). Opposition is not a Trojan horse of sorts. It cannot be easily manipulated by authoritarian incumbents. The perception that autocrats are somewhat magically gifted with adaptive capacities to turn constraints into opportunities defies the opposition's own determination, cleverness, and abilities. This perception also ignores the fact that autocrats can fail, as we could witness in the fall of Mubarak. The opposition does not generally have an *intention* to support autocracy. Some individual figures might actually do so; in this case, one would not necessarily grasp them as a political opposition in the proper sense. In any case, it will remain difficult, if at all possible, to identify analytically the possible "hidden agendas" contradicting the public discourse of opposition groups and individuals.

It is not the aim of this book to account for such conspiracy theories. I assume that political opposition figures generally mean what they communicate in challenging incumbents, regime policies, and processes. Authoritarian incumbents will apply their adaptive capacities and abundant containment strategies to engage with political opposition; but, more often than not, incumbents will look down on the opposition with some goodwill so long as it plays by the rules of the political game. At the same time, an opposition's regime-supporting character will usually remain an unintended outcome of the very existence of political groups, but it is contradicted by the opposition's readiness to bother state incumbents. From the regime's perspective, political opposition is a rose, that is, a beautiful flower with a thorny side—and these thorns might well puncture a regime losing its adaptive and/or coercive capacities to contain societal discontent.

The January 25, 2011 uprising is the very obvious indicator for the dangers embedded in the establishment of a liberalized autocracy. This holds true even though the institutionalized opposition analyzed in this book has not contributed much to the fall of Mubarak. It has rather indirectly contributed to a political environment that facilitated the factors leading to the "revolution": the revolutionary youth groups have learned from the errors of some opposition movements organizing street protests; several constituencies (e.g., workers) have played out the practical experiences developed in their previous political skirmishes with state authorities; the "barrier of fear" broke down completely with the occupation and defense of iconic Tahrir Square, but it had already eroded in the last years of Mubarak's rule as a consequence of the opposition's piecemeal transgression of formerly well-established red lines for public political action. The opposition described in this book has not caused the January 25 uprising (rather, it has sometimes operated against it in the initial days of January 2011), but it has worked to establish the political infrastructure for the uprising.

In so doing, the opposition in Egypt came to play a much more prominent role than they would have ever anticipated, quite magically as a result of an uprising they did not engineer. The Muslim Brotherhood has cashed in on its superior organizational strength and public support to become the dominant player in electoral politics, witnessed in the first-ever competitive parliamentary elections in Egypt between November 2011 and January 2012. The Islamist current was strengthened by a number of new parties and movements in the more conservative, Salafist spectrum, also winning a considerable number of parliamentary seats. Both Salafis and the moderate Muslim Brothers have entered the race in the presidential elections resulting in the takeover of the presidency by Brotherhood member Mohammed Mursi in June 2012.

Apart from the Islamists, liberal, leftist, and nationalist parties and individuals have also gained in political prominence: as a parliamentarian bloc smaller than the Islamists, but more substantial than in any electoral rounds since the 1980s; as intellectuals representing a political current in the transitory political institutions (such as in the Supreme Council of the Armed Forces' (SCAF) "advisory council," a constitutional college created in March 2012 in order to write a new constitution); as representatives in informal gatherings between the military rulers and civil society; and as a voice in political discourses that has a significant impact owing to its media presence, and despite its limited support in society.

The former opposition's role in the post–February 11 phase in Egypt reminds us of the "sitting-on-the-table" rationale described by Jennifer Gandhi and Adam Przeworski: "For the opposition, participation in legislatures provides an opportunity to pursue its interests and values within the framework of a dictatorship, to transform the dictatorship from within. When the opposition sees no chance to overthrow a dictator in the foreseeable future, it may prefer limited influence to interminable waiting" (Gandhi and Przeworski 2006, 14); and once an opportunity arises, one would want to add, the opposition would be ready to take over a more prominent role than it was meant to play.

Apart from the more recent developments that mirror an authoritarian regime in transition, we are also able to identify a side of the political opposition that contains direct challenges toward incumbents, policies, and procedures under persisting authoritarian rule. Generally we identify an idiosyncratic political opposition that makes use of, and plays on, the equally idiosyncratic nature of a liberalized authoritarian regime, floating between pluralism and control, concession and coercion, and co-optation and the granting of autonomy. Oppositions have repeatedly applied different entrapment strategies in order to challenge the regime. Jason Lyall said that "strategically minded activists can wield a form of rhetorical coercion by exploiting contradictions within official rhetoric to inflict costs on a regime and its leaders for failing to uphold prior rhetorical commitments" (Lyall 2006, 383). Most important, an opposition can play against the fundamental internal contradiction of liberal authoritarian regimes: the "liberalization trap," that is, the regime's promise of a seemingly pluralist and liberalized political order—and political institutions governing this order—despite its firm commitment to stay in power. Opposition actors make use of political institutions crafted to allocate a measure of political legitimacy, well aware of the fact that their open containment and the regime's foul play will not only discredit the respective political institutional body, but also those who have created and managed it.

Part of the cat-and-mouse game between incumbents and opposition is the struggle over the judiciary. The establishment of a seemingly effective judicial apparatus is central to a regime's modernization project; and the claim to have established the rule of law looks good on a liberalized authoritarian regime's business card.[11] The *litigation trap* is an opposition's usage of judicial bodies—most important, the higher courts' ruling over politically relevant cases—for their own purposes: to challenge the decisions of the authorities blocking opposition groups and organizations; to raise awareness, both in the country and abroad, of an authoritarian regime's foul play and human rights violations; and to protect their personal integrity from coercive practices.

Since the Egyptian judiciary, addressed more intimately in chapter 5, belongs to the more efficient apparatuses in the nondemocratic world, the litigation trap can be quite effective. When oppositions walk out of the courtrooms victoriously, regime incumbents will be asked to decide whether to bow to the rulings of a sometimes independent judiciary or accept the blame of having violated the state's institution it claims to have erected for the development of the country. The significance of the judiciary's role in the regime's philosophy of a modern Egyptian state, and in it being a channel for opposition-incumbent struggles, is indicated by the fact that the Mubarak regime constructed a parallel judiciary system of special courts, legally based on an emergency law in effect since Mubarak's takeover in 1981. Through this parallel legal system, the regime could quench its thirst to execute politicized litigation to its liking without openly violating the regular judiciary's decisions too often. The fact

---

11. Tamir Moustafa (2007) has argued that the modern judicial apparatus—and in particular the Supreme Constitutional Court—contributed to the regime's quest, since the early 1970s, to attract a measure of foreign private capital that would require a solid legal basis for significant investments.

that the regular judges have been regularly sidelined by state security and military courts speaks for their independence as well as for the opposition's determination to use the judiciary as a viable channel to charge incumbents and their policies.

An *institutional entrapment* strategy can also be performed through the opposition's penetration of those "imitative institutions" that have been created to mimic a modernized, representative, and democratic political order: namely, parliament, trade unions, and professional syndicates (Albrecht and Schlumberger 2004, 382; see also Gandhi and Przeworski 2007). Designed as an institutional infrastructure of legitimation and control, political oppositions can pin down regimes on their promise to allow for greater societal interest representation.

The publicity of parliamentary politics promises a prominent stage for oppositional engagement as well as a degree of protection from authoritarian countermeasures. Opposition parties can count on an authoritarian regime's principal readiness to allow for limited, but protracted access to this political arena, because incumbents in a liberalized authoritarian regime cannot afford a parliament-without-parties without losing credibility in the eyes of the public. This is evidenced by the 2010 parliamentary elections in Egypt, which have seen the ruling party claiming 94.7 percent of the seats. Disillusioned by the closure of the parliamentary process, Egyptians abandoned institutional politics and took to the streets to have their voices heard (on the 2010 parliamentary elections, see El-Ghobashy 2010; Albrecht and Kohstall 2010). In retrospect, with the January 25 uprising unfolding only few months after the "sham elections" of 2010, the NDP's decision to monopolize parliament was a failure of authoritarian strategizing (if it was the result of a centrally planned strategy at all); but the alternative, that is, a significant presence of the opposition in parliament, also did not appear very attractive for the incumbency, commemorating the opposition parties' success in the 1980s and the Muslim Brotherhood's success in the 2005 election.

A third strategy pursued by an opposition under authoritarianism refers to the co-optative arrangements by which regimes attempt to integrate strategically important parts of society in the state apparatus. *Co-optative entrapment* takes place when oppositions penetrate the societal support base of authoritarian regimes. This is evidenced in the opposition's almost complete takeover of professional syndicates that were once established to bind professional guilds (physicians, teachers, lawyers, etc.) to the state apparatus. These syndicates slipped out of state control since the 1980s, when representatives of the opposition—both Islamist and secular—identified elections to the boards of these organizations as relatively free and competitive. Similarly, student unions have become a playground, already since the late 1960s, for the engagement of younger opposition cadres. The Egyptian regime has traditionally referred to the urban, educated middle classes as its support base, rendering the Nasserist reference to workers and peasants a trivial and hollow promise. Though this social support base has grown increasingly disillusioned with the depoliticized, eclectic, and arrogant manner in which political decision making was executed in the late Mubarak years. Whereas activists have favored an engagement in opposition parties and movements over the promise of acquiescence, they have made ample use of those institutions established by the regime for their corporate organization.

Finally, political oppositions in and under authoritarianism engage in a *discursive challenge* of regime incumbents. Both a liberalized authoritarian regime's own modernization discourse and a track record of broken promises facilitate the radicalization of an authoritarian opposition's discourse. More often than not, political oppositions can engineer radical, sometimes anti-systemic political narratives without being punished by the authoritarian incumbents. This includes the tenacious calls for democracy, human rights, and justice, but also the announcement to implement shari'a law and the reference that "Islam is the solution" prominent in the public discourse of Islamists. The reason is that, on the one hand, regime incumbents themselves would actively engage in these narratives. On the other hand, narratives radicalize because the oppositions themselves are not expected to deliver on their promises. Giovanni Cappocia found that "anti-system parties feel they can promise anything in the knowledge that they will never be called upon to make good on their pledges" (Cappocia 2002, 16).

In general, a government will tolerate an opposition's radical and anti-systemic public discourse if it believes that the opposition has marginal power to realize its aims, or if it detects a difference between the opposition's claims and promises, on the one hand, and the expected decisions, on the other hand—that is, a fundamental difference between political *discourses* and political *action* on the side of the opposition. Autocracies create an inverse relationship between the quality of an opposition's claim and its threat potential. As a rule of thumb, a weak opposition (in terms of public support, financial capacities, and organizational autonomy) will be able to exaggerate discursive claims because it has no implementation capacities. In Egypt, NGOs, small opposition parties, and even small protest movements such as Kifaya, have routinely employed radical (from an authoritarian regime's perspective) discourses surrounding democracy and human rights because none of these groups have commanded over significant public support. The question was how far singular opposition groups and representatives could go without triggering coercive countermeasures. Such limits are often difficult to diagnose owing to the regimes' obscure red lines; and the fate of several individuals from this spectrum of political opposition indicates that weakness alone does not offer this opposition the license for unrestricted action.

On the other hand, a strong opposition (in terms of public support and thus the leverage to push for the materialization of their aims) will refrain from formulating fundamental and radical demands. In order not to provoke the regime's fierce coercive reactions, the opposition would engage in an auto-limitation of its discourse. This would either lead to the identification of petty demands, such as those formulated by appearances of a contentious workers' movement: higher wages, the materialization of statist economic promises, and reforms in the corporatist body of workers' representation (the Egyptian Trade Union Federation, ETUF). Those were not necessarily less political demands than the call for democracy and social justice; but they were limited enough to allow an authoritarian regime to consider concessions, rather than to unleash its full coercive potential that it would not hesitate to use in the case of mass-backed fundamental demands. Auto-limitation in discursive practice can go as far as witnessing an opposition force hiding its aims behind a veil of empty gestures and promises. The Muslim Brotherhood's protracted limitation, in practiced political discourse, to the quite vague promise that "Islam is the solution," should not be interpreted as an indicator for the group's lack of programmatic substance. Rather, it is evidence for an authoritarian regime that was not ready to accept its strongest challenger to advance a more meaningful narrative of an alternative social project.

2

Loyal Opposition

The Opposition Party Cartel

Party politics in Egypt is a rather new phenomenon compared with other political systems in the region.[1] Egypt under Mubarak had a non-competitive multiparty system that has emanated from political liberalization initiated by Anwar Sadat in the second half of the 1970s. This process was accompanied by liberalization in the economic sphere that has come to be remembered as the *infitah* era ("open-door policy"). In the center of political liberalization stood the breakup of the former single party, the Arab Socialist Union (ASU). Having become a rather monolithic block, the ASU had proven unable of representing important parts of society and, at the same time, co-opting them into the political arena, a mission that had become the party's raison d'être ever since its inception under Gamal Abdel Nasser (see Baker 1978; Waterbury 1983; Brownlee 2007, 84–93).

The reason for the breakup of the single-party system was that the political elite in the early days of Sadat's tenure has experienced a remarkable transformation and reconfiguration, both in social and ideological terms. New elite members and vocal parts of the intellectual community had a technocratic and professional background (economists, engineers, physicians, etc.) and formed a new stratum of the "state bourgeoisie," complementing a former more homogeneous political elite that had long been dominated by people with a military background (see Hinnebusch

---

1. Neighboring Jordan, for instance, had a multiparty system already in the 1950s, with political parties having a large basis of popular support (see Lust-Okar 2001).

1985, 109–21; Piro 2001). Apart from the social background, ideological differentiation was also decisive. The political program of Gamal Abdel Nasser had featured Arab nationalism, a socioeconomic revolution, and state-led development as its major traits. Nasserism did not disappear as an attractive programmatic point of reference from politics when Sadat, upon his takeover of power, took action against the Nasserists in an attempt to distinguish himself from his predecessor and internal rivals. With the rise of Sadat, Nasser's ideological legacy was complemented with the introduction of other political ideas that found their way into the new intellectual circles. As a consequence, conservative-Islamist, liberal-Western, Marxist, pan-Arabic, populist-etatist, and capitalist views stood in opposition to one another in a political elite organized in the ASU that resembled a "melting pot" of competing views rather than a homogeneous ruling party (see Abd al-Wahab 2005).

The Challenge of Pluralism

Stretched to its very limits, the ASU was no longer capable of containing, as a single ruling party, an ever-growing number of political and ideological factions in the regime. Its breakup would later come to be seen as a potential harbinger of democratization, but it was rather meant to adapt to changing sociopolitical and economic circumstances (see Pawelka 1985, 76). In order to guarantee its mission as the regime's most important political mass organization, a political outsourcing of segments of the heterogeneous political establishment became necessary.

    Recent scholarship sheds light on the logic behind the breakup of the single-party system in Egypt. An authoritarian regime's willingness to embark on a distinct path of political liberalization does not fully explain it. Rather, out of an authoritarian logic, a multiparty system can be established with the aim of broadening and outsourcing co-optation. As Gandhi and Przeworski noted, "a single party may not suffice to coopt a sufficient range of the opposition. Multiple parties can be an effective instrument of dictatorial rule if they can be tightly controlled by the dictatorship." Gandhi and Przeworksi go on to argue (analyzing the Polish opposition under communist rule): "One way to think of this 'multipartism' is that it represented a menu of contracts, allowing people characterized by different political attitudes (and deferring degrees of opportunism) to sort themselves out. Membership in each party entailed a different degree of identification with the regime. . . . In exchange, these memberships offered varying amounts of perks and privileges, in the same order" (Gandhi and Przeworski 2006, 15).

The Egyptian regime followed such a manual and created, in 1978, the National Democratic Party (NDP)—since then the ruling party— along with the Liberal Party (LP, Hizb al-Ahrar) on the Right and the National Progressive Unionist Party (NPUP, Tagammu) on the Left of the formerly monolithic block of the Arab Socialist Union. These parties were first established in 1977 as "platforms" (arab.: *manabir*) within the ASU, and they participated as such in the first parliamentary elections in that same year. In addition to these three "platform parties," the Umma Party gained legal recognition through a court ruling in 1978; however, it did not significantly influence Egyptian politics in the years to come (see Springborg 1989, 187–215; Makram Ebeid 1989b; Wille 1993, 52–82; Fahmy 2002, 56–98). The NDP quickly rose to become the successor organization of the ASU in that it became the most important political arena for the Egyptian ruling elite. The two other ASU-factions soon seemed to have broken away from direct government control and forged a block of loyal opposition parties complemented by the newly established Socialist Labor Party (SLP). In 1983, the pre-1952 Wafd Party was reestablished as the New Wafd Party; the Arab Democratic Nasserist Party (ADNP) came into being in 1992 (on the Tagammu Party see Hinnebusch 1985, 187–98, and Karawan 2001, 161–74; on the New Wafd Party see Hinnebusch 1984 and Springborg 1989, 202–7; on the Nasserist Party see Abd al-Hafiz 2005).

These five parties formed the nucleus of opposition party politics in Egypt until the early years of the new millennium. Sadat's breakup of the single-party system can thus be seen as the hour of birth of the institutionalized political opposition in the country. Some noteworthy differences among these parties notwithstanding, a number of common features and properties deserve further mentioning. First and foremost, all of these parties were part and parcel of a loyal opposition that "played a role in helping to define the terms of political debate and in raising the big issues of public policy. But influencing this policy was something else" (Hinnebusch 1985, 170).

The political opposition parties have suffered, until today's post-Mubarak transition period, from a historically inherited shadow of the past that had a significant effect on their self-image: the foundation of the Egyptian party system—and thus of the main opposition parties—was not caused by societal pressure from below, but rather by an initiative from above, that is, Sadat's decree. As the result of a disintegration of a formerly monolithic, etatist mass party, the opposition parties were creatures of toleration rather than autonomous societal demands. From the very beginning of their existence, their role was not to confront the Egyptian rulers, but rather to complement the president's ruling party NDP. This had palpable consequences for the self-image of the opposition parties' strongmen. Having been politically socialized within the regime in the 1950s and 1960s, the leaders of opposition parties had seen their task as a duty by which they were to serve their country.

If we look at the biographies of the founders or elder leaders of the opposition parties, one will recognize that they had played important roles in the regimes of Gamal Abdel Nasser and/or Anwar Sadat. For instance, Mustafa Kamil Murad, founding party leader of the Liberal Party, was a military officer and former chairman of a public sector enterprise; the Labor Party's Ibrahim Shukri had been a former minister in Sadat's cabinet (Hinnebusch 1985, 165–67). The party's associate leader in the first years, Mahmoud Abou Wafia, was a brother-in-law of Anwar Sadat (Makram Ebeid 1989b, 33). The Tagammu's first party leader, Khaled Mohey Eddin, running as the party's elder statesman in the 2010 parliamentary elections, was a former member of the Free Officers and the Revolutionary Command Council in the 1950s (Koszinowski 1999, 102). The Nasserist Party's Diaa Eddin Dawoud was a state minister under Nasser and remained the party's president until his death at the age of eighty-five in April 2011 (author's interview with Diaa Eddin Dawoud; see also Stacher 2002, 226).

Clearly, when they had the chance to establish their party organizations, these people did not come to ask: how can we remove Sadat or, later, Mubarak from political power? Rather, one may imagine an unwritten code among them that their political struggle was about relative gains, in opposition to political leaders and elites who have remained under the umbrella of what would become the new leading force in the political realm: the National Democratic Party. Therefore, opposition party leaders found it apt to ask: "How significant was the margin of action permitted by the regime? How much of the state's monolithic and repressive power could realistically be expected to wither away as the new political experiment evolved?" (Karawan 2001, 162).

On the other hand, soon after the establishment of the Egyptian party system, the small opposition parties shifted away from direct government control and emerged into a tolerated, regime-loyal opposition. The term "toleration" implies that, in the early 1980s, the political incumbency put something at stake for political contestation and opened up a measure of space for political action outside of direct government intervention. During this decade, the opposition parties gained some prominence in a distinct phase of institution building that saw the establishment of a system of multiparty elections and parliamentary representation. Among outside observers as well as parts of the political establishment in Egypt, much hope was put into the breakup of the single-party system as a catalyst for democratization, and research on opposition has focused primarily on its assumed role in that very process (see, for instance, Makram-Ebeid 1989a; Wille 1993). Developments in the following two decades have proved such hopes unfounded.

In the process of political liberalization during the first decade of Mubarak's rule, the small opposition parties have hoped to play at eye level with the ruling NDP. The New Wafd Party was identified as the organization embracing the most comprehensive organizational capacities, and this party was designated to lead the legalized opposition camp. The leader of the Wafdist movement, Serag Eddin, was, in his inaugural speech in front of the lawyer's syndicate, quite outspoken in his criticism of Sadat and the 1952 revolution in general, even to an extent that observers were not sure why the party had been tolerated at all (see Hinnebusch 1984, 99, 115). In contrast to the opposition parties that have emerged as distinct platforms of the former one-party system, the New Wafd Party, revitalized in 1983, had existed already before the 1952 takeover of the Free Officers and led the nationalist struggle in the pre-Nasserist period. Accordingly, the New Wafd Party has been associated among the Egyptian public with the famous leader in the country's nationalist struggle against foreign domination, Saad Zaghloul, with a liberal political program, and with "men of substance" (Hinnebusch 1984, 105). Those were wealthy, bourgeois, and well-respected people who, on the one hand, had been sidelined from the inner circles of the political regime during Nasser's reign and, on the other hand, chose not to follow Sadat's infitah project politically by joining the relevant organizations of political co-optation, most important the ASU and later the NDP.

Restrictions on Party Politics

Expectations that the opposition parties would form a vehicle for democratization have proved unfounded. One major reason is that parliamentary elections under Mubarak have remained subject to massive engineering and fraud. Unfair legislation and their observation by the security forces have further restricted the activities of opposition parties. There was a plethora of measures in place to confine the activities of political parties, formal and informal (see Kienle 2001; Kassem 2004, 49–86). Apart from the restrictions enforced by the vast apparatus of military and security services, which is part of a standard repertoire of authoritarian control, the legal framework governing party activism has been primarily regulated—among other laws—by Law No. 40, of 1977. The law implied that political parties could only obtain legal recognition when their programs vary from programs of already existing parties and offer "something new" to party life. It does not need much imagination to understand that such a vague formulation could always be used to the liking of the authorities. Second, the law prohibited the recognition of a party "based on religion," an aspect primarily used to bar the legalization of the Muslim Brotherhood and other political forces from the ambit of a growing Islamist movement. This restriction against religious parties seemed to contradict article 2 of the 1971 constitution, which said that legislation in Egypt was based on the *shari'a* (Islamic law).

After all, the parties' law was not created with the aim of inspiring a flourishing party life, but rather of controlling activism through several restrictive regulations that were overseen by a state body, the Political Parties Committee (Lagna Shu'un al-Ahzab, PPC). The PPC has reported to parliament's second chamber, the Consultative Council (Maglis al-Shura), and its members were recruited among key regime figures: the head of the Consultative Council; the three ministers of justice, the interior, and the People's Assembly (PA); and three judges handpicked by the president. The law was amended in 1992 in a larger context of political deliberalization, thus exerting further restrictions on party activism (see Kienle 2001, 68; Fahmy 2002, 67–68; Stacher 2004, 220).

Money was also decisive. Several measures adopted by the regime since the emergence of opposition parties have imposed substantial restrictions on the financial capacities of parties. Such measures include, for instance, the proscription to accept funds from foreign sources. While this came as a much more severe constraint to the "poor" opposition parties—such as the Tagammu, the Nasserists, or the SLP—compared to the "wealthy" parties—such as the New Wafd Party or later the Ghad Party—these differences in degree were marginal in comparison to the overwhelming financial resources that the ruling party NDP had control of (see Kassem 1999, 93).

Apart from the confinements imposed on the opposition parties, there were a number of internal problems that have pictured the parties as weak and inefficient in the eyes of many observers (see Stacher 2004; Langohr 2004). In general, the small opposition parties lacked popular support, internal democratic structures, and coherent programmatic incentives. Concerning programs and ideological footings, political parties in Egypt were very difficult to grasp, let alone to classify, a problem that became all the more imminent in the post-Mubarak period, that is, when party politics mattered in a competitive transition environment (Albrecht 2012).[2] Their political, social, and economic programs were often unclear and subject to quick changes. Several political parties were ideologically heterogeneous

2. For an early attempt at analyzing parties in a framework of secular, social-revolutionary, religious, and conservative alignments, cf. Pawelka (1985, 87–90).

in that they hosted members of differing orientations. The reason is that the parties—irrespective of their initial programmatic ideals—competed for the more or less same popular constituency: the urban, professional middle and upper-middle classes of society (Yadlin 1989, 19). The main consequence of the parties' limited constituency (compared to both the regime and the Islamists) was fierce competition among the opposition parties themselves, which decreased their capacities (and willingness) to compete with the ruling party.

Power struggles within the organizations led to internal fragmentation in most parties. These power struggles were very common in times of leadership change, but there were also often subliminal conflicts between ageing leaderships and a younger generation of activists (usually in their forties and fifties; the term "young" in the Mubarakist era did not necessarily refer to the active youth). The party organizations have adopted clear hierarchies. The helm of the organizational body was occupied by a mighty chairman who would rule the party either until death or until being more or less involuntarily replaced by an internal competitor. Below the chairman usually came a secretary-general, a deputy chairman (sometimes more than one), and the editor of the party's mouthpiece. The latter position used to be, prior to the advent and spread of electronic media, quite influential in party politics because, owing to the lack of grassroots campaigning opportunities and limited presence in parliament, the party newspapers were often the only effective means to speak to the public.

Personal disputes and competition between the opposition parties, and particularly between their leaders, prevented them from forming alliances—despite several failed attempts between 2002 and 2005 (Rey 2005, 29–33; Kraetzschmar 2010)—that could have become an effective force in parliamentary elections. As Josh Stacher summarized, the parties' internal weakness and external pressure handed down by the regime led to the "demise of Egypt's opposition parties" (Stacher 2004).

Mapping the Landscape of Opposition Parties

After a decade of political deliberalization in the 1990s, causing more pressure and restrictions on the opposition parties, the parties were either politically marginalized or virtually defunct. When drawing a picture of the multiparty landscape during the late Mubarak years, organizations can be grouped into four categories: (1) "weak-but-working parties," (2) "legal-limbo parties," (3) "internally divided parties," and (4) "empty-shell parties."

The most prominent party of the first category was the National Progressive Unionist Party (NPUP), generally referred to as Tagammu (Alliance). In a nutshell, the party was weak with respect to electoral output, but its organization has functioned well compared to most other opposition parties. Generally, Tagammu representatives have been more confident about their ideological background and the party's program. The Tagammu did not always trade their ideological convictions for tactical concessions. Most important, the Tagammu has declined, under any circumstances, to cooperate with Islamist organizations and individuals, in particular with the Muslim Brotherhood. The objections against the Islamists might be interpreted as the party's consistent reference to its secular-leftist leanings, but it was also presumably the consequence of its chairman's strong personal antipathy to the Islamists.[3]

The party was often accused, by fellow opposition figures, as being too close to the regime and coordinating with the authorities on several occasions. Its history of defection started with boycotting the boycott, to which all other opposition parties agreed ahead of the 1990 parliamentary elections. The boycott came as a response to what the mainstream opposition establishment perceived as an unacceptable degree of restrictive measures imposed by the regime (see Kienle 2001, 52–56). Ever since this incident, fellow opposition forces have insisted that the Tagammu was open to forging "special deals" with the regime and the security forces—speculations

---

3. Rif'at Sa'id was an outspoken leftist who endorsed the protracted refusal to collaborate with the Muslim Brotherhood. After his takeover of the chairmanship, the party's leadership crew comprised Farida Naqqash (member of the party's "political bureau"), secretary-general Husayn Abdel Razeq, and Medhat al-Zahet, editor in chief of the party's mouthpiece al-Ahali; Khaled Mohey Eddin has continued to represent the party as a well-respected "elder statesman" and was a candidate (though unsuccessful) in the 2010 parliamentary elections. The party's Gouda Abdel Khaliq was appointed Minister of Social Solidarity in the post-Mubarak transition period.

that were not even explicitly denied by Tagammu officials (author's interview with Tagammu party official). Prior to the January 25 uprising, the Tagammu was blamed for its initial explicit rejection of the demonstrations: the party had openly discouraged people to participate in the planned demonstrations on the grounds that it refused mass rallies on official holidays.[4]

In 2005, however, the Tagammu declined the regime's invitation to participate in what has come to be known as the first-ever "pluralistic" presidential elections in Egyptian history (see Hassabo 2006; Kassem 2006). Party leader Rif'at Sa'id was very outspoken in arguing that the presidential "elections" had been designed as a mere window-dressing adventure of the regime, exploiting the participating opposition figures for the purpose of legitimacy seeking in times of increasing pressure from abroad, particularly from the US administration (author's interview with Rif'at Sa'id).

Owing to this refusal to trade in ideological foundations for success in elections and parliamentary representation, the party has remained weak in terms of political effectiveness, at least when the latter is measured through electoral success. Considering that the party's organization was probably the most coherent among Egyptian opposition parties, it is striking to see that only one Tagammu representative, Muhammad Abdel Aziz Shaaban, was elected to the PA in 2005. However, the party has functioned relatively well and has not suffered from internal frictions as much as other opposition parties. For instance, the change in leadership from party founder Khaled Mohey Eddin to his successor, Rif'at Sa'id, in December 2003 differed remarkably from such processes in other parties that have been generally characterized by substantial infighting. More often than not, succession crises brought the respective parties to the brink of breakdown—and sometimes also beyond

---

4. January 25, 2011, was to be celebrated for the first time as a "Police Day," which came as a welcome provocation for the organization of public protest, the initial aim of which was the renunciation of police brutality and human rights violations rather than the fall of the regime (El-Ghobashy 2011).

that brink. This holds true also in the aftermath of the 2005 elections when the party leadership around Rif'at Sa'id and Husayn Abdel Razeq came under pressure from party ranks because of the party's dismal performance.

We find a second category of opposition parties having operated in a legal limbo, most prominently the Socialist Labor Party (Hizb al-Amal al-Ishtiraki, SLP) and the Liberal Party (Hizb al-Ahrar, LP). The SLP has been internally divided ever since its participation in an electoral alliance with the Muslim Brotherhood in the 1987 parliamentary elections. As a consequence of this alliance, the SLP had traded in its leftist leanings for a rather bizarre ideological mixture of Islamism and socialism (see Shubki 2005). Protracted internal power struggles during the 1990s saw the aging party founder Ibrahim Shukri virtually sidelined by younger firebrands under the leadership of socialist-turned-Islamist Magdi Husayn. Magdi Husayn has gained some prominence when he became one of the most outspoken critics of government members and policies during the 1990s. He rose to prominence as the editor in chief of the party's newspaper, *al-Sha'b*, which was closed down in the wake of the regime's freeze order on the party. He and opposition peers had launched public campaigns against, among others, the state ministers of interior and agriculture (author's interviews with Magdi Husayn and the party's deputy chairman, Magdi Qorqor; see also Kienle 2001, 99 and 103–4). Obviously, the regime found this activism unacceptable and "froze" the party in summer 2000 (Abd al-Al 2004, 7–26).

This strategy of "party freezing" was a unique containment strategy in that it established a protracted legal uncertainty on the party. It is a good indicator of an authoritarian regime's "fine tuning" of soft-repression tactics; and it shows that legality cannot necessarily be addressed as a yes-no question. The ambiguous legal status had a negative impact in particular on the financial capacities of the party and therefore on its campaigning and societal outreach.[5] On the other hand, the regime refrained from dis-

---

5. In personal communications with the author, party representatives have identified the lack of financial resources as the most severe consequence of the authorities'

solving the party altogether. The SLP has never been judged "illegal," and the party members have not been legally prosecuted for their membership; Magdi Husayn himself has maintained an office on Roda Island in the heart of Cairo, where party activism was coordinated.

Whereas the party was virtually defunct regarding electoral and parliamentary participation, public appearance was sustained in two ways. First, whereas open campaigning was not tolerated by the regime, since 2002 party members have met in al-Azhar mosque every Friday following religious prayers in order to listen to political speeches delivered by Magdi Husayn, other party members, or fellow Islamists. This has continued at least until 2005. While supporters and listeners seldom exceeded a few dozens in numbers, the very fact that the gatherings of the SLP were allowed to happen in al-Azhar's iconic mosque is noteworthy because al-Azhar as a religious institution was tightly controlled by the state and has, in many instances, shown its readiness to support the regime rather than provide a platform for outlawed opponents. The fact that the regime allowed the SLP to hold its meetings in the mosque did not mean that it ignored its activities. Rather, I have observed a massive presence of security personnel both outside and inside of al-Azhar mosque, the latter in plainclothes but easily discernible (author's personal observation and interviews with Magdi Husayn and Magdi Qorqor).

A second form of activism was launched by Magdi Husayn and fellow party members following the emergence of the Kifaya movement of street protest. Whereas public rallies under the SLP banner have remained inhibited by the security services, Husayn has capitalized on Kifaya's public visibility by hiding under its banner during demonstrations. This free-rider tactic was tolerated by the security forces that, however, made it clear that a return to the political arena as an official and legalized party

---

freeze order. It is obvious that the Labor Party differs remarkably from the "rich," centrist opposition parties, such as the New Wafd and al-Ghad parties. Those included a whole number of wealthy business people among their members. In general, the leftist parties Tagammu, SLP, and the Nasserists did not have many such affluent patrons among their ranks who could channel substantial funds to the party organizations.

remained barred. Between May 2000 and November 2001 alone, the party had received eleven rulings from different courts in Cairo judging that the ban on the party had to be lifted (author's interview with Magdy Qorqor). Yet, the rulings have not been implemented by the authorities. A SLP representative claimed that a meeting took place in November 2004 between SLP members and the regime's NDP bigwig Safwat Sherif, who underscored that the Labor Party freeze was seen as a political case rather than a legal one; and, therefore, a reestablishment could not be achieved through legal means (author's interview with a SLP representative who asked to remain anonymous).

The saga of the Liberal Party is similar to that of the SLP with respect to the causes of internal fragmentation that ultimately led to its freeze by the authorities, too. The LP also participated in the 1987 electoral alliance with the Muslim Brotherhood only to escape this adventure in ideological tatters: originally starting as a centrist movement, Islamist sentiments have also become widespread among its members. The LP is a good example for the high degree of "ideological flexibility" that is innate to political parties in authoritarian settings. Ever since the party's founder and first chairman Mustafa Kamel Murad passed away in 1998, internal struggles between competitors over its leadership have literally torn the party apart. Media reports claimed that thirteen party affiliates have struggled with one another over the vacant post, thereby holding their own party congresses and submitting independent bids to the PPC to be recognized as party chairman. In 2005, the authorities accepted the request of one of the contenders, Helmi Salem, and recognized him as party chairman only to revoke this decision in April 2006. Whereas a unified organizational body ceased to exist, the LP kept a measure of presence on the political scene with irregular appearances and announcements of one of the more prominent party affiliates, the late Anwar Sadat's nephew Tal'at Sadat.[6]

6. Tal'at Sadat had publicly communicated his ambitions to run in the 2005 presidential elections, but his initiative was dismissed by the "official" party chairman, Salem. He was convicted and sentenced, in October 2006, to one year imprisonment for insulting the Egyptian army and passed away in November 2011.

Another prominent member of the LP was Ragab Helal Hemeida. Having been dubbed an Islamist (and even former member of the militant group Takfir wa al-Hijra), Hemeida was one of the most active opposition figures in the 2000 parliament. He was ousted from parliament in March 2003—officially for voting irregularities in his Abdeen constituency—and joined the Ghad Party when it was established in late 2004. As one of the few party candidates who made it into the People's Assembly after the 2005 elections, Hemeida stripped off his Islamist credentials and subsequently has represented the "liberal" Ghad Party in parliament.

A third category of opposition parties in Mubarak's Egypt can be identified by substantial internal ruptures and divisions. These parties, however, have remained formally accepted other than those mentioned above, which have received a freeze judgment by the authorities. Most important, the New Wafd Party has suffered from internal frictions and power struggles ever since its resurrection in 1983. As Robert Springborg put it, the ability to be a "masterful political infighter" (Springborg 1989, 203) had become a necessary precondition to accede to the post of party leader and to keep on top of the organization. This was apparent in the mid-1980s, in particular following the parliamentary elections in 1984, when Fuad Serag Eddin struggled to consolidate his grip on the party's leadership.

History repeated itself when Serag Eddin passed away in 2000 and his post went to his close associate Noman Gomaa. Obviously, Gomaa's role in the party's infighting in the mid-1980s had acted as a training course, preparing him well for the struggles over the leadership (Springborg 1989, 202–7). At that time, prominent members, such as the Wafd's representatives in parliament Ayman Nour[7] and Mohammed Farid Hassanein, defected from the New Wafd Party in 2001, claiming that their own ambitions had been crushed by Gomaa's takeover of power (author's interviews with Ayman Nour and Mohammed Farid Hassanein).[8] Mohammed Farid

7. Ayman Nour later became famous as the founder of the Ghad Party and a candidate in the 2005 presidential elections; see in more detail below.

8. Along with Nour and Hassanein, Saif Eddin Mahmoud and Mahmoud al-Shazli are other Wafdist MPs who resigned from the party minimizing the Wafd's representation in the 2000 parliament from initially seven to a mere four members.

Hassanein was a businessman and prominent opposition figure. As a student leader in the late years of Nasser's reign, Hassanein split with the regime when Sadat came to power. Ever since, he has been a colorful figure in the Egyptian political establishment. In the 2000 parliament, he became one of the fiercest critics of President Mubarak and participated in street protests.

Discontent with Gomaa's leadership style grew within the New Wafd Party and culminated in a successful effort of second-rank party members to oust Gomaa in January 2006. He was succeeded by his former deputy chairman, Mahmoud Abaza, who became the party's leader in June 2006. Abaza was escorted by secretary-general Mounir Fakhry Abdel Nour, a prominent Coptic businessman who was appointed Minister of Tourism in the post-Mubarak cabinet. Ousted party leader Gomaa has repeatedly tried to regain his post. In a Wild West-like coup attempt, he struggled, on April 1, 2006, to recapture by force the party headquarter in Cairo's quarter Doqqi, accompanied by a group of armed followers. Gomaa's "troops" were fought off, leaving a total of twenty-eight people wounded. Despite the turmoil in the late-Mubarak period, the New Wafd Party has remained an important, legally operating opposition party. It has internally consolidated under the new leadership of businessman Sayed al-Badawi, and—as a prominent exception among the opposition parties—could rely on a more solid electoral constituency in the post-Mubarak period.

A fourth type of opposition party in Egypt appeared virtually as an empty shell. A good example is the Arab Democratic Nasserist Party (see Abd al-Hafiz 2005). Established in 1992 and led by the former cabinet member Diaa Eddin Dawoud, the programmatic incentives of this leftist-nationalist party basically appeal to those who continued to commemorate the intellectual legacy of the leader of the 1952 revolution, Gamal Abdel Nasser. Dawoud was at the time of the writing of this book in his early eighties, but has repeatedly hindered younger cadres from rising within the party, which led, in 1996, to the walkout of prominent younger activists and, in 1999, to the formation of the Karama (Dignity) movement (author's interview with Hamdeen Sabahi). Karama was led by Hamdeen Sabahi, a popular opposition figure in the 2000 parliament, who has represented, in the eyes of many politically aware Egyptians, the modern

Nasserist movement even though Karama was not officially recognized as a political party. Nevertheless, Karama members have participated in elections as independent candidates, often more successfully than the Nasserist Party. As a consequence, the Nasserist Party under the leadership of Diaa Eddin Dawoud was seldom referred to as the organization effectively representing Nasserism in the political arena. In the 2012 presidential elections, Sabahi successfully presented himself as an alternative candidate between Islamists and old regime figures.

Apart from Karama, a number of independent intellectuals and opposition figures have referred to themselves as "Nasserists," such as Mohammed al-Badrashini (member of the 2000 parliament), the Bar Association chairman Sameh Ashour (returned to the Nasserist Party in early 2007), and Mustafa Bakri (independent member of the 2005 parliament and editor in chief of *al-Usbou* newspaper). Both Ashour and Bakri came to play a more prominent role in the post-Mubarak transition period in that they have forcefully represented nationalist-leftist ideas as an alternative vision to the rising Islamists. They have also been affiliated with the post-Mubarak military leadership.

In the 2000 parliament, only two out of seven Nasserists have affiliated themselves with the Nasserist Party, the remainder running as "independent" Nasserists. The Nasserist Party's headquarter in downtown Cairo was in fact to be reanimated only at certain occasions, for instance when a press conference was announced that usually featured the chairman's statements on recent political developments. Other forms of party activism have not been observed, let alone any substantial outreach to the Egyptian public.

To sum up this glimpse on Egyptian opposition parties, many of their problems were homemade and inherited from the fact that they came into being as loyalist platforms of an authoritarian, single ruling party. Their founders and leaders have been politically socialized as members of the previous hegemonic political structure. The degree of institutionalization and internal accountability (of party leaders to the rank and file, and of the parties toward their electoral constituencies) remained weak. The opposition parties have adapted comfortably to the prevalent patrimonial structures of organizations, including a clear hierarchy at the helm of which

would be a mighty party leader who ruled out intraparty democratic procedures in order to stay on top. Internal crises within the parties have
corresponded with leadership crises triggered by the death or the aging of
the respective party founders and leaders being confronted with a younger
generation of aspiring activists. The degree of such internal infightings in
all opposition parties has substantially increased owing to their embarrass-
ing performances in the 2005 parliamentary elections. Less than twenty
members of the 2005 parliament were members of one of the opposition
parties. Considering that the 2005 elections were among the most open
in the country's authoritarian past, this result was certainly an indicator of
the parties' weakness rather than the regime's electoral engineering.

Continued Fragmentation in Party Politics

Statist restrictions have obstructed party life considerably during the
1990s. Only since 2004 did the political regime take a more liberal
stance toward the opposition parties and eased restrictions on party activism. In a surprising move in late 2004, the authorities legalized two new
parties in less than a month: the Free Social Constitutional Party (FSCP)
and the Hizb al-Ghad (Tomorrow Party). After a long period of political
stagnation and having turned down sixty-three requests (including previous ones from the FSCP and al-Ghad), the Political Parties Committee
(PPC) responded positively to their applications. According to al-Ghad
founder Ayman Nour, the authorities had turned down three previous
attempts of the party to be legalized (author's personal communication
with Ayman Nour). Restrictive passages in the Egyptian constitution
served as a legal tool, widely used by the authorities, to bar the formation
of new parties.

This move was surprising for two reasons: first, the PPC had not
accepted any requests for legal recognition since 1992 (the foundation of
the Nasserist Party); second, it was clear that the toleration of the Ghad
Party would mark the first entrance of a new serious player into opposition
party politics. Since the Wafd's reintegration in formal politics in 1983,
only minor fractions have gained legal recognition. With the Nasserist
Party as a more prominent exception, groups such as the Future Party,

the Green Party, or the Social Equality Party have not come to exert any significant influence in Egyptian party politics. Neither did the FSCP, founded by the lawyer Mamdouh Qenawi and counting a mere 192 founding members, have any significant impact (Rey 2005, 37). The formal toleration of al-Ghad, however, came as a minor earthquake to many observers. This new party has immediately played at eye level with the well-established parties, that is, the Tagammu and the New Wafd Party.

Al-Ghad was established by Ayman Nour, a dynamic lawyer, then in his mid-forties, who rose quickly in the Egyptian political establishment to become one of the most active opposition figures in the 2000–2005 parliament. Nour was a member of parliament since 1995. He became a prominent opposition member by initiating a number of hearings on corruption and economic mismanagement (author's personal communication with Ayman Nour). Until 2001, he was a member of the New Wafd Party, which he left after Noman Gomaa outplayed his internal rivals and took over the party's leadership. Thus, the Ghad-initiative came primarily as a response to the quarrels within the New Wafd Party; and the driving force of the initiative were those people who had seen their own expectations and political ambitions vanish with Noman Gomaa's consolidation as the New Wafd's leader.

Ideologically, the Ghad Party did not add a new dimension to Egyptian politics because Ayman Nour made it clear from the very beginning—and outlined his vision in several programs that varied only marginally in previous attempts at legalization—that the party would be one of a liberal type (author's personal communication with Ayman Nour). Concerning its program and, for instance, in pronouncing the memory of Saad Zaghloul, al-Ghad was difficult to distinguish from the New Wafd Party. The fact that the parties' law required distinction as a necessary precondition for party recognition triggered speculations about the regime's rationale of tolerating the Ghad Party because, quite obviously, the party has not contributed anything new to the landscape of opposition parties. Accordingly, early critics of the Ghad Party have speculated about a "secret deal" between the party and the authorities. Whatever the substance of these speculations, there is no denying the fact that the inclusion of the Ghad Party contributed to the further fragmentation of the party system, and the liberal corner of party politics in particular, with the New Wafd Party as the main victim.

What is remarkable about the Ghad Party is that, despite Ayman Nour's outstanding role and in contrast to many other parties, it was in the immediate aftermath of its legalization not a one-man show. Rather, al-Ghad attracted a number of other prominent opposition figures, such as its secretary-general, the university professor and former MP Mona Makram-Ebeid, or the former bigwig of the Liberal Party, Ragab Helal Hemeida. The party had become a leading opposition group in parliament, almost overnight, with six members of parliament affiliated with the group.

In the more illiberal post–2005 period, however, the Ghad Party experienced a similar fate as the older opposition parties. A serious internal crisis erupted after the regime—obviously disturbed by the party's activism and Ayman Nour's personal ambitions—put a sudden halt to the honeymoon period of party politics and took severe action against al-Ghad. Nour was at the time perceived in Egypt as much as in the West as a young, dynamic, and charismatic opposition leader with a potential to challenge the authoritarian regime of Hosni Mubarak. Nour has frequently attempted to fuel and confirm these expectations in the run-up to the presidential elections in 2005. In his campaign, he bluntly capitalized on associations with the Ukrainian Orange Revolution by using orange banners and posters at demonstrations and public speeches.

While a larger Egyptian public did not seem very impressed, the political regime obviously felt that Ayman Nour had crossed a red line, which triggered a harsh answer. On January 29, 2005, Nour was arrested on charges of forging signatures in the party's registration procedures. Moreover, the party's mouthpiece, al-Ghad newspaper, was closed down and Nour himself was stripped of his parliamentary immunity. On December 24, 2005, Nour received a prison sentence of five years. Apart from the question of whether the action against Nour was justified, his prison sentence caused serious rifts within the party itself and the dismissal of forty members shortly after Nour's arrest. In addition, conflict broke out between the party's deputy chairman, Mustafa Moussa, and the editor of its mouthpiece, Ibrahim Eissa. Secretary-general Mona Makram-Ebeid had already declared her resignation on May 29, 2005 hinting at internal party struggles. Ayman Nour's wife, Gamila Ismail, was also involved in what became a rather confusing situation. Internal splits within the Ghad Party culminated, on November 6, 2008, in the failed takeover of Ayman Nour's office at Tal'at Harb Square in downtown Cairo by a group led by Mustafa Moussa. Nour's apartment had been used as the party office despite his absence and caught fire in the wake of clashes between the party factions.

The realm of centrist parties is an intriguing example for the high degree of fragmentation that has plagued, and continues to plague, Egyptian party politics. By mid-2007, four distinct groups (whether represented in parliament or not) could be identified as opposition movements competing with one another in similar ideological fields and about the same constituency: the New Wafd's "official" section; the Gomaa-group, which was sidelined from the New Wafd; the Ghad Party; and a new party that was licensed by the authorities on May 24, 2007. The Democratic Front was led by the veteran politician Yahia al-Gamal and the prominent political columnist Osama al-Ghazali Harb. Harb was a former member of the NDP's Policies Committee (since 2002), which had come to be referred to as the ruling party's "reform faction" led by the president's son, Gamal Mubarak. The Democratic Front has attracted business people and members of the Coptic minority. There is reason to believe that the regime's rationale for the party's legal approval came as an attempt to strengthen the liberal, loyal opposition in order to counter the Muslim Brotherhood.

Opposition Parties between Contestation and Regime Support

The political opposition parties in Egypt before the January 25 uprising can be described with Gunther and Diamond as *cartel parties* "in which public financing of parties and the expanding role of the state induce party leaders to restrain competition and seek primarily to perpetuate themselves in power to avail themselves of these new resources" (Gunther and Diamond 2003, 169). They were also *elite-based parties* "whose principal organizational structures are minimal and based upon established elites and related interpersonal networks within a specific geographic area" (175).

Needless to say, Egyptian opposition parties differed from political parties in democracies concerning their capabilities and their role within the political system. They were "leadership organizations with low levels of internal differentiation where solitary bosses command diffuse followings" (Schedler 1996, 301). Statist repression and containment have prevented them from constituting serious contenders in a competitive game for political power. They have been agents utilized to draw the picture of a multiparty system that existed only on formal grounds to hide a dominant-party regime, controlled by the National Democratic Party. As to their self-image, the opposition parties have been aware of their own status. Party leaders have not been as naïve to believe that their organizations were players in a democratic game; nor have they pushed for the rapid advent of democracy. By contrast, the opposition parties adopted their actions comfortably to clientelist authoritarian arrangements and came to the tacit agreement that Egypt was not yet "ripe" for democracy. This was the formula that has long been shared by the opposition parties, actors of civil society, and the so-called reform faction within the government. The "Islamist threat" was the common denominator for them to perceive the sudden advent of democracy as the second-best option compared to a step-by-step development.

Apart from their internal weakness and dubious intentions, the opposition parties have played an important role in the Mubarak era in that they have preserved an institutionalized political arena for the representation of ideological factions sidelined under Mubarak and his predecessor. The representation dimension is not to be underestimated despite the parties' weaknesses. The parties have remained an arena in which liberal, nationalist, and socialist positions could be voiced and nurtured—ineffective in terms of the share of parliamentary seats, but loud enough to constitute a counterposition to the growing Islamist movement that has had, for some time prior to the January 25 uprising, the potential to represent a significant part of Egyptian society. The opposition parties, while continuously unsuccessful in their "natural habitat" of electoral politics, have continued to represent the liberal-secular positions in the media and intellectual discussion circles. They have done so quite successfully, indicated by the fact that the liberal-secular camp has continued to play an important role in post-Mubarak politics, despite the Islamist movements' overwhelming victory in new electoral, representative procedures, such as in the parliamentary elections of late 2011.

The opposition parties in Mubarak's Egypt have been able to survive politically not because they had the power to do so, but because the regime incumbents willed them into protracted existence. No other form of opposition is as attractive to incumbents as an opposition party cartel of the sort we have witnessed under Mubarak. The opposition parties have, through their very existence, contributed to the political system, a liberalized authoritarian order. In the post-1990 era of democracy, expectations in a modern polity would include the existence of electoral politics and multipartyism as necessary conditions. However uncompetitive the electoral processes would be (and elections in Mubarak's Egypt have been entirely uncompetitive), the persistence of contenders to ruling parties and candidates would be seen as a better-than-nothing option compared to closed hegemonies. Whereas power was never put at stake, the Egyptian incumbency needed opposition parties in their quest for legitimacy, both external and in front of their own population.

The legitimacy dimension of the opposition parties' raison d'être, however, rendered the incumbents vulnerable to an institutional entrapment strategy executed by the parties. Since opposition parties were needed to bolster the picture of multiparty politics, their share of parliamentary representation beyond insignificance was a valid expectation. Despite their generally poor performance in popular outreach and representation, opposition parties would be assured a share in parliamentary seats—until 2010, when the NDP's leadership succumbed to internal pressure and allocated 94.7 percent of the seats to the ruling party (see El-Ghobashy 2010; Albrecht and Kohstall 2010; Lesch 2012). Infamous for its degree of electoral fraud and vote rigging, only compared to the 1995 elections, Mona El-Ghobashy observed "that the Mubarak regime abandoned what is thought to be its trademark asset, namely the calibration of election rigging to let in some legislative opposition, polish its image and thereby stabilize its hold on power" (El-Ghobashy 2010). Only a few weeks later, in January 2011, it became clear that the main casualties of the regime's hegemonic turn were not the opposition parties, but rather Hosni Mubarak.

3

Tolerated Opposition

Civil Society and Public Protest

Opposition parties have constituted the landscape of regime-loyal opposition activism in Egypt. There was a clear modus vivendi for the relationship between the regime and the respective opposition actors. The rules, both formal and informal, of that activism were quite established, though subject to adaptation and orchestration from above. In general, authoritarian incumbents have a preference for this type of political opposition because they can observe and control it well. One observer of Egyptian politics said: "The government is not principally against the opposition; they are all part of the family" (author's interview with Hazem Mounir).

The Egyptian incumbents liked "their" opposition—and perceived it as part and parcel "of the family"—when it was performed in the backrooms of institutions (parties, associations, committees), in the print media, and in the halls of parliament. The main rationale for the regime's readiness to accept these forms of activism was that they did not imply an outreach toward larger parts of society: parties, parliaments, associations, committees, and unions—in short, the formal landscape of politics—constitute the realm of the politicized parts of society, that is, urban-based and of middle- to upper-class origin. This political arena, however, did not necessarily represent larger parts of the population in Egypt: the poor, illiterate, and non- or undereducated. Hence, the organizations performing in the formal arena of politics were not the main channels of political participation for the majority of the Egyptian people (Albrecht 2008, 22).

Three forms of opposition activism have emerged in the 2000s that were disloyal to the regime in different ways. Human rights groups and protest movements have challenged the Egyptian incumbents, who have, however, not resorted to bluntly repressing this form of opposition. Rather, they have been granted a significant measure of toleration. Human rights groups represented the politicized part of a larger body of civil society organizations and challenged the execution of coercive control.

Whereas these organizations did not pose a major threat to the regime, two movements of street protest were a potential threat to the regime's control over the public sphere at a much greater extent: an urban, elitist protest movement that came to be known as Kifaya; and a workers' movement representing primarily public-sector employees and industrial workers. It is well-known that authoritarian regimes dislike oppositional street politics. If it occurs anyway, expectations abound that the respective regime may lose control over the power to rule. Geoffrey Pridham argued that "street demonstrations are the demonstration that the most sacrosanct of authoritarian values, order itself, has been violated" (Pridham 1995, 60).

Even before the dramatic events in early 2011, some forms of opposition activism have emerged in Egypt with which the regime was not as comfortable as it presumably was with their opposition parties: the expression of dissent and dissatisfaction on public streets and squares.

These movements differ from one another considerably in terms of aims and discourses, their constituencies, and the degree of popular support. Their main commonality is that they have not been regarded by the incumbents as an immediate threat to their rule. Whereas the human rights business remained insignificant in the number of organizations and activists, the street protest movements did not seem troubling so long as the urban intellectuals in Kifaya would not unite with the lower middle class that was making the workers' movement: an unlikely prospect that magically materialized in the January 25 uprising.

The Human Rights Business

Whereas the 1980s saw the advent of an electoral multiparty system, the 1990s were the decade of politically relevant NGOs and civil society. In Egypt, estimates claim that sixteen thousand associations had come into existence by the early years of the new millennium. This is close to the number of NGOs and PVAs that had registered with the Egyptian authorities. When we add many informal initiatives that did not officially register, the gross number of civil society organizations might have been substantially higher. Some estimates put the possible number at between twenty thousand and thirty thousand (Abdelrahman 2004, 121). This number sounds impressive; but a closer look at the organizations reveals that the vast majority of them existed only on paper: around one thousand were active; of those, only about two hundred had a thematic agenda that could be held as politically relevant.[1] The bulk of the remaining organizations consisted primarily of local self-help organizations and, in particular, Islamist associations. Also, one should keep in mind that NGOs and PVAs did not constitute a new phenomenon when they emerged throughout the 1990s. Rather, Egypt looks back at a long history of the establishment of voluntary groups and movements, both of a religious origin—Coptic and Islamic, the latter often based on the principle of *zakat* (religious alms)— and also of a secular nature (see Hussein 2003, 200–202; Abdelrahman 2004, 123–29).

In a narrow sense, the number of NGOs that are relevant for the perspective in this book was small. Civil society organizations as a form of political opposition comprised a limited number of NGOs and PVAs: those that have a human-rights agenda. They were advocacy groups that formulated the aim to protect the universal rights of individuals in society and the general sociopolitical framework governing such rights in an authoritarian regime. These organizations were rather distinct within the overall landscape of Egyptian NGOs and PVAs. They were urban-based, located in Cairo, and run by educated middle-class people with a liberal-leftist ideational background.[2] The oldest NGOs of this kind were the

1. Estimates are by Haggag Ahmed Na'il, executive director of the Arab Program for Human Rights Activists (APHRA) (author's interview with Na'il). Maha Abdelrahman cites estimates according to which one-third or half of the registered NGOs are actively working (Abdelrahman 2004, 121–22).

2. The vast majority of PVAs and NGOs spread over the country and in more rural areas consisted primarily of members of wealthy upper-class families (Abdelrahman 2004, 154).

Ibn Khaldoun Center (IKC), founded by the Egyptian sociologist and human rights activist Saad Eddin Ibrahim, and the Egyptian Organization for Human Rights (EOHR). Both organizations were among the most acknowledged human rights groups in Egypt, active primarily in minority affairs, the denunciation of the practices of the Egyptian security services, and the supervision of elections.

Saad Eddin Ibrahim, who is a renowned social scientist and carries an Egyptian and a US passport, appeared at the center of international attention when he was sentenced to seven years in prison by a state security court on July 29, 2002. Whereas the real reason for this harsh treatment remained obscure, rumors among Cairo's political establishment held that Ibrahim had overstepped a red line when criticizing the sons of President Mubarak. This had provoked the lifting of the protective hand of the president's wife, Suzanne Mubarak, that Ibrahim had enjoyed for many years. However, there is also some credit to Ibrahim's claim that the IKC's performance in supervising the 2000 elections had aroused serious concerns among the authorities and triggered this strong reaction (author's interview with Saad Eddin Ibrahim). As a consequence of international pressure, Saad Eddin Ibrahim was released from prison on a final judgment of the Court of Cassation on March 18, 2003.

The EOHR was founded in 1985 and is the oldest independent human rights group in the country. It has a history, during the comparatively illiberal period in the 1990s, of criticizing the government, but not too harshly. Hafez Abu Saada followed the prominent human rights lawyer Negad al-Boreʻi as secretary-general of the EOHR in 1996. He claimed to have turned to the benches of the "dissidents" when he was imprisoned for one week in 1998 on charges that the EOHR had accepted foreign funding. The real reason behind it was presumably that Abu Saada had reported, in spite of explicit warnings from the security services, on bloody incidents of sectarian strife in Upper Egypt in January 2000 that have become infamous as the "Kosheh affair" (author's interview with Hafez Abu Saada; see also Kassem 2004, 119–24).

Other Cairo-based human rights groups were the Cairo Institute for Human Rights and the Arab Program for Human Rights Activists. Some NGOs have specialized in providing legal assistance to individual people haunted by the authorities in one way or another. They have gained prominence in the last decade because the opposition has increasingly, and quite successfully, made use of the opportunity to challenge the authorities through the judicial system. The most recognized of these NGOs were the Center for the Independence of the Judiciary and the Legal Profession (CIJLP) and the Hisham Mubarak Law Center (HMLC). Other, more specialized NGOs include the Human Rights Center for the Assistance of Prisoners, the New Women Research Center, and the Nadeem Center for the Rehabilitation of Victims of Violence. Since some prominent Egyptian human rights activists have established more than one NGO, I estimate that the total of such human rights organizations did not exceed twenty to twenty-five independent bodies by the end of Mubarak's rule.[3] These few organizations have formed the nucleus of a realm of political contestation that has come to the center of attention. Western governments and observers have often referred to exactly this minuscule part of the landscape of PVAs and NGOs when reflecting on Egyptian civil society.

There were marked differences among NGOs with respect to their relationship to the political regime. My personal impression is that, for instance, the CIJLP belonged to a majority of human rights organizations that were "sanctioned" by the authorities and, in turn, have refrained from challenging the regime to the extent that they would trigger a severe reaction. The Egyptian Organization for Human Rights (EOHR) and the Arab Program for Human Rights Activists (APHRA) may also fit into this category of "co-opted" organizations. The APHRA was established in 1997, like many other political NGOS, as a nonprofit company (*sharika madania*), based on Law No. 32 of 1964. The Ibn Khaldoun Center may have switched from a co-opted group, representing the "loyal" opposition until the late 1990s, to an opposition of principle in the wake of Saad Eddin Ibrahim's prosecution. Accordingly, the HMLC and the Land Center for Human Rights (LCHR) were among the "troublemakers" that defied, more often than not, the unwritten rules and guidelines established by the security apparatus.

3. Vicky Langohr supports this estimate (see Langohr 2004, 201).

The HMLC was one of the most outspoken and stubborn human rights groups among Egyptian NGOs. Established as a law firm and led by the lawyer Ahmed Saif al-Islam, the HMLC has repeatedly entered politically sensitive no-go areas, for instance when it coordinated a court file openly accusing interior minister Habib al-Adli and even President Mubarak of responsibility for human rights violations in the wake of the anti-Iraq war demonstrations in 2003. The HMLC has put much energy into the observation of the security and military raids in al-Arish on the Sinai Peninsula. Those had come as the state's response to the bomb attacks in Taba (October 2004), Sharm al-Shaykh (July 2005), and Dahab (April 2006) carried out by a group with an Islamist background (author's interview with Ahmed Saif al-Islam; see also International Crisis Group 2007; Human Rights Watch 2005).

Whereas such an assessment is certainly highly intuitive—and possibly subject to changes, as the Ibn Khaldoun case indicates—the membership of an organization's chairperson at the National Council for Human Rights may serve as a viable indicator for his or her readiness to co-optation. In this regard, the EOHR has come to be repeatedly criticized because its chairman, Hafez Abu Saada, has remained a member of this institution that is perceived as one of the main bodies of statist co-optation (Stacher 2005, 4). Other signals include the organizational and financial equipment that individual organizations had at their disposal. Given that the control over financial resources was key to the regime's strategy of confining and, if necessary, disciplining human rights NGOs, a "poor" organization may have hinted at the regime's readiness to hinder its activities and therefore at the respective human rights group's determination to take its mission more seriously.

Responding to International Expectations

How can we explain this development of the adoption of a human rights agenda in Egypt? Contrary to the assumption that a global wave of civil society had reached the Arab world in general (and Egypt as one of the most important countries in the region in particular) as a harbinger of democracy, other explanations sound more plausible. Brian Grodsky found, by looking at post-communist developments in Uzbekistan, that opposition parties under authoritarian regimes adapt their organizational structures according to changing opportunity structures (Grodsky 2007). Similarly in Egypt, the growing opposition in the 1980s underwent a process of learning and adaptation, understanding quickly that the multiparty system would not provide unrestricted opportunities, not only because of the restrictions of the authorities but also because of the dynamics of hierarchical and undemocratic internal procedures in the parties. The proliferation of civil society institutions as a mass development (in terms of the sheer number of registered organizations) was encouraged by a fundamental change in the opportunity structure for opposition politics. As has been mentioned in the previous section, oppositional activism within the party system had become increasingly difficult because the opposition parties had moved to the center of statist contention strategies. The increase of exclusionary politics toward the parties became a decisive push factor for the involved opposition actors to search for other organizational forms of contentious politics.

Western expectations and ideals acted as a pull factor, that is, as another positive incentive to engage in the form of the emerging NGO business. Caught in the Huntingtonian dictum of "third-wave" global democratization, Western governments found it apt to connect expectations of "development"—in both political and socioeconomic terms—to the existence of civil society. For a variety of reasons, funds have been promised to civil society organizations that promised to engage in "democratization" and "good governance." In Egypt, the regime as well as societal actors responded quickly to such demands and opportunities and met respective expectations: if the West needed a civil society in order to sustain its development assistance—and keep a generally positive assessment about sociopolitical developments in the respective country—it should have exactly that (see, in support of this argument, Brouwer 2000; Carapico 2002; Albrecht and Schlumberger 2004; Kienle 2007; Cavatorta and Elananza 2009).

In an instructive anthropological piece of research, Julia Elyachar has shown how a group of craftsmen in a Cairene neighborhood organized and, in this process, adapted to changing national and international circumstances. When the interests of the craftsmen involved the necessity to address the Egyptian authorities, the craftsmen's association was referred to as a *rabta* (association). However, when things changed and the international arena became more important (e.g., for such a group's fund-seeking endeavors), the "dominant mode of discourse to refer to civic associations had changed to one in which notions of development organized around NGOs were paramount" (Elyachar 2003, 572). More generally, grassroots social organization was not a new phenomenon in Egypt. This contradicts assumptions about the novelty of civil society in Egypt that one could easily hold when reading the mainstream literature on the emergence of Western-style civil society organizations during the 1990s. Rather, irrespective of the question of whether it is helpful to adopt the term "civil society" at all, the phenomenon of social organization itself was deeply rooted within Egyptian society already before the advent of the discourse on Egyptian civil society. Thus the novelty is the branding, not the phenomenon itself.

Whereas the opposition found a new playing field in activism in the "civil society business," the regime smoothly adopted containment strategies similar to those employed toward "partyism" (see Ismail 1995, 43). First, Maha Abdel Rahman found empirical evidence to believe that, similar to the intra- and interparty quarrels, Egyptian "civil society" organizations more often than not struggle with one another rather than challenge the regime (Abdel Rahman 2002). Second, similar to the political parties, the NGO-related "human rights business" is controlled by a mixture of co-optation, legal restrictions, and repression (see Abdelrahman 2004, 120–50). Until Law No. 84 of 2002 replaced all previous legal provisions for the registration of NGOs, many of those perceived as politically sensitive by the security services operated in a legal limbo because they were denied legal recognition as private voluntary associations. Previously, NGOs had to register with the Ministry of Social Affairs on the basis of Law No. 32 of 1964 that was designed to exert tight control over PVAs. Many political NGOs thus registered as nonprofit companies; those active in a politically relevant framework often registered as law firms. In May 1999, Law No. 32 was replaced by a new Association Law (No. 153) that was found unconstitutional by the Supreme Constitutional Court in 2000 and replaced again by Law No. 84 of 2002. According to this new law, all NGOs had to register by June 4, 2003.

Indeed, this legal framing established a settlement of legal affairs for NGOs. All but two applications for registration under the new law have been accepted by the authorities: the applications of the New Woman Research Center and the Land Center for Human Rights (LCHR) were turned down, reportedly "for security reasons." According to Karam Saber, executive director of the LCHR, the Ministry of Social Affairs was entrusted with registration procedures and complied with orders from state security forces (author's interview with Karam Saber). However, the law was still criticized for its restrictive nature and for being a mere "carbon copy" (Kassem 2004, 122) of the previous legislation. Some NGO representatives warned that their organizations would come under even more direct control from the Ministries of Social Affairs and Interior. A small number of NGOs did not even apply for registration and have remained vulnerable to crackdowns by the authorities. One prominent example is the HMLC. According to its chairman, Ahmed Saif al-Islam, the HMLC chose to remain a law firm because the group estimated its chances to be registered to be remote. Saif al-Islam also refused to comply with the law's legal framework and control exerted by the authorities (author's interview with Ahmed Saif al-Islam). The legal framework for the human rights groups has not improved during the transition period after the January 25 uprising. In April 2012, the draft of an even tougher NGO law, which might curtail human rights activities even further, was heavily criticized by domestic and international human rights activists.

Apart from these legal provisions, NGOs and PVAs have been subject to the standard repertoire of control as much as the political parties. The security apparatuses have communicated to them quite openly what was tolerated and what not.[4] This holds particularly true in those cases when the regime perceived that the PVAs and NGOs had an Islamist background. To cite only one example, a former MP for the Muslim Brotherhood claimed that his failed attempt to found an apolitical NGO was caused by the security apparatus's exertion of pressure on his fellow

---

4. This was affirmed in several personal interviews with representatives from Egyptian human rights and advocacy groups.

would-be founders, who subsequently withdrew from the project (author's interview). The emergency law, in effect since 1981, and the affiliated judicial framework of state security and military courts, served as effective tools of intimidation and prosecution. Not very surprisingly, the removal of these authoritarian institutions has been on top of the agenda of most human rights organizations during the 2000s.[5]

The regime's stance toward the political NGOs, however, is based on dialogue and co-optation much more than on direct intervention and oppression: the establishment of the National Council for Human Rights (NCHR) on June 16, 2003, as a consultative committee does not indicate the regime's practical adoption of human rights principles but rather a mere window dressing and blatant attempt to institutionalize co-optation. Dennis Sullivan reported that "virtually all participants in and observers of NGO activity in Egypt recognize that these organizations are far from being independent of the government and many in fact are creations of that government" (Sullivan 2000, 12). Sheila Carapico (2000) argued that NGOs and PVAs are sometimes even established by the state. According to the chairman of the APHRA, Haggag Ahmed Na'il, several special departments within the regime's bureaucratic body have been responsible for the dialogue with human rights groups: in the Ministry of Interior, the Ministry of Justice, and—quite tellingly—in the Ministry of Foreign Affairs (author's interview with Haggag Ahmed Na'il). The fact that the latter ministry was involved in a domestic matter hints at the importance of an external perspective (particularly from the West) and the issue of external funding. Other nonpolitical groups in civil society had to report to statist organizations within the relevant ministries, such as the Health Ministry's Central Administration for Nongovernmental Organizations and Licenses.

NGOs also have communicated constantly with the state security forces (*amn al-dawla*) that set the limits for the NGOs' engagement. Issue

---

5. The "state of emergency" was proclaimed in 1981 in an immediate response to the assassination of Anwar Sadat. It was initially designed for the temporary suspension of civil and human rights but proved to become a useful tool in the hands of the Mubarak regime to deal with opposition forces (Allain 2003).

areas considered sensitive were the president of the republic and his family, the armed forces, national unity and minority affairs (Copts), relations with Saudi Arabia, and religious issues. NGOs have generally been aware of the margins of political expression. They would have criticized human rights violations to a certain degree, and they would have also attacked government representatives. Since the first half of 2003, for instance, some NGOs have increasingly criticized the emergency law and the affiliated judiciary procedures (state security and military courts).

These issues constituted the necessary political playground for the NGOs, making them heard among the Western community. While the NGO business remained the "natural" partners for development assistance, it did not pose a political threat to the regime because it never gained much support from the Egyptian public. "Democracy," "political reforms," and "human rights" were key words that sounded appealing in the ears of secular parts of the intellectual elite. The NGOs' discourses, however, did not fall on fertile soil in Egyptian society at large. This is not to say that Egyptians did not care about politics or about the issues and problems associated with those catchwords. The January 25 uprising's grand narrative, in which the people demanded "freedom, dignity, and justice," has ultimately proven otherwise. Before the explosion of the popular will on Tahrir Square, however, the "avenues of participation" for ordinary Egyptians—and the means of achieving their goals—were based on informal personal relations and networks; and, more often than not, the people would care about material goods instead of political participation, all the more so in times of economic crisis. As Diane Singerman opined, "the state has reduced formal politics to the issue of distribution, and participation to the realm of consumption" (Singerman 1997, 245).

Most active support for political NGOs originated from Western governments and international organizations, emphasizing their perceived importance in an anticipated democratization process. However, this support was a blessing as much as a curse for the Egyptian human rights community. First, the regime has repeatedly seized the opportunity to discredit human rights groups in the eyes of the Egyptian public by accusing them of "selling out" national interests when they accept Western funding; and the fact that NGOs were often financially dependent on foreign funding has made them vulnerable to the authorities' legal prosecution (see Carapico 2002, 391–94).

In an ironic twist, it was after the fall of Mubarak, and thus in the midst of the transition period to a presumably democratic political order, that human rights groups were hit hardest by such accusations. In 2011 and early 2012, forty-three NGO employees including sixteen foreign representatives of political foundations have been accused of illegal foreign funding of unregistered NGOs. Reportedly engineered by the then Minister of International Cooperation Fayza Abul Naga (who had served in several positions under Mubarak), the accusations played on nationalist emotions revitalized through the "Egyptian revolution." The saga ended abruptly with a heavily debated and criticized ruling of the Cairo Appeals Court headed by Abdel Moez Ibrahim and the subsequent departure of foreign NGO workers on bail of approximately US $330,000 each. Whereas all but one foreign representative left the country to avoid legal prosecution, relations had already soured with the United States, which made it clear that the disbursement of its yearly assistance of approximately US $1.3 billion would depend on a satisfactory solution of the case. More important for the domestic Egyptian context, the incident also increased a feeling of insecurity among both foreign and Egyptian NGOs. Fears that human rights NGOs would remain under close scrutiny of the authorities were reinforced on April 23, 2011, when the licenses of eight US-based NGOs were revoked by a court ruling.

Even before these incidents, showing the protracted great degree of suspicion thinly veiled under a national-security discourse, during Mubarak's authoritarianism Western organizations have been very cautious regarding the funding of human rights organizations because of the possible implications that an accusation to have intervened directly into Egyptian internal affairs would entail. Western support has always been a double-edged sword for Egyptian human rights groups. It could also bring about some protection from harsh repression by the regime, at least in prominent instances. One example is the case of Saad Eddin Ibrahim, who was released from prison presumably on protracted diplomatic pressure of the United States.

Kifaya: Enough of Mubarak!

On December 12, 2004, a group of around three hundred political activists squeezed together at the main entrance of a court building in downtown Cairo surrounded by hundreds of security personnel. Two aspects raised particular attention at the time: first, the very fact that an unauthorized demonstration happened in Cairo under close scrutiny but without being dissolved by the security forces. Second, the demonstrators' message—in short: *Kifaya* (Enough!)—which expressed the outright demand to put an end to President Mubarak's rule. The term "Kifaya" also included outright opposition to a possible shift of power to his son Gamal. The declared aims of Kifaya were in line—beyond the withdrawal of Mubarak and his son—with the usual claims to end the state of emergency, introduce free elections, and pass constitutional reforms that would guarantee a "real" democracy. A new movement of street politics was born, and "Kifaya" was the term under which it became familiar to observers (see Vairel 2006; Meital 2006, 267–69; Al-Sayyid 2009; El-Mahdi 2009). Kifaya's activities increased rapidly over the year, 2005, that witnessed an "atmosphere of contestation" (Hussein 2005; see also Albrecht 2007). Since January 2005, more demonstrations have been launched at strategic locations in order to attract widespread public attention, for example, at the Cairo Book Fair, on university campuses, and on Cairo's iconic Tahrir Square. A new quality of street politics in Egypt was reached when Kifaya demonstrations spread out from the capital. One instance is striking: on April 27, 2005, anti-Mubarak demonstrations were launched in fourteen cities simultaneously (see *Al-Ahram Weekly*, no. 742, May 12–18, 2005).

In 2005, Egyptian street politics as represented by Kifaya was unique in two ways: first, it has become a new form of contestation; and, second, it was—as a form of social protest—distinct from any other means of the expression of dissent observable in the pre-2011 history of the Middle East.

As to the first matter, Kifaya's appearance is remarkable because it has involved the protracted crossing of former limits firmly established by the regime's incumbents. First, the politics of toleration was always severely limited when contentious activism took to the streets; more often than not, street politics had triggered massive repressive actions by the security services. What is more, Kifaya contested the widely held claim that opposition politics in Egypt was primarily performed in the comparatively liberal press; as one intellectual said before the advent of Kifaya, "there is opposition, no action" (author's interview with Gamal al-Banna)—an assessment that seems to have been seriously challenged by the mere appearance of Kifaya irrespective of its power to engineer change.

Second, before the advent of Kifaya the authorities had always clearly communicated to the opposition—usually informally through direct warnings of the security services—that the man at the helm of the polity was not to become the subject of any criticism. Even among the independent foreign-language press in Egypt, which have benefited from a relatively liberal stance compared with the Arabic media, two issues had to be accepted as red lines, the crossing of which would likely have triggered negative consequences: on the one hand, the president and his family, and, on the other hand, the military and security forces (author's interview with Paul Schemm). The rather sudden change of red lines was materialized in the nonintervention of the security forces. They were well aware of Kifaya's demonstrations and showed a strong physical presence on the spot, but in the majority of cases they remained observers to the demonstrations.

Kifaya was also unique concerning its form of protest compared with those seen previously in the Middle East. Asef Bayat distinguished between six forms of social activism: urban mass protests, trade unionism, community activism, social Islamism, NGOs, and quiet encroachment (Bayat 2002, 3). Kifaya does not match any of these expressions.[6] Similar to urban protest movements, Kifaya's expression of discontent has focused primarily on a single issue: the end of Mubarak's hold on power. Thus, Egypt's street politics lack an elaborated programmatic profile, quite like bread riots or other mostly economically induced upsurges. Those are a

6. There were other instances when opposition movements have used the "enough" metaphor to directly attack the power center of nondemocratic political orders. For comparisons with cases outside of the Arab world, look at the *Trop-C'est-Trop* movement in Burkina Faso (Hagberg 2002) or the *Kmara* movement in Georgia's "Rose Revolution" (Karumidze and Wertsch 2005).

widespread phenomenon throughout the Middle East but lack the organizational capacities that were at the disposal of Kifaya and helped the latter endure in contrast to other outbursts of popular discontent (see Sadiki 2000). Retrospectively, it is striking to observe the discursive similarity between the Kifaya movement 2005, which dissolved in 2006 mainly because of the lack of public support, and the uprising between January 25 and February 11, 2011, which was successful in rallying millions of people under a political battle cry that the Kifaya movement had invented a few years earlier.

Whereas Kifaya's discursive practice should prove successful in the long run, its member structure was a far cry from a mass-based grass roots phenomenon. Kifaya had a decidedly elitist character, contrary to its claim to reach out to the popular masses. Kifaya was an informal movement because it never pursued legal recognition as a political party, pressure group, or NGO. On the other hand, it did possess decisive organizational capacities in that it relied on the intellectual capacities of its members and other formal institutions traditionally used by the opposition: NGOs, professional syndicates (in particular the Press Syndicate and the Bar Association), and student groups at universities.

While the majority of Kifaya members were liberal and leftist human rights activists, Kifaya was—at least at the time of its inception—remarkably open toward different ideational trends. One would have found in the movement's first "coordinator," George Ishaq, a Coptic human rights activist, along with a great number of people with leftist leanings such as Nabil al-Hilali (an independent communist), the journalist Ibrahim al-Sahhari, Muhammad al-Alim (an independent leftist with Tagammu leanings), and the university professor and human rights activist Aida Saif al-Dawla.

In an unusual display of unity among opposition forces, Kifaya has also attracted some prominent representatives of the Islamist current: Abu al-Ela Maadi, the former Muslim Brother and head of the Wasta would-be party, was one of the initiators of Kifaya; Magdi Husayn was the secretary-general of the then "frozen" Socialist Labor Party. Even Abdel Mun'eim Abul Futuh, then a Muslim Brotherhood bigwig and post-Mubarak presidential candidate, has referred to himself as affiliated with Kifaya (Aclimandos 2006, 86). Whereas Islamists remained alien to the dominant leftist-liberal background in Kifaya, it did not come as a complete surprise that the Islamists have initially declared sympathy with Kifaya. Whereas they were certainly sympathetic with Kifaya's one and only goal, they would also see an opportunity to appear in public without being prosecuted. However, the Islamists have never actively supported Kifaya's mobilization efforts, mainly because there was a joint understanding among all members involved in the movement that it would become the target of the security forces. Nevertheless, the Islamists' involvement led to internal rifts that certainly contributed to the movement's demise in 2006. Magdi Husayn and six fellow Kifaya members with Islamist leanings clashed in December 2006 with the majority of liberal and secular members over the movement's "official" stance—to be communicated on its website—to support an anti-veil initiative of Minister of Culture Farouk Husni. The quarrels reportedly led to the withdrawal of Kifaya's coordinator, Copt George Ishaq, only a few weeks later.

Kifaya was incoherent not only with respect to the ideational profile of its members, but also with respect to their degree of dedication and strategic interests. From this perspective, one can distinguish between four different types of Kifaya members: (1) the "protest pro," (2) the "rising star," (3) the "free rider," and (4) the "young gun." As to the first category, it is obvious that the spearheads of the Kifaya demonstrations have been veteran street activists, such as Kamal Khalil, Abdel Halim Qandil, and Ashraf Ibrahim, who would not let go the chance to occupy a public stage to spread their leftist and nationalist political formulas.

The second category, the "rising star," refers to those Kifaya members who had not played a prominent role within the overall landscape of opposition before the advent of the movement, for whatever individual reason. For intellectuals, such as George Ishaq and the *al-Ahram* journalist Mohammed Sayyed Sa'id, Kifaya was an opportunity to enter politics outside of the realm of the regime *and* the severely discredited opposition parties, yet on a prominent stage well-covered by the media both in Egypt and abroad. Kifaya was a prominent opportunity for risk-averse political intellectuals to vent their anger at both the authoritarian incumbency and the then established opposition organizations that were obviously neither capable nor willing to engineer significant change. The "free rider" category refers to those Kifaya members who have also perceived the movement as a special opportunity of activism given that—to them—other forms of activism have been forestalled. Magdi Husayn, the head of the dormant SLP, is a good example. With his party and its mouthpiece *al-Sha'ab* frozen by the authorities, an appearance at Kifaya demonstrations was certainly a better-than-nothing option to make him heard among the public.

The fourth category of Kifaya member, the "young gun," refers to those younger activists who have called themselves the "Youth for Change" and formed the bulk of demonstrators in 2005. Muhammad al-Sharqawi was among the most outspoken younger firebrands who have attracted some coercive responses by the security services, in particular since early 2006. For them, Kifaya as a street movement was a matter of heart, possibly to a greater degree than it was for its founding members. For the youth, Kifaya became a chance to become active in politics at an occasion where the pervasive hierarchical structures that have characterized political parties, NGOs, and other organizations would not apply.

Retrospectively, the younger activists' engagement in the Kifaya movement had a strong impact irrespective of the movement's virtual disappearance from the streets since 2006. The youth's engagement, while small in number, led to the politicization of a younger generation of political activists who quickly understood that the movement itself would not be a viable vehicle for continued activities. Rather, Kifaya served as a catalyst for the politicization of a younger generation, quite like the country's universities in the 1970s, which had provided a platform for the political socialization and learning of today's *gil al-wasat* (middle generation) of activists.[7] At the time of Kifaya, they were in their late fifties and sixties when they came to dominate the oppositional organizations, both among the parties

7. Dina El-Khawaga (2002) used the term "generation seventies" to describe a generation of activists who, through the introduction of new means of political engagement, introduced modern civil society activism in Egypt.

and the NGO business. The *gil al-wasat* learned how to engage in politics under Sadat, and so did the younger generation of Kifaya activists in 2005. When street politics ceased to be an option, they found virtual space—in blogs, Facebook groups, etc.—to reorganize and finally trigger the January 25 uprising.

The Sociology of Protest under Mubarak

The significant impact that Kifaya had in the longer term warrants a closer look at the social fabrics of protests under Mubarak. There were two social bases of Kifaya: some—from the political regime's perspective—notorious oppositional "troublemakers," and a number of intellectuals who have provided the necessary organizational background. In general, the form of political activism that was offered by Kifaya was attractive for many figures in Egyptian opposition politics because of the lack of a hierarchical organization. For the majority of activists, an engagement in formal organizations remained unattractive because the top positions in the established opposition parties and NGOs were usually occupied, and fiercely defended by those who had made it to the top of these organizations. A majority of political parties and NGOs somewhat resembled the Egyptian state in that the upper echelons of the respective organizations were monopolized by a small group of individuals.

The fragmentation of the political landscape is one important consequence, and the majority of the politicized, urban parts of society learned to participate in opposition politics as "free agents." Thus, prior to Kifaya's formation there existed a network of individual "troublemakers." These "troublemakers" did not share a common programmatic footing and organizational platform. Most of them were middle-class intellectuals politicized in the late Nasserist years or during the 1970s. As a rule of thumb, they have operated as individuals and struggled with the regime as much as with fellow opposition figures; they have contested sensitive issues and the red lines established by the regime's security services at irregular intervals; usually, they were financially independent and quite familiar with the conditions in Egyptian jails, however, none of them has shared the

Islamists' experience of protracted incarceration; finally, their immediate political impact and leverage was limited because of their lack of popular mass support.

To give but a few examples of individuals who may fit into this category: Abdel Mohsen Hammouda was called by Mona El-Ghobashy "a fierce campaigner against executive overreach who has made an art out of administrative litigation" (El-Ghobashy 2008, 1601). Hammouda was a veteran political activist with Wafdist leanings who has used the judicial system to confront the regime on a regular basis. In June 2001, he received a ruling from the Court of Cassation proving that his son's death in custody was caused by torture; following a court file by Hammouda, on April 2, 2003, the Supreme Administrative Court (SAC) reaffirmed the constitutional right of holding demonstrations (*Cairo Times*, June 5–11, 2003).

Mohammed Farid Hassanein, parliamentarian for the New Wafd Party in the 2000 parliamentary elections, broke the regime's unwritten rules (at the time) by carrying politics to the streets: he participated in the antiwar demonstrations on March 20–21, 2003, which slipped out of government control and triggered massive interventions by the security forces. He was, like Kamal Khalil, a veteran leftist "troublemaker" and has never awarded great merits to his party affiliations. During his political career, Hassanein had been member of the Nasserist Party, the SLP, and the New Wafd Party, and broke with each organization citing their lack of democratic principles (author's interview with Mohammed Farid Hassanein).

Kifaya did not appear out of the blue. Apart from the social basis that was provided by individual opposition figures, several attempts at organizing public dissent preceded the movement. Some of the initiators of Kifaya had already appeared on the scene of street politics as the organizers of the Committee in Solidarity with the Palestinian Intifada (CSPI), founded on October 13, 2000, in support of the Al-Aqsa Intifada in the occupied Palestinian Territories. The CSPI was quite similar to the later Kifaya initiative in that it attracted a number of "troublemakers" of quite different political colors: next to Nasserist Hamdeen Sabahi (Karama movement) stood Islamist Magdi Qorqor (SLP) and leftist intellectuals such as Kamal Khalil and Farid Zahran. Apart from smaller demonstrations staged by the CSPI—for instance on April 1, 2002, leading to fierce street battles with security personnel—a real test run of the pre-Kifaya demonstrations was staged in 2003: triggered by the US-led military intervention to replace Saddam Husayn in Iraq, massive antiwar demonstrations took place in Cairo in February and March 2003. During these demonstrations, the regime faced a highly politicized populace mainly because the events in Iraq coincided with a devaluation of the Egyptian currency, the cutting of subsidies, and subsequent price rises of consumer goods only three weeks before the US military campaign. Interestingly, some slogans heard at these mass gatherings moved from international to domestic political affairs. Demonstrators shouted: "We are not a kingdom, we are a republic!" which can only be understood as a critical call against a possible shift of power from Hosni Mubarak to his son Gamal (author's interview with Farida Naqqash). In retrospect, the political situation in 2003 showed some remarkable similarities with the moment prior to the January 25, 2011, uprising; demonstrations took place amid economic hardship and slipped out of the control of the security forces, at least temporarily. The main difference was that, during 2003, public criticism of domestic politics was heard only as insulated calls, whereas it became the dominant frame in the 2011 uprising.

The Kifaya initiative in December 2004 was different concerning the subject of demonstrations and the regime's reaction. As to the latter aspect, the regime handed down a massive repressive reaction on the antiwar demonstrations in 2003. After running battles, the security forces finally dispersed the crowds using excessive violence and incarcerated a number of demonstrators and organizers both during and after the demonstrations. The forces did not even step back from physically assaulting opposition members of parliament, including Mohammed Farid Hassanein (then MP for the New Wafd Party) and Hamdeen Sabahi (then independent MP affiliated with the Karama movement, later candidate in the presidential elections of 2012), thereby violating their parliamentary immunity (author's interviews with Hassanein and Sabahi). Only two years later, in 2005, Kifaya demonstrations were, by and large, spared from such massive coercive interventions.

There were, however, exceptions indicating that the regime had drawn new red lines. First, the regime did not allow the holding of street demonstrations outside of the capital, where they could be observed and contained more easily. Consequently, the security forces stepped in when Kifaya launched demonstrations in fourteen cities all over the country on April 27, 2005. Second, the regime was obviously nervous on election days and, for instance, used a more coercive tactic against Kifaya demonstrations on May 27, 2005, the day when the constitutional referendum allowing for multicandidate presidential elections was passed. In general, Kifaya suffered, since early 2006, from a more restrictive and deliberalized political environment similar to other opposition forces, in particular members of the Muslim Brotherhood and journalists.

Whereas the individual "troublemakers"—quite naturally—formed the core of Kifaya's street appearance, they needed a second group of political activists who were able to establish the necessary organizational capacities of the movement. In the course of 2003 and 2004, several gatherings took place among intellectuals of different political leanings. George Ishaq asserted that the foundation stone for Kifaya was laid as early as November 2003, at a meeting of several opposition figures in the home of the moderate Islamist and leader of the would-be Wasat Party, Abu al-Ela Maadi (author's interview with George Ishaq). In the subsequent political calls and communiqués, the political narrative turned from foreign to domestic affairs and the Egyptian presidency moved to the center of criticism. At these gatherings, the notorious human rights group Hisham Mubarak Law Center, the moderate Islamist Abu Ela Maadi (Wasat movement), and the Nasserist Abdel Halim Qandil, among others, were the driving forces. In a communiqué following a meeting of opposition figures on August 7, 2004, the catchword "Kifaya" appeared for the first time, as well as the name under which the movement would also become commonly known, Egyptian Movement for Change (Haraka al-Misriyya min agl al-Taghir) (Vairel 2006, 113). Thus, behind street demonstrations featuring the notorious Egyptian "troublemakers" stood an organizational structure of "back room activists" consisting of a forty-member coordinating committee, a seven-member steering committee responsible for day-to-day actions, a spokesman, and a coordinator.

The spokesman was Abdel Halim Qandil, an independent Nasserist and editor in chief of the oppositional *al-Karama* newspaper. The movement's first coordinator, human rights activist George Ishaq, stepped down on January 27, 2007, and was followed by the liberal intellectual Abdel Wahab al-Messiri (he passed away in July 2008). The decision-making circles within the organizational branch of Kifaya convened in the seven-men steering committee, which was reportedly dominated by opposition figures of leftist and Nasserist leanings (see International Crisis Group 2005, 11, footnote 75). Whereas the sources of financial capacities remained obscure, rumors abound that the publisher and businessman Hisham Qassem has provided substantial funding for Kifaya activities.

Without any doubt, by 2005 it had become en vogue to be part of Kifaya, which essentially turned into a catch-all term to denote the activities of multiple factions: the "Egyptian Movement for Change," the "Popular Campaign for Change," and the "National Front for Change." Moreover, in several professional syndicates "Engineers" or "Doctors for Change" have seen the light of day. While the term "Kifaya" was routinely employed in the media and implied a homogeneous movement, protest politics had by spring 2005 become as fragmented as party politics and thus mirrored one of the major flaws of opposition activities at large. Moreover, it was never obvious where "change" would lead, given the lack of programmatic coherence and common interest among the different opposition groups beyond the very term that united them.

Concerning Kifaya's immediate impact on Egyptian politics, the crossing of several red lines previously upheld by the regime is noteworthy, although the claim to reach the popular masses did not materialize. Rather, Kifaya activities were limited to a few hundred participants. Kifaya fits Robert Tucker's term "charismatic coterie-movement" (Tucker 1968, 738), or a movement encapsulating "pocket protest"; that description, coined by Jason Lyall for the antiwar movement in Putin's Russia, describes the activism of the Egyptian Kifaya well. Lyall said that "the movement's own culture . . . dictates the use of tactics and slogans that have little mass appeal. Preferring symbolism to practical politics, and emphasizing strong face-to-face contacts rather than weak ties among potential supporters, the antiwar movement has undercut its own ability to 'scale-up' and pressure the regime" (Lyall 2006, 379–80).

Kifaya's limited immediate impact on Egyptian politics—that is, in essence its weakness—explains why it was able to push the limits set by the regime to an extent unprecedented in Egyptian state-society relations and fairly unexpected by observers. In historical retrospect, Kifaya should not be equated with those movements that triggered fundamental change in Eastern Europe or Lebanon—and a few years after Kifaya's emergence in the Arab world. Under the impression of Kifaya's demise in 2006, Karen Kramer wrote: "The Western media may love Egypt's Kifayah movement, but a hundred or so protesters in a country of 79 million is hardly a revolution in the making" (Kramer 2006, 160). The events of 2011 beg for a slightly different interpretation. Whereas Kifaya itself was never a revolutionary movement, it helped to construct the social and organizational infrastructure for a revolution in the making: by showing that street protest was possible, by providing an opportunity for the politicization of a younger generation of activists, and by providing an example for both success and failure in street politics and mobilization tactics that contributed to learning and experience of the opposition. Finally, by stretching the red lines and limits of authoritarian control, Kifaya provided an early example of breaking the barrier of fear. Tarek Masoud described Kifaya's achievements as "to serve as the training ground for and gateway to political activism for many of the individuals who would lead the protests" in the January 25 uprising (Masoud 2011, 21).

It was a younger generation of political activists who triggered the events during those eighteen days in early 2011. With Kifaya's demise in 2006, the retreat of these younger activists from street politics was only temporarily, to regroup in social media: Facebook groups, Twitter networks, blogs. Not quite political activism in the strict sense, the retreat to the cyber world did not indicate the depoliticization of the younger generation of urban, educated, upper-middle classes. Rather, other forms of contestation have emerged with which, quite obviously, the authorities could not deal well. One Internet initiative attempted, on April 6, 2008, to organize a general strike in the industrial city of Mahalla al-Kubra, thereby paying reference to an ongoing struggle of the workers (see below). The April 6 Movement, founded by Ahmed Maher, failed to unite with the workers and achieve its goals—partly because of the authorities' repressive containment, partly because of the workers' ignorance of what they perceived to be a group and a political cause alien to their own struggle. But the movement's attempt alone to unite a larger cross-class constituency for the struggle against the state was indicative of its initiators' dedication, politicization, and awareness of new means of communication and contestation. The movement's website quickly grew into one of the most dynamic sites of critical political discussions for Egypt's younger generation.[8]

Equally important for the buildup of a revolutionary infrastructure was the Facebook group Kulluna Khaled Saeed (We are all Khaled Saeed). Founded by Wael Ghoneim, Google's marketing head in the MENA region and later icon of the January 25 uprising,. the Facebook group's name paid reference to a young man from Alexandria who was beaten to death by the police on June 6, 2010. In disclosing police brutality and thereby using explicit media footage, the group played on the emotions of the people and was therefore able to decry police brutality and human rights violations much more effectively than the NGOs could have ever done (Shehata 2012).

Labor and the Economy

In essence, the Kifaya movement is a good indicator to assess changes in incumbent-opposition relations at a window of opportunity of limited political liberalization. On the other hand, there is another movement of street protests that has gone largely unnoticed by international observers until the January 25 uprising. Yet, it has increased dramatically since the early years of the millennium and had a substantial impact on Egyptian politics and state-society relations even before the 2011 uprising.

In December 2006, up to twenty thousand workers and their sympathizers participated in a wildcat strike. They blocked the Misr Spinning and Weaving Factory in Mahalla al-Kubra and demanded higher annual bonuses that had been promised for allocation at the end of that year. In the following months, protests endured in the textile sector and saw a total

8. The movement's website is: http://6april.org/ (retrieved May 25, 2011).

of around thirty thousand workers on the streets in several factories in the Nile Delta and in Alexandria (see Beinin and el-Hamalawy 2007).[9] In the first half of 2007, the protests in Mahalla al-Kubra spread to other sectors in the economy; strikes shook the automobile industry, cement factories, and the food industry (see Lübben 2007). The catalyst of the unrest was, in the majority of cases, the plan or announcement to privatize the respective establishments.

Unlike Kifaya, labor protest was not a new phenomenon in Egypt. Compared to other countries in the Middle East, Egypt has seen in its history several phases of industrialization starting in the first half of the nineteenth century during the reign of Mohammed Ali. Industrialization witnessed a boost in the wake of the modernization and development project of Gamal Abdel Nasser.[10] Therefore, labor and blue-collar workers comprise an integral part of modern Egyptian society, and the political incumbents have always had to deal with the political impact of an emerging working class. For authoritarian incumbents, labor is a double-edged sword. Jennifer Gandhi and Wonik Kim held that "the extent to which the economic life of a country requires the use of domestic labor indicates not only the extent to which workers constitute a potential threat, but also the extent to which regimes must solicit cooperation to govern" (Gandhi and Kim 2005, 6). Whereas Nasser enjoyed a great measure of support for his etatist and socialist program, both of his successors had to deal with labor as a potential or manifest source of contestation that—from an authoritarian logic of power maintenance—needed to be carefully controlled.[11] The

9. A dose of caution should be applied concerning the numbers of participants at such demonstrations communicated in the press. The Egyptian media, from where these numbers are taken, and observers alike—let alone participants—tend to overestimate numbers at demonstrations. Nonetheless, there is no doubt that numbers of participants at labor protests exceed by far the numbers of, for instance, Kifaya gatherings or any other politically motivated demonstrations before the January 25 uprising.

10. For a history of industrialization and state-labor relations in Egypt, see Joel Beinin and Zachary Lockman, *Workers on the Nile* (1988).

11. I admit that this is a simplification of a far more complex phenomenon. Occasionally, Nasser had some difficult times with workers' demands and protests, particularly

case of Egyptian workers—and the differences between the Nasser regime and the regimes of his successors—approve the assumption that populist outreach at mass participation can be a double-edged sword for authoritarian incumbents.

In the Nasser era, several measures were introduced in order to control the workers, the most important of which was the reconfiguration of corporatist participation into a system of corporatist control. This was organized in the official labor unions; at the top of its hierarchy was the General Federation of Trade Unions (GFTU) (see Pripstein Posusney 1997, 94–113). However, Sadat's political "correction movement" of 1971 and his private-capital oriented, socioeconomic *infitah* project (economic "open-door policy"), which was sustained and reinforced by Mubarak from 1989 onward, led to the worsening of labor-state relations, which have been characterized through conflict rather than cooperation and support ever since.

Roger Owen has observed that "in Egypt, as elsewhere, groups of workers were often able to obtain sufficient independence from official control to organize strikes and sit-ins or to develop a local leadership which was independent of the official union structure" (Owen 2000, 39). This was manifest, for instance, in the late Sadat years when labor and the GFTU sided with the newly established leftist wing of the opposition party structure, in particular the Tagammu Party. Food riots in 1977 were also seen as part of labor protests against the economic policies of the state. As a consequence, labor and its leaders became subject to fierce repression especially in 1979 and 1980. But Mubarak also had to face a challenge from the labor movement in the first decade of his tenure. Particularly in the textile sector and in heavy industries, massive strikes that came to be known as the "Kafr al-Dawwar Uprising," the "ESCO Strike," and the "Mahalla Strike" impaired state-labor relations. Textile workers are said to be among the most active in Egypt. Their propensity to engage in protest is due to the

---

in the immediate aftermath of the Free Officers' takeover that witnessed a large-scale strike at the Kafr al-Dawwar textile mills, and also during the last years of his reign (Pripstein Posusney 1997, 80–93).

fact that they have suffered tremendously from socioeconomic reordering under neoliberal auspices under Sadat and Mubarak. Faced with the challenge of thousands of workers on the streets, the regime responded with little compromise (see El Shafei 1995, 22–36; Beinin 2006).

Not much was heard from the workers in the 1990s. This is, at a first glance, quite astonishing considering that the neoliberal economic reform project under the auspices of the International Monetary Fund, the World Bank, and the Paris Club was to materialize to the detriment of labor, and in particular of the workers employed in the public sector (see Albrecht, Pawelka, and Schlumberger 1997; Paczynska 2006). Surveys reveal that in the period 1990–2005 the average annual growth rate of labor employment (2.63 percent) did not match the average annual growth rate of GDP (4.2 percent) (Kheir El-Din and El-Laithy 2008). One should expect that reforms involving large-scale privatization efforts and economic hardship especially for the lower middle classes would possibly trigger massive protests from the workers.

Several factors explain why the protests did not take off during the 1990s. First, with a declining public sector, the informal sector of the national economy absorbed a large proportion of the workforce in the 1990s (El Mahdy 2002). According to Nihal El-Megharbel (2008, 181), the workforce in the informal economy increased from 2.4 million in 1976 to over 2.9 million in 1986 and to 4.8 million in 1996. The problem is that informal employment in the economy does not support large-scale mobilization, which is necessary to launch contentious activism. Second, potential labor protests were deterred during the 1990s, first by the memory of coercive measures during the 1980s and second by a general climate of political deliberalization. While the right to organize a strike was granted in the 1971 constitution, it has been de facto impeded by the security forces. According to the Unified Labor Law of 2003, strikes had to be approved by the GFTU. However, "since the federation, along with the sectoral general unions and most enterprise-level union committees, are firmly in the grip of the ruling National Democratic Party (NDP), all actual strikes since 2003 have been 'illegal'" (Beinin and El-Hamalawy 2007, 2).

Notwithstanding several measures and reforms that came to the detriment of labor, during the 1990s the situation did not initially deteriorate for workers as much as one may have expected, at least not compared to the majority of the population: urban and rural poor without a formal contract in the public or private economic sectors. Contrary to the assumption that labor was entirely on the losing side of labor-capital conflicts in times of neoliberal economic reforms, Agnieszka Paczynska found that Egyptian workers have indeed been able—at least in part—to influence these very reforms by means of the formal organizations, the labor unions (Paczynska 2006; see also Pripstein Posusney 1997, 10–11; Bayat 2002, 6). Especially the public-sector workers have indeed managed to preserve some benefits and advantages compared to their colleagues in the private sector (El-Megharbel 2008, 195). The most severe problem of labor in the 1990s was thus not the representation of the interests of those who managed to find a job, but increasing unemployment or the push of workers into the informal economy.

Economic policy analyses have shown that the logic of authoritarian regime maintenance has prevented the Egyptian regime from embarking on a clear path toward establishing a liberal market economy (see Wurzel 2004). What did happen was the protracted dismantling of the public sector. While not being liberalized in a strict economic sense, the sale of public sector enterprises and assets to the regime's political "cronies" entailed similar effects for the employees as "real" market reforms: increasing unemployment, dropping real wages, and—since the late 1990s—cutting privileges that public sector employees and workers had enjoyed for many decades. In this context of liberalization under "crony capitalism," the privatization of public enterprises has become a meaningful part of the economic reforms only since 1996, which marked the starting point for a substantial change of state-labor relations (author's interviews with Saber Barakat, Ahmed Saif al Islam, and Ali Khaled). Most important, an independent workers' movement reemerged outside of the official corporatist organizations.

The Reemergence of Labor Protest

Like the Kifaya movement, the recent wave of labor protests, increasingly covered by the media, did not appear out of the blue. This movement was fuelled by an emerging cohort of young, educated, but economically underprivileged people who were hit hardest by increasing unemployment during the 1990s. Ragui Assaad found that "open unemployment in Egypt continues to be concentrated among educated youths under the age of 30, with the highest unemployment rates being experienced at the intermediate levels of education" (Assaad 2002, 33). The new lumpen intelligentsia merged with an "older" politicized generation of workers in the public-sector enterprises who had been involved in strikes, protests, and sit-ins during the 1980s to provide the social basis of labor protest (author's interview with Saber Barakat).

Asef Bayat cited Egyptian press reports indicating that around five strikes or sit-ins per week occurred on average during 1999 (Bayat 2002, 6). Workers' activism has increased dramatically since 2002 (author's interview with Ahmed Saif al-Islam). The Land Center for Human Rights reported that a total of 202 incidents of protest happened in 2005: 90 gatherings, 53 sit-ins, 43 strikes, and 16 demonstrations (LCHR, Press Release, January 26, 2006; see also Hussein 2005). One of the particular incidents that came to the attention of the media was the rally of former workers from the Aura-Misr asbestos factory in Cairo's satellite industrial city 10th of Ramadhan. Having been closed by the authorities, the factory's workers demanded outstanding wages and compensations for health problems in front of the GFTU headquarter in Cairo. In the first half of 2006, the LCHR reported 18 strikes, 15 demonstrations, 31 gatherings, and 43 sit-ins throughout the country and across all sectors of the economy (LCHR, Press Release, July 17, 2006). The Land Center's data reveal that there was a culture of protest among workers already a number of years before the January 25, 2011 uprising.

What was the dimension of this wave of labor protest in Egypt? In general, the overall number of protests throughout the country had not increased remarkably in 2006. According to a press release of the Land Center for Human Rights of February 7, 2007, 115 protests occurred in the second half of 2006 compared to a total of 202 in 2005. Of these 115 incidents, 41 were gatherings, 26 sit-ins, 29 strikes, and 9 demonstrations. In plain numbers, this is not a significant increase compared to the protests that the LCHR had reported in the previous years. Rather, what came to the attention of observers in 2006 was that the numbers of participants increased dramatically.

In an explanation of this phenomenon, Saber Barakat indicated that a critical mass of ready-to-protest workers was reached only in 2006, contributing to the already existing wave of protests. As a consequence of the deteriorating conditions for the workers—in particular concerning payment and the threat of unemployment—a point of no return was reached for many workers who had remained silent prior to 2006 out of fear for their jobs. According to Barakat, a "new working class" (employed during the 1990s under unfavorable contracts and largely depoliticized) joined the "old workers," who were experienced in the protest wave during the 1980s, to trigger the wave of labor strife (author's interview with Saber Barakat). Indeed, there was a high burden set up by the state as an employer of many disenfranchised workers: since 1985, the Egyptian government had stopped issuing permanent contracts to state employees and workers (see Kassem 2001, 64). Possible unemployment had become a decisive disincentive for the concerned workers to engage in open protest against the state; and this disincentive had kept many workers at home so long as they perceived their jobs as valuable assets.

A second aspect refers to the organizational capacities of the independent labor movement. During the first half of the 1990s, an independent workers' movement was impossible because of the severe repressive state responses toward mass protests in the previous decade. Another detriment to the workers' cause was that those political parties with familiar ideological foundations (such as the Tagammu, the SLP, and the Nasserists) did not represent the workers' interests in practice; rather, they had turned party activism basically into backroom, intellectual discussion circles (author's interview with Abdel Rahman Khair).

The increasing number of protests since the turn of the millennium did not attract broader attention because they were largely seen as singular instances without a common strategy, aim, or ideological background; and the numbers of incidents and participants remained small at the beginning. In the course of this smoldering labor unrest, however, a small number of organizations saw the light of day, which grew into an independent source of coordination and information. These clandestine organizations have not been in the focus of civil society observers, presumably because their discourses did not adapt to the terminology common among civil-society observers and human rights practitioners.

Examples of these clandestine organizations included the Coordinating Committee for the Rights and Freedoms of the Syndicates and Labor (CCR, al-Lagna al-Tansiqiya li al-Huquq wa al-Hurriya al-Niqabat wa al-'Amaliya), the Center for Trade Union and Worker Studies (CTUWS), the National Committee for the Defense of Workers Rights (NCDWR), or the Center for Socialist Studies (CSS). The CCR was led by Saber Barakat and Mohamed Abdel Sallam; the founder and head of the NCDWR was Ahmad Sharif, who had also been active in the independent workers' movement in the 1980s. The CSS was directed by the renowned leftist opposition figure Kamal Khalil. In accordance with the recent wave of Kifaya movements, a "Workers for Change" group was not missing. Another, though virtually defunct, organization ran under the banner Workers Committee for Political Parties (Lagna al-'Amal bi al-Ahzab al-Siasiya) (author's interview with Karam Saber).

The CCR has long been the most active and effective independent organization representing labor interests and could rely on its working relationship with two NGOs: the Land Center for Human Rights has collected information on workers' affairs, and the Hisham Mubarak Law Center has provided space in its Cairo headquarters for the Committee's meetings. These organizations have provided assistance in legal cases and information on labor issues; they have also published reports on labor conflicts. The CTUWS was led by Kamal Abbas and Adel Zakariya and was closed down by the security forces in April 2007, presumably because its leaders had begun to establish offices in those enterprises and industrial cities most affected by the protest waves (see *Middle East Times*, April 26, 2007; *Al-Ahram Weekly*, no. 843, May 3–9, 2007).

The leaders of these movements had a common biographical background: they all belonged to the "old working class"; they have been politicized in the workers' movement in the late Nasser and early Sadat years and suffered from statist repression when Sadat broke with his predecessor's political program. Contrary to fellow workers' leaders who have accepted their integration in the top-down etatist system of labor corporatism, at the head of which stands the GFTU, they became the initiators of an independent protest movement already in the late 1970s and during the 1980s (see Pripstein Posusney 1997).

The corporatist labor unions had come under increasing pressure during the recent wave of protests, even before its executive board was dissolved in the immediate post-Mubarak period. Economic demands—for example, for higher salaries and bonuses—were mixed on several occasions with an outspoken criticism of the unions. The protesting workers have accused them of negligence and inability to represent their interests and support their demands vis-à-vis the political decision makers. Apparently, the authorities' interference in labor union elections increased dramatically in the years prior to the 2011 uprising, which severely discredited these organizations in the eyes of the workers (author's interview with Mohammed Sayyid Sa'id). The workers criticized that union elections were generally rigged in favor of pro-government candidates. For example, during the Mahalla al-Kubra strike in December 2006, addressed above, which became a catalyst for the following protest wave, workers demanded the removal of "their" representatives in the union (see Beinin and El-Hamalawy 2007). These attacks even led to frictions within the corporatist union structure because a number of factory-based representations of labor unions gave in to the workers' pressure and started to support their demands, putting them at odds with the upper echelons of the GFTU. This happened on several occasions: in the Helwan-based Portland Cement Factory over the factory's privatization plans; in the Aura-Misr asbestos factory in summer 2005; and at Samuli Company, one of the few private enterprises that allowed the emergence of a workers' union in 2003 (author's interview with Ali Khaled).

Four indicators suggest that the wave of protests since late 2006 resemble in many respects the heydays of labor activism in the period 1977–1989. First, protests erupted in exactly those economic sectors and singular enterprises that have a history of contestation: in the textile sector and in the industrial enterprises in Kafr al-Dawwar and Mahalla al-Kubra. Second, strikes and sit-ins have become a regular phenomenon and have turned into mass protests that easily matched the numbers of the protests in the 1980s. Third, like in the 1980s, a clandestine network of organizations has been built independent of the official GFTU. The CCR and the CTUWS were the successor organizations, for instance, of the Committee for Defending Public Sector Workers, established in 1983, or the Popular Committee for Combating the Sale of the Public Sector; the workers' mouthpiece *Awraq al-Amalya* (Workers Papers) had a parent in 1986–1989, the *Sawt al-Amal* (Workers Voice) (author's interview with Saber Barakat; on the older organizations see Pripstein Posusney 1997, 225–30). Fourth, in order to contain the workers' uprising, the regime incumbents seem to have reinvigorated their scare-and-promise tactics successfully employed during the 1980s (see El Shafei 1995). When attempts failed to suppress an uprising at the very beginning, the three statist bodies that came into play there have often been employed in a "good cop, bad cop" manner: the security forces (*amn al-dawla*; *amn al-markaziya*) have remained a constant threat to the insurgent workers; the Ministry of Manpower acted as the official representation of the state and offered both threats and concessions; and the respective labor union officially represented workers' interests, but de facto it usually came into play as a negotiator in the conflict (author's interview with Mohammed Sayyed Sa'id).

Despite these similarities, the labor protests during the last decade also showed differences in comparison to labor activism in the 1980s. Most important, the labor force today has a much greater share of private-sector employees and laborers than in the 1980s. Khaled Ali, a human rights activist and presidential candidate in 2012, also claimed that the solidarity of workers was more distinctive in the 1980s. Singular strikes and actions had then, more often than not, triggered sympathy and the participation of workers from other factories (author's interview with Khaled Ali). Retrospectively, both the regime incumbents and the workers' activists might have underestimated the potential of the movement to induce change beyond the material interests of the sectoral constituencies of singular protests. Dina Bishara and Hesham Sallam did not claim that the workers triggered the January 25 uprising; but with their pro-revolutionary activities increasing in early February, they have strongly contributed to Mubarak's fall (see Sallam 2011; Bishara 2012).

Public Protest between Contestation and Regime Support

Tolerated opposition has taken different forms in Mubarak's Egypt: a number of human rights NGOs, the elitist, short-lived protest movement Kifaya, and a workers movement drawing significant mass support. Despite their obvious differences, all these movements have challenged a number of rules and procedures of the Egyptian authoritarian regime; they have used distinct entrapment strategies and, at the same time, have been used by the regime incumbents to bolster their image as representing a relatively liberal authoritarian polity.

The human rights NGOs, while small in numbers, have primarily acted against the institutionalized coercive mechanisms of authoritarian rule: the emergency law, human rights violations, and the authorities' foul play during elections. Their main strategy was a legal entrapment of the regime. They made abundant use of the judiciary system in which they invested a lot of trust, besides the fact that its autonomy was always put under siege by the authorities. As I will discuss below, the Egyptian judiciary had developed a spirit of independence, which made the court system a relatively promising playing field for human rights activists. In fact, given their relative insignificance (in numbers, popular support, and financial capacities), the human rights NGOs have been quite successful in the strategy of litigation.

These groups' full dedication and trust in the judicial system was revealed by some striking evidence after the fall of Mubarak when representatives of the human rights business defended presumed political opponents from what they perceived as unjust and illegal treatment. The Egyptian Organization for Human Rights officially criticized a parliamentary draft law, the idea of which was to bar former regime figures from participating in the presidential elections of May and June 2012. The EOHR's position was that the law was unconstitutional because neither the 1971 constitution, nor the interim constitutional declaration, issued by the Supreme Council of Armed Forces (SCAF) in March 2011, allowed for the exclusion of any individual from rallying for political office, for whatever reason. The law was finally endorsed by SCAF on April 24, 2012.

Equally striking was the personal involvement of the longtime human rights lawyer Khaled Ali in the defense of presidential candidate Hazem Saleh Abu Ismail. As a lawyer with strong leftist leanings, a human rights activist for the independent labor movement, Ali did not seem to have much in common with Abu Ismail, the Salafi candidate in the 2012 presidential elections. Moreover, Ali himself was a candidate in the presidential race, making the two direct competitors. Nevertheless, Khaled Ali won a verdict in front of the Administrative Court in Cairo to reinstate Abu Ismail's candidacy, who was later barred from the race on the grounds that his mother had allegedly held a foreign passport.

With its trust in legal procedures, the human rights activists have, on the one hand, achieved some political leverage that exceeded their limited influence and capacities. On the other hand, through their very existence, the human rights NGOs have supported the incumbents' claim to represent a relatively open and liberal political order. They have therefore contributed to the legitimacy dimension of authoritarian opposition politics.

The Kifaya movement has also challenged core rules and procedures of the Mubarak regime. Despite its discursive framing in targeting Mubarak, Kifaya's main impact was not that of an anti-system opposition because—owing to its lack of popular mass outreach—it did not constitute a counterhegemonic force that would have directly challenged the incumbents' hold on power. Rather, its main direct impact on politics concerned the regime's policy of strict red lines implemented by the security forces. Before the advent of Kifaya, the phenomenon of street politics and the targeting of the "Pharaoh" in popular opposition were tactics beyond the imagination of the opposition. Ever since Kifaya's appearance, the concept of red lines was not completely abandoned. There were still journalists censured and legally sentenced for their critical reporting on the president; and demonstrations have been dissolved by force. But the red lines as well as their implementation were subject to a great deal of insecurity; and the violation of assumed red lines, formerly well-established by the security forces and largely accepted by the opposition, became a feature as common as the prosecution of these violations.

Whereas Kifaya conducted a discursive entrapment strategy toward the regime, it also provided the incumbents with some good reasons for toleration. Kifaya members have contributed to the incumbents' menu of control in that they have channeled popular discontent among the urban, upper-middle-class intellectuals. Kifaya was seen, during a moment of political liberalization, as a harmless political happening of intellectuals, both young and old, who could vent their anger with the regime's policies. At the same time, the protest movement contributed to the fragmentation of opposition politics because, first, it was itself a fragmented movement, and second, it has distracted attention from the political parties for which Kifaya was in fact a greater challenge than for the incumbency, at least during 2005.

It is worth comparing the two protest movements discussed above, Kifaya and the independent labor movement. Contrary to elitist movements like Kifaya, workers do have strong contentious capacities because they represent a mass constituency. Therefore, and because worker strikes can hurt the country's economic performance, labor protests contain an imminent political threat for the incumbents, whereas Kifaya did not. On the other hand, labor protests have a difficult task in sustaining organizational capacities; such protests tend to come to the fore as singular upsurges rather than an institutionalized opposition. Lack of organizational capacities was not the main problem of the "backroom" elitist troublemakers of Kifaya.

With respect to the materialization of the goals of the two types of protest movements, the workers have been more successful than Kifaya. Ironically, the usually economic nature of the workers' claims made the movement a greater challenger to the political incumbents than the anti-incumbent discourse of Kifaya. The workers' movement played on a co-optative entrapment strategy in that its constituency—since Nasser considered a segment of society providing regime support—threatened to defect from the corporatist structure of the state. The labor movement comprised singular upsurges that raised *petty demands*: higher wages, the workers' stake in a process of privatization, compensation in the course of an enterprise's liquidation. They have been usually addressed positively by the regime during negotiations. However, concessions were often successful in that they prevented sustained and protracted contestation. The incumbents' reactions to the events in Mahalla al-Kubra on April 6, 2008, was telling: on Labor Day, May 1, 2008, President Mubarak announced a substantial raise of the salaries and wages of public-sector workers and employees. The politics of concessions have not been a possible strategy with the *universal demands* of Kifaya: democratization and Mubarak's removal from political power. This proved detrimental for Kifaya in 2006—and for the regime in February 2011, when it did not have the capacities in hand to engineer concessions toward a popular movement reiterating Kifaya's demand but comprised of a mass constituency.

4

Anti-System Opposition

The Islamist Challenge

The Islamist movement constitutes the strongest political force in Egyptian politics. Political Islam in Mubarak's Egypt was composed of three forms of movement organizations: a moderate Islamist mass movement based on strong popular backing, a number of clandestine groups and would-be parties that have been loosely associated with the Brotherhood-dominated mainstream political Islam, and radical groups that have engaged the state in militant activism between the mid-1970s and 1997. Whereas the Muslim Brotherhood and the smaller mainstream organizations composed an anti-system opposition to the ruling incumbents, the militant movements offered a form of political resistance that was not based on a minimum degree of mutual acceptance between the relevant Islamists and the incumbency.

The Muslim Brotherhood

Some observers of Egyptian politics held that the core organization of politically relevant Islamic activism, the Muslim Brotherhood, was the only "real" opposition in the country. The Muslim Brotherhood (al-Ikhwan al-Muslimun, MB) was founded in 1928 by Hassan al-Banna, and was, at that time, the first organized form of Islamic contentious activism not only in Egypt but in the whole Muslim world. The MB quickly emerged as a powerful movement in pre-1952 Egypt. Most groups and movements in other countries, from the ambit of political Islam, trace their roots back, in one way or another, to the Brotherhood (see Ansari 1984a; Lia 1998; Gerges 2000; Munson 2001; Aclimandos 2002).

The Muslim Brotherhood has been, since its inception, the main source of trouble for those who controlled the state in Egypt: the British administration until 1952 and the different Egyptian authoritarian regimes afterward, including the Supreme Council of Armed Forces, which took over power from Mubarak. In order to account for the rapid rise of the movement, one should keep in mind that two ideological traits highlighted by the Brotherhood happened to be particularly appealing to the populace in Egypt: the movement's call to apply Islamic principles for the transformation of society, culture, politics, and the economy; and its struggle against the British occupation of the country.

The Nasserist coup in 1952 marked a first decisive turning point for the Brothers: they initially welcomed the end of the British occupation, but quickly found themselves caught in a fierce power struggle with the new regime of the Free Officers. Gamal Abdel Nasser won this fight by resorting to blunt repression and by incarcerating thousands of Islamists. This, in turn, led to the radicalization of parts of the Islamist movement. Inspired by radical thinkers, of whom the most influential was Sayyid Qutb, Islamist radicalization triggered the emergence of militant groups and splinter factions of the Muslim Brotherhood. Such underground extremist movements included the *Islamic Jihad* (Struggle), the *Jama'a Islamiya* (Islamic Group), and the *Takfir wa al-Hijra* (Excommunication and Flight). These groups quickly turned away from the Brotherhood and resorted to a militant struggle with the aim to overthrow the Egyptian regime, lasting from the late 1970s to 1997.

The Muslim Brotherhood, however, denounced violence as a means of political action in the early 1970s and entered the political scene again when Nasser's successor, Anwar Sadat, discretely encouraged the Islamists in an attempt to counterbalance secular opposition from Nasserist, Marxist, and nationalist circles. In an ironic twist, the Islamist resurgence encouraged by Sadat in the 1970s proved to become a genie that escaped the bottle in 1981 when Sadat was assassinated by the Islamic Jihad. With this political move, Sadat laid down the origins for the demise of the secular opposition forces and, at the same time, for the strengthening of Islamism in Egypt at large. The country's universities became the harbor for the resurgence of Islamist activism and the birthplace of a new generation of activists. Those members of the MB that joined the organization as university students in the 1970s have formed the so-called middle generation of activists (*gil al-wasat*) or the generation of the 1970s (*gil al-saba'inat*). Interestingly, this new generation of activists appeared on the scene in the 1970s as members of those student organizations that formed the nucleus of the Jama'a Islamiya. Before it radicalized and its activists went underground, some of its members decided to join the mainstream organization of political Islam, the Muslim Brotherhood. Whereas this new generation contributed to a profound reorientation and politicization of the Brotherhood, the organization—and the processes and experiences associated with the necessary bargaining and compromise within it—led to the moderation of these younger fellows.

Often referred to as the younger generation in relation to an aging leadership, the *gil al-saba'inat* were, at the time of writing this book, in their late fifties and early sixties. From the late 1970s onward, they were responsible for the politicization of the Muslim Brotherhood, which embraced the demand to participate in the formal political institutions, particularly in parliamentary elections and in the professional syndicates (see Al-Awadi 2004; El-Ghobashy 2005; Utvik 2005). Prominent members of this strata include Abdel Mun'eim Abul Futuh (who defected from the MB shortly after Mubarak's fall and was a candidate in the 2012 presidential elections), Essam al-Irian (one of the most prominent members of this generation), Mahmoud Ezzat (who lost in prominence after a leadership reshuffle in early 2010), Mohammed Habib (former deputy head of the MB, resigned in 2010), as well as the Wasat Party founder Abu al-Ela Maadi.

A deep social transformation under Sadat led to the marginalization of parts of the middle classes, which proved to become a constant source of societal support for the Islamists. As Carry Wickham has shown in her seminal study *Mobilizing Islam* (2002), Islamist outreach fell on fertile soil within Egyptian society at large. While diffuse support among the rural and urban poor has been difficult to evaluate in the absence of free and fair elections, the Brotherhood can certainly count on large popular support from the urban lower middle classes of society.

As of today, the MB stands out, compared to other political forces in the country, with respect to the strength of its organizational capacities.[1] The movement is tightly organized along hierarchical arrangements, at the top of which stand the Supreme Guide (*murshid al-'amm*) and his two deputies. During much of the late Mubarak years, the leadership of the MB was occupied by Mohammed Mahdi Akef, the last *murshid al-'amm* out of the older generation of MB leaders who experienced the repressive period under Nasser. Akef was a MB member since 1950 and was sentenced to a twenty-year prison term for the alleged involvement in an attempt on Nasser's life. Contrary to his predecessors, such as Mustafa Mashour (*murshid al-'amm* until his death, November 14, 2002) and Ma'mun al-Hodaybi (until January 8, 2004), who have been criticized for their authoritative leadership styles, Akef has adopted a more open, politicized, and confrontational course that has long been advocated by the middle generation of activists who have subsequently occupied most of the posts in the *maktab al-irshad*. Akef's deputies, Mohammed Habib and Khairat al-Shater, were chosen from the younger cadres of the organization.

Akef was replaced, in a silent internal coup in late December 2009, by Mohammed Badie. In a subsequent reshuffling of the internal leadership, the group around Mohammed Habib, Abdel Mun'eim Abul Futuh, Essam al-Irian, Mahmoud Ezzat, and the university professor Abdel Hamid al-Ghazzali lost influence in the organization. Whereas Badie and a number of low-profile members would represent the Muslim Brotherhood as a social movement, its political wing would be represented by businessman Khairat al-Shater (the MB's strongman behind the scene after the ousting of Mubarak), Saad El-Katatni (speaker of the first post-Mubarak parliament), and Mohammed Morsi (the MB's official candidate in the 2012 presidential elections and chairman of its Justice and Development Party); Essam al-Irian has remained an influential figure in the organization.

The MB's sixteen-members-strong Guidance Bureau (*maktab al-irshad*) selects the organization's leadership and functions as its executive

---

1. The reader will find a very insightful empirical account on the Muslim Brotherhood's organization and social outreach in Munson (2001).

board. It is supported by a consultative council that is, together with the Guidance Bureau, supposed to elect the organization's leader. At the lower organizational strata, the Muslim Brotherhood maintains offices and representatives not only in every governorate of the country, but also in all bigger cities and even in smaller villages and settlements. Two documents provide a legal basis for the organization of the Brotherhood: the Basic Order, issued after the meeting of a General Assembly on September 8, 1945; and the General Order, issued on July 29, 1982 (Rashwan et al. 2007, 169). The organization's working agenda is reflected in special departments in which day-to-day work on specific issues is coordinated. For instance, there is a "political section" subdivided into the "political," "economic," and "information unit." The "technical section" supervises activities in the professional syndicates and comprises several subdivisions, like the "labor unit," the "women section," and the "social section" (author's interviews with Abdel Hamid al-Ghazzali and Mohammed Habib).

Clearly, the Brotherhood's organizational structures and capacities stand out among political forces in Egypt. Emad Shahin maintained that the Brotherhood had the most efficient and well-performing political apparatus in the country (author's interview with Emad Shahin).[2] This holds true despite obscure regulations concerning the election of the *murshid al-'amm*, which led, at several times, to internal struggles and leadership crises after the death of the Brotherhood's leaders (see Rashwan et al. 2007, 165–71). Yet, in contrast to other Islamist factions, the concept of a viable organizational body (*tanzim*) has remained central in the thinking of the Muslim Brotherhood. Despite the legal restrictions established by the authorities, outreach toward the public was engineered in this organizational network that has literally reached every corner in the country and facilitated the coordination of the Brothers' work in the professional syndicates, schools, universities and student unions, clubs, and charity organizations. As concerns active support, the Muslim Brotherhood (and other

2. See also Shehata and Stacher (2006) for the Brotherhood's performance in the 2005 parliament. The most in-depth account on the organizational body of the MB is by Richard Mitchell (1969, 163–80).

Islamist groups) built up its basis during the 1970s in the country's public universities. From the end of the 1980s onward, the Brothers controlled the student unions in all major universities including those in Cairo, Alexandria, Mansura, and also al-Azhar universities (Al-Awadi 2005, 64).

The strong capacities of the Brotherhood's organizational machine could be witnessed in the competitive electoral contests of the post-Mubarak era, in particular a constitutional referendum on March 19, 2011, in which the MB helped to endorse nine constitutional amendments in a popular vote by 77 percent. The result is a remarkable indicator of the MB's mobilization capacities because the amendments were highly contested in public debates prior to the vote. In the following parliamentary elections of late 2011 and January 2012, the Muslim Brotherhood's new Freedom and Justice Party (Hizb al-Hurriya wa al-'Adala, FJP) secured around 45 percent of the seats, making it by far the strongest single force in the immediate post-Mubarak era. And in the presidential elections of June 2012, Mohammed Morsi—at the time a comparatively low-profile MB member—acceded to the presidency, yet by a low margin in comparison to his competitors.

Even in the Mubarak years, when the Muslim Brotherhood has been the main target of statist containment strategies, singular instances reveal the popularity and mobilization capacities of the movement—in conjunction with its readiness to show strong performances, particularly in parliamentary elections. The most striking example was the Brotherhood's success in the 2005 elections that witnessed the group to occupy eighty-eight seats (20 percent of total seats), even though it had only contested 170 seats.

The spectacular performance in 2005 would not have been possible without this efficient organizational body and the high degree of personal determination on the part of MB activists. The focus on organizational coherence has guaranteed, for a long time, a high degree of stability and homogeneity among the MB's ranks. This, however, has not prevented the occurrence of rifts between competing factions. Fissures within the organization have persisted between moderate and more radical proponents, between different generations of activists, and between social-movement oriented members and a more politicized faction of activists (author's interview with Diaa Rashwan; see also El-Ghobashy 2005, 385–87). Yet, the siege put upon the organization by the state's security apparatus has prevented these fissures from turning into open conflict. Internally divided, the Muslim Brothers have successfully drawn a disciplined picture until the breakdown of the Mubarak order. Only on rare instances has internal dissent emanated in the split of factions, as was the case with the Wasat Party in 1997.

With Mubarak's fall, and the subsequent political opening in the transition period, the state's repressive straightjacket was stripped of, and internal cohesion was put to a test. Several key figures, such as Mohammed Habib and Abdel Mun'eim Abul Futuh, left the Muslim Brotherhood and formed rivaling organizations. Moreover, the movement's youth, among which Abul Futuh enjoys strong support, has become increasingly critical of the MB leadership. A number of prominent youth members, among whom were Mohammed al-Kassas and Ahmed Abdel Gawad, broke with the MB after Abul Futuh was dismissed from the organization and formed their own party, the Egyptian Current Party (al-Tayyar al-Masry), to back the MB dissidents Abul Futuh and Habib.

In addition to its organizational capacities, two intertwined dimensions determine the success of the Muslim Brotherhood's quest for popular support: the provision of ideational and material incentives. Concerning the content of the Brotherhood's ideology, it should be noted that its political program has remained vague. Using the Islamic concept of *da'wa* (call), the Brotherhood fell short of offering a comprehensive political program, but called, in very general terms, for the re-Islamicization of Egyptian society and the application of Islamic law, *shari'a*, to law and politics. Other Islamic concepts include the call for the payment of religious alms, *zakat*, which has been developed as an important source for financing a parallel Islamic economic sector. The principal of *umma* (Muslim community) pronounces the quest for an outreach transcending national borders. Since the early 1990s, internal discussions on the relationship between Islam and democracy—often referring to the Islamic principle of *shura* (consultations in the realm of authority)—have intensified, and so did the politicization of discourses among the Brothers. This culminated in the formation, in September 2007, of a draft political program that was primarily designed to indicate the MB's dedication for parliamentary presentation and eventually party formation.[3] In April 2011, Khairat al-Shater announced, as part of his presidential bid (later turned down by the authorities), a new program of sorts, called *Nahda* (Renaissance) Project, which introduced a technical, economic terminology. It is a clear signal of the MB's preparedness to accept a major role in the governing procedures of the post-Mubarak era. That the movement's political ideology has remained largely vague, as of the fall of Mubarak, was in large part due to the fact that the organization was never called on materializing its visions. But there is no doubt that the Brotherhoods' political and social agenda would systemically alter public life in Egypt if they ever came to fully take over executive power.

The moderate Islamist current has, in the course of the 2000s, smoothly adapted to the dominant political debates, inspired by a secular discourse on civil rights and freedoms, the abolition of the emergency law and human rights abuses, and free and fair elections. Already in the 1990s, the reformist discourse figured prominently within the Islamist current, particularly among a growing moderate-centrist faction of the movement called *wasatiya* (see Baker 2003). More recently, the Muslim Brothers have adapted their discourses on central political-programmatic traits—such as the source of law and rule making, the exertion of state power, the protection of civil rights and liberties, and popular participation in politics—to the thinking of moderate Islamist intellectuals, the most important of whom are Yusuf al-Qaradawi (based in Qatar), Tareq al-Bishri (a well-respected former judge), Salim al-Awwa (a prominent Wasat Party intellectual and presidential election candidate in 2012), and Ahmad Kamal Abul Magd (see Rutherford 2006).

The new dynamic took root primarily among the younger generation of Islamist activists, in particular at the country's universities. Islamist thinking was increasingly associated with Western ideas of modernity,

---

3. The draft program introduced an idiosyncratic mixture of basic democratic principles and Islamic-fundamentalist positions including the establishment of shari'a-based legal punishment (see Lübben 2008).

efficiency, and management. This ideological reorientation among the younger Islamists has gained particular momentum through the appearance of the celebrated "secular" preachers, such as Amr Khaled. Khaled's outreach represented a new form of "Islamic televangelism." Apart from spreading the new tones via satellite TV, the Internet and social media became the prime source of outreach for the younger generation. In the political arena, the Wasat Party remained, according to Patrick Haenni, "the clearest political manifestation of the new thinking" (author's interview with Patrick Haenni).

These new tones indicated not only substantial intellectual revisions within the Muslim Brotherhood, but also more politico-strategic considerations: it was one aim of the MB to strive for a revision of the Western (and specifically the American) perspective on Islamist movements in general and the Egyptian Brotherhood in particular. Indeed, following the 2005 elections and the MB's presence in parliament, a careful rethinking may have commenced on the side of US foreign policymakers who have become increasingly open to engage in dialogue with the moderate Islamists. In 2007, several meetings had occurred between US government officials and MB representatives. Whereas the Egyptian regime was obviously not amused about these meetings and continued to emphasize that the Brotherhood was an "illegal" and "terrorist" organization, a modus vivendi was reached by emphasizing that meetings were held informally with independent parliamentarians. Nevertheless, the warming up of relations between the MB and the US administration contained a substantial challenge to the Egyptian regime's strategy to legitimize repressive countermeasures toward the Brotherhood by referring to its "illegal" and "fundamentalist" stature.

Surprisingly or not, the Brotherhood's programmatic fuzziness did not harm its appeal toward the populace. One decisive reason for the popularity of political Islam is that rival ideologies of Western origin, such as socialism, Marxism, capitalism, or nationalism, were severely discredited in the 1980s and gave way to an ideology that was perceived as autochthonous and based on Arab-Islamic roots. Islamic ideology was also accompanied by the movement's provision of social security services that the Egyptian regime had set up in the Nasser era and during the early

Sadat years but could not maintain any longer in times of economic crisis. Financed by a parallel Islamic economic sector, the Muslim Brotherhood has capitalized politically on the proliferation of services, jobs, and material benefits through private mosques and Islamic voluntary associations. The organization has provided jobs, education, and healthcare as well as hardship funds and other charitable services.

The extent of financial flows through Islamic channels is unknown. However, we may reasonably speak of a parallel economic sector, as it is largely uncontrolled by the state (see Wickham 2002, 100; Utvik 2006). Sources to finance charitable services include Islamic banks and investment companies, Egyptian residents in the Gulf countries, the profit-making activities of Islamic associations, and donations from wealthy Egyptians, such as millionaires Khairat al-Shater (a businessman with trade ties in the entire MENA region) and Hassan Malek, or the "MB-financiers" Youssuf Nada (a Swiss-based businessman of Egyptian origin) and Abdel-Rahman Saudi (owner of a chain of supermarkets). As Emad Shahin maintained, however, the central source of power for the older generation within the Muslim Brotherhood was comprised of small- and middle-scale donations from private individuals, mostly economically successful, semi-educated middle-class people (author's interview with Emad Shahin).

A whole plethora of private mosques and religious endowments (*awqaf*) have served as the main transmission belt for the provision of social services. Estimates claim that, in 1993, 170,000 mosques existed in Egypt, of which only around 30,000 were sanctioned and controlled by the state; roughly half of all PVAs were supposedly religious foundations (Wickham 2002, 98–99). Whereas we cannot equate the entirety of the parallel Islamic sector with the Muslim Brotherhood, the latter is by far the largest and most important single organization of Islamist social outreach. Other organizations and associations were of an apolitical nature, and the militant groups have also provided social services (Toth 2003).

The Egyptian regime has been on high alert with the growth of this parallel Islamic sector since it lost credibility and, as a consequence, political legitimacy to the Islamists. Clearly, when Hosni Mubarak came to power in 1981, he did not face an easy task in coping with the Islamist movement awakened under his predecessor. His regime was confronted with the challenge of both radical underground groups and a moderate Islamist mass movement that was independent from government control and deeply rooted within society. It does not come as a surprise that the regime's repressive reflexes against the Muslim Brotherhood have been more intense compared to secular opposition groups. This "siege" by the state security forces was not caused by radical Islamist views expressed by the Muslim Brotherhood but by the regime's perception that this organization was the only potent, autonomous social force outside of regime control. In the words of Eberhard Kienle, "the conflict was less about ideology than about power and the spoils associated with it" (Kienle 2004, 74).

On the other hand, the Brotherhood has been particularly accommodating as concerns its means of political action. Ever since the devastating experience under Gamal Abdel Nasser, the Muslim Brothers have tried to escape harsh repression to the extent that they have been extremely cautious not to provoke the regime. Nabil Abdel Fattah observed a general "transformation of the Islamist phenomena from the political field to social, cultural, and symbolic markets" (author's interview with Nabil Abdel Fattah). The focus on social work was certainly a response to the harsh treatment of the group following its victory in the 2005 parliamentary elections. Starting in 2006, the security forces' reactions resulted in several thousand MB members' serving prison terms.

Despite the often coercive treatment, the Brothers have refrained from confronting the regime openly and, instead, have employed a more gradual agenda. For instance, in the turbulent times of spring 2005—when the regime was aware of increasing opposition activism and the MB became a likely target of coercion—the Brotherhood tried to placate the regime in that it announced to even support Hosni Mubarak in his hold of the presidency (Aclimandos 2006, 84). The Muslim Brothers have made only limited use of their social mass support in order to confront the regime openly. Instead, they have followed a more discrete strategy of infiltrating political institutions over which the regime had lost control, at least temporarily. Examples here are the Brothers' successful engagement in student unions and the professional syndicates (see Wickham 1997;

Fahmy 1998; El-Ghobashy 2005, 380). Since the fall of Mubarak, the Brotherhood has capitalized on the new political freedoms and revised its stance to refocus on political matters proper, clearly indicated in Khairat al-Shater's *Nahda* Project.

The Regime and the Brothers: Conflict and Containment

The conflict between the Mubarak regime and the Muslim Brotherhood was not a struggle between two ideologically distinct camps, that is, between a *secular* state and *religious* fundamentalism. True, Muslim Brotherhood representatives have expressed (and continue to do so) fundamentalist views, but so did parts of the incumbency. During the 1990s, most Islamist campaigns against liberal intellectuals were launched by pillars of the state (al-Azhar) or by established political parties (New Wafd Party, Socialist Labor Party), but not by the Muslim Brotherhood. The reason for the regime's harsh reaction toward the Muslim Brotherhood is simple. Not only by the regime but also in the eyes of the majority of the secular opposition and intellectuals, the Brothers were perceived as a dangerous threat because it has enjoyed a solid basis of popular support.

In order to contain the Islamist movement, Mubarak's regime employed a two-sided strategy. Whereas the radical Jihad and Jama'a Islamiya were put under heavy-handed pressure through the security apparatus, the moderate Muslim Brotherhood was given some opportunity to become a player in the political institutions. As discussed above, political liberalization during the 1980s had led to the emergence of a multiparty system and elections, the creation of "civil society" organizations, and the politicization of professional syndicates. Thus, a playground emerged for those among the Muslim Brotherhood who have advocated activism in these political institutions. In the first decade of his rule, Mubarak conceded to the Islamists' demands for political inclusion to some degree. The Brothers' activities, however, have been closely observed from the very first minute they entered the political arena. Most important, the regime did not tolerate the creation of a political party. The Brothers were allowed to participate in the elections of the parliament and professional syndicates only as independent candidates.

In the 1984 and 1987 parliamentary elections, the Brotherhood formed alliances with secular opposition parties. Cooperation among opposition groups in the 1984 and 1987 elections was incentivized by the election law that required political parties to pass an 8 percent threshold in order to be represented in parliament. In 1984, the Brotherhood formed an alliance with the New Wafd Party; in 1987, members of the Muslim Brotherhood and other Islamist associations joined with the Socialist Labor Party and the Liberal Party to form the Islamic Alliance. From 1984 to 1987, they increased their seats in parliament from around ten seats to approximately thirty-six (see Abed-Kotob 1995, 328; Ghadbian 1997, 91).

The Brothers' activities in the professional syndicates were also significant and successful. Between 1987 and 1992, Islamists took over the majority in the boards of the engineers', the doctors', and the lawyers' syndicates. The Muslim Brotherhood's success in Egypt's political life could no longer be ignored after the Brothers' sweeping victory in the board elections of the Bar Association in September 1992. This syndicate had always been a traditional stronghold of liberal forces (see Wickham 1997; Fahmy 1998).

The parliamentary elections in the early 1990s marked a decisive turning point in the regime-Brotherhood relationship. Since then, the "honeymoon period" of the 1980s was over and the Muslim Brotherhood has come under siege from coercive containment emanating in a policy of minimal toleration (see Lust-Okar 2005, 140; Al-Awadi 2005; Albrecht and Wegner 2006). In the early 1990s, the Egyptian regime was alarmed by the Algerian experience where Islamists challenged the military-backed government in elections to an unprecedented extent, later triggering a military coup d'état, followed by a decade of civil war. While the Egyptian regime has always differentiated between the moderate Muslim Brotherhood and the more radical groups, such as the Jama'a Islamiya and Jihad, the latter's militant initiative during the 1990s has almost certainly impaired opportunities for the Brothers since it has increased diffuse fears on the part of the regime of an Islamist revolution.

Neither the organization itself nor the Brotherhood's mouthpiece *al-Da'wa* was legally recognized by the authorities on the formal grounds that the Egyptian constitution prohibited political parties based on religion. MB members have been subject to regular observation and harassment by the security forces; coercive measures of the state included the arbitrary arrest of the Brotherhood's rank and file and also prominent activists, particularly in the run-up to the parliamentary elections in 1995 and 2000. Members of the Brotherhood felt "besieged" at the time, according to Essam al-Irian, one of the prominent members of the organization's middle generation held in custody between 1995 and 2000 (author's interview with Essam al-Irian). Prominent members of the *gil al-wasat* who have spent terms in prison between 1995 and 2000 were Abdel Mun'eim Abul Futuh, Essam al-Irian, Mahmoud Ezzat, and Mohammed Habib. In total, the security roundup led to the sentencing by a military court of thirty-eight Brothers to five years and fifty-seven to two years in prison.

Islamist candidates have been severely hampered during election campaigns and also in the course of parliamentary sessions. Among those who succeeded in winning a seat, some Islamists have been removed because they have been seen as too active and critical. One of the most prominent examples here is the case of Gamal Heshmat. An active member of the medical syndicate and Brotherhood bigwig in Alexandria, Heshmat was ousted from parliament in January 2003. Heshmat claimed to be among the most active opposition figures in the 2000 parliament but emphasized that he had not deliberately crossed a red line (author's interview with Gamal Heshmat). Azab Mustafa, from Giza governorate, was another Muslim Brother removed from parliament.

The Muslim Brotherhood was also barred from the political dialogue with other opposition forces in the country (i.e., legalized political parties and the human rights NGOs). Any liaison between the Muslim Brotherhood and another opposition force has been, since the late 1980s, under suspicion by the security forces (author's interview with Mohammed Habib). On the one hand, it was therefore discouraging for the secular opposition to coalesce with the Brothers in an attempt to form a broad support base against the incumbents. On the other hand, communication between the Brothers and the regime has been, until the fall of Mubarak, maintained almost exclusively via security channels (*amn al-dawla*), a clear indication of the authorities' perception of the MB as a security threat. Informal communication channels between single Brothers and regime members have been maintained in the corridors of parliament, some professional syndicates (particularly the press syndicate), and universities (mainly Cairo University) (author's interviews with several MB members).

The fact that the regime's political representatives ignored the MB is noteworthy because they did communicate with other opposition forces, including Islamists. One striking example is a meeting between Safwat al-Sherif and members of the socialist-turned-Islamist SLP in November 2004, during which the un-freezing of that party was discussed (author's interview with SLP representative who asked to remain anonymous). The Socialist Labor Party had an Islamist background too, but it was obviously not perceived by the regime as a security threat. The fact that the incumbents did communicate with the SLP, but not with the Brotherhood, supports the judgment that they did not have any principal prejudices against Islamists as such, but perceived the MB as its one and only serious political rival.

Whereas the Muslim Brotherhood has formally remained an illegal organization and was subject to decidedly higher degrees of coercion than the secular opposition, there were some signs that repression was never the regime's sole answer toward the movement. On the toleration side of the game, the regime never made the attempt to destroy the organizational capacities of the movement. Despite substantial restrictions throughout the 1990s, the MB formed the largest opposition block in the 2000 parliament with seventeen members, all formally independent but affiliated with the Muslim Brotherhood. It was also allowed, as an officially "illegal organization," to maintain two Cairo offices on Roda Island: one main office of the organization (run by Mohammed Habib) and another one regulating the activities of the movement's parliamentary group (headed by Saad Katatny). The MB also has quite openly maintained dependencies in other cities in the country; and the coordination of activities has been organized in the professional syndicates, the boards of which were under the control of the Brothers. The organization has occupied some public space in the media, in particular in the electronic media,[4] although

4. The organization's own website is www.ikhwanweb.com; another prominent source is www.islamonline.net.

its own print organ, *al-Da'wa*, has been banned from publishing. On some very rare occasions, the regime has even cooperated actively with the Muslim Brotherhood, for example when they jointly organized a public rally against the US-led military campaign against Saddam Husayn's Iraq on March 27 and 28, 2003 (author's interview with Farida Naqqash; see also *Cairo Times*, April 3–9, 2003).

As mentioned above, the Brotherhood was usually reluctant to make full use of its popularity and challenge the regime openly. During the last decade, however, this low-key policy was replaced by a more confrontational stance. In the course of 2005, which came to be known as the year of the "Cairo spring" owing to a more liberal window of opportunity offered by the regime, the Brotherhood's leadership decided to join in the street politics invented by Kifaya, mobilizing its supporters to launch demonstrations of their own. The Kifaya phenomenon was an opportunity for the MB. Clearly, the decision to take to the streets marked a fundamental change in the Brotherhood's stance toward the regime. The latter had always communicated to the Brotherhood that it would not accept any public demonstrations by the Islamists on domestic issues. The movement had given in to these demands, making no use of its large societal backing. The Brothers have previously organized mass demonstrations, but they were either of an apolitical nature (e.g., at the funerals of late leaders) or sanctioned by the state, such as the aforementioned anti-Iraq war rally of April 2003. Things can change: a first rally was held in downtown Cairo on March 27, 2005, cordoned off by a massive security presence. In the following weeks, demonstrations took place in the capital and other governorates of the country. Contrary to the Kifaya demonstrations, the Brotherhood has mobilized crowds of up to ten thousand participants (see Aclimandos 2006, 85–86).

Concurrent with the movement's limited appearance on the Egyptian street, the Muslim Brotherhood joined in the debate on political reforms. In March 2004, the organization launched a reform initiative comprising eighteen articles that was important in two ways (see Rashwan et al. 2007, 184): first, it underlined the Brotherhood's willingness to accept the principles of democratic governance, such as political pluralism, freedom of speech, and the rotation of power at regular intervals. Second, the very fact that the organization issued such a statement made it clear to observers, followers, and the political regime alike that the Muslim Brotherhood had entered a clear path toward participating in politics proper, irrespective of whether the foundation of a political party would be authorized or not. In late April 2005, MB representatives in parliament raised their voices against the constitutional amendments to article 76 of the Egyptian constitution. Soon thereafter, the organization announced its boycott of both the electoral referendum on the amendments and the presidential elections of September 2005.

In late 2005, the Brotherhood scored its biggest electoral success in the Mubarak era: in the parliamentary elections, the Islamists won eighty-eight of 444 seats, although they had contested only around 170 seats. Two main factors account for this astonishing success of a movement that was always subject to a high degree of statist repression. First, the MB took the elections, in contrast to the presidential referendum, extremely seriously; thus, its performance reflected careful planning, ample organizational and financial capacities, and the decision to trade in its history as a social movement for a new identity as a serious political player and would-be party. The MB leadership emphasized, already in December 2004, that they had no intentions to participate in the presidential elections in mid-2005 (author's interviews with Mohammed Mahdi Akef and Mohammed Habib). The focus was entirely on the parliamentary elections. Whereas, ahead of the elections, other opposition forces and the NDP were still engaged in intensive discussions on the opportunities and legal framework as well as on the appropriate electoral strategy, the Brotherhood had already developed different agendas and scenarios that could be applied according to the legal framework and political circumstances ruling the electoral process.

Second, the Brothers benefited from a political window of opportunity. Driven by international pressure and internal rifts within the ruling party, the regime was ready to grant a degree of openness in the elections unprecedented in Mubarak's Egypt. Consequently, after the Islamists' success in the first two electoral rounds (on November 9 and 20, 2005), the authorities established countermeasures against the Brotherhood in order to make sure that its presence in parliament would not grow any larger.

Out of their total share of eighty-eight seats, the Brotherhood managed to win only twelve seats in the last electoral round held on December 8. This third round was marked by the usual degree of violence and ballot-rigging, and left several people dead and wounded along with an alleged thirteen hundred Brotherhood supporters in custody (see Meital 2006; El-Ghobashy 2006). This was followed, in the years 2006 and onward, by a substantial shift in regime policies toward the MB that witnessed an increasingly coercive stance unseen in Egypt since the second half of the 1990s: during several security round-ups, thousands of MB activists and supporters were arrested, the most prominent of whom were Essam al-Irian, Mahmoud Ezzat, and Khairat al-Shater. On April 15, 2008, a military court handed down severe jail sentences on twenty-five members of the Brotherhood for up to ten years. The most prominent victim was the MB's number three, Khairat al-Shater, who received a sentence of ten years.

The prominent representation of the Muslim Brotherhood in parliament since the 2005 elections had a significant consequence also on the internal stakes of the MB organization. While not formally recognized and legally tolerated, the Brotherhood has established organizational structures of a mass-based political movement that shows in essence every sign of a political party. Another important step in this direction came in spring 2007: the issuance of a political program by the Brotherhood's parliamentary group and under the guidance of Essam al-Irian, which presented a political, social, and economic agenda.

With the ongoing politicization of the Muslim Brotherhood came about the creation of parallel proto-party structures (see Ferrié 2006). This process had already started with the representation of the MB in the 2000 parliament, which hosted seventeen "independent" members who were in essence MB members, the largest opposition block in that parliament. Whereas this move was not legally recognized, the Brotherhood was quick to establish a parliamentary group within its own organization. The group's speaker, Mohammed Morsi, became a second, unofficial spokesperson of the Muslim Brotherhood mainly in political affairs. Morsi, who would replace Khairat al-Shater as the MB's official candidate in the 2012 presidential elections, was succeeded after the 2005 elections by Hamdi Hassan and, later, Saad al-Katatni. These proto-party structures and the experience of the Muslim Brotherhood in parliamentary politics during the 2000s certainly facilitated the formation of the Freedom and Justice Party after Mubarak's fall and the Muslim Brotherhood's rise to the country's strongest political force.

During the Mubarak years, however, one should not overestimate the impact of this parliamentary group because those Brotherhood figures with the greatest influence within the organization often refrained from campaigning for a seat in parliament. This was a consequence of the experience in the 1990s: in the run-up to the 1995 and 2000 elections, the authorities' detention of MB candidates was a common feature. With the candidacy for parliament becoming a potential personal sacrifice to the MB's overall cause, the organization decided to protect its most influential members from prison.

The fall of the Mubarak regime had a tremendous impact on the Muslim Brotherhood. Previously a closed, coherent, and tightly organized movement, dedicated preachers and politicians alike, the organization has experienced two processes that might fundamentally alter the internal stakes of the Muslim Brotherhood. First, the MB is on a clear path from a social movement to a political organization, with the FJP becoming a considerable force in the country's political institutions. In the immediate transition period after Mubarak's fall, the top brass of its leadership has appeared on the political scene and strives to enter political institutions with the aim of occupying executive positions.

Second, the MB as a social movement has experienced its disintegration into different organizational units, the interrelations of which remain uncertain. Whereas the Freedom and Justice Party and the MB as a mother organization have remained tightly knit in the immediate transition period, the movement has experienced a significant number of defections among its youth as well as its top personnel. In addition, a Salafi movement—hitherto mainly apolitical—has quickly emerged into a significant political force, represented by several political parties (the Nour Party being the most efficient) and individuals (the preacher Hazem Salah Abu Ismail becoming a charismatic political figure during his campaign for presidency in early 2012). With the Islamic Bloc (al-Kutla al-Islamiya), a coalition of Salafi parties and the Jama'a Islamiya, winning almost 28 percent of the votes in the 2011 parliamentary elections, the Muslim Brotherhood has clearly lost its monopoly to represent the Islamist current in politics and society.

The Wasat Party

Apart from the new Salafi movement, which was in the process of formation and institutionalization at the time of writing this book, other groups in the ambit of political Islam existed prior to Mubarak's fall. There were a number of small groups and movements that were either breakaway factions of the MB or independent political groups with an Islamist background. An important point of distinction can be made with respect to the degree of militancy that characterizes political action: on the one hand, there was a number of groups that complemented the realm of moderate mainstream Islamism dominated by the Muslim Brotherhood; on the other hand, a number of small radical groups have come into being that have engaged the regime into a civil-war like scenario during the 1990s.

Examples of smaller groups of mainstream Islamism were the Socialist Labor Party and the Wasat Party. As mentioned above, the SLP started as a party with leftist and Marxist credentials but picked up decidedly Islamist leanings when it entered into a strategic coalition with the Muslim Brotherhood in the parliamentary elections of 1987. Whereas even the Muslim Brotherhood seemed to have acknowledged that the SLP was part of the Islamic sector,[5] the party has been internally divided broadly between a "secular" faction and a stronger Islamist faction led by its secretary-general, Magdi Husayn. Husayn emerged as one of the most outspoken critics of the government and launched several press campaigns against government ministers during the 1990s. As mentioned above, the

5. In historical retrospect, the MB has evaluated the alliance with the New Wafd Party in the 1984 elections as a purely tactical move in order to overcome an 8 percent electoral threshold, which has incentivized party alliances. On the other hand, the coordination with the Liberal Party and the SLP in 1987 was seen by MB representatives as a "real alliance" among Islamist forces (author's interview with Mohammed Habib).

SLP and its mouthpiece *al-Sha'ab* were "frozen" by the authorities in May 2000, but some party representatives have remained politically active.

The Wasat Party (Hizb al-Wasat) came into being in January 1996 as a breakaway faction of the Muslim Brotherhood. Initially, some prominent, middle-aged MB activists attempted to gain official party status. The Wasat has been one of the most well-known attempts of the politicized parts of the Muslim Brotherhood to engineer a decidedly political agenda. As Olav Utvik put it, the Wasat initiative "marked the first distinct crystallization of the religious-political outlook of the 1970s generation" (Utvik 2005, 294). This initiative was understood by the regime incumbency as an attempt to create a party under the control of the MB; and it was therefore repressed despite its liberal stance. The security establishment acted quite uncompromisingly even though the movement did not necessarily look like a mere MB-outlet: only forty out of seventy-four founding members were from the Brotherhood (Hatina 2005, 173). After two attempts to be officially recognized had failed, most of the founding members returned to the Muslim Brotherhood, including Abdel Mun'eim Abul Futuh and Essam al-Irian. The movement, however, did not disappear but remained an independent group headed by Abu al-Ela Maadi, a moderate Islamist intellectual and former MB bigwig from the *gil al-saba'inat*. A second prominent Wasat figure was Salim al-Awwa, who launched a presidential campaign of his own in 2012, though he was not endorsed by the Wasat as its official candidate. Other intellectuals in the ambit of moderate "*Wasatiyya* Islam," who were, however, not closely associated with the party itself, were the Qatar-based Yusuf al-Qaradawi or Tareq al-Bishri, a former judge and highly respected intellectual in Egypt.[6]

The Wasat Party has gained prominence particularly among observers in the West because it was seen as a platform for a discourse about the modernization of Islam, its compatibility with democracy, and dialogue

---

6. Al-Bishri later came under widespread criticism for his personal involvement as head of a military-appointed committee to engineer some limited constitutional amendments in March 2011 (see Brown and Stilt 2011).

with the West.[7] Accordingly, representatives from the secular opposition in Egypt have been open to establishing contacts with the Wasat. As Mona El-Ghobashy put it, "Madi and his associates became darlings of the secular intelligentsia" (El-Ghobashy 2005, 387). One aspect that has been consistently raised in appraisals of the Wasat's liberal nature was the fact that the organization also hosted Coptic members such as the writer and sociologist Rafiq Habib (see Hatina 2005, 173).[8] The Wasat Party was not taken very seriously by the regime because it was an entirely elitist and intellectual movement that did not pose a political threat to the incumbents. What is more, the Wasat's relations with the Muslim Brotherhood have soured during the late Mubarak years, mainly over the representation and interpretation of Islam and religious principles.[9] Yet the authorities refused to grant it formal status as a political party because they feared the takeover of the Wasat through the Muslim Brotherhood once it would be legally recognized. Since 1996, three attempts have been made to achieve legal recognition as a political party. With all attempts turned down, Abu al-Ela Maadi created two NGOs, Egypt for Culture and Dialogue (founded in 2000) and the International Center for Studies (founded in 2003) (author's interview with Abu al-Ela Maadi).

The Wasat has remained a platform for discussions among open-minded Islamists and between themselves and secular intellectuals. In this respect, its importance has increased in the post-Mubarak period. The Wasat Party was finally recognized through a court ruling on February 19, 2011, that is, only one week after Mubarak's fall. In the highly

7. Much has been published on the Wasat Party, often with particular reference to the question of whether or not political Islam might be compatible with democratic rule (see Lübben and Fawzi 2000, 267–81; Stacher 2002; Wickham 2004; Hatina 2005; Utvik 2005).

8. Habib was later chosen by the MB's Freedom and Justice Party as a vice president. Without any real leverage in the organization, Habib's selection was an attempt to improve the image of the FJP as an open and liberal political organization.

9. The former MB's *murshid al-'amm*, Mohammed Mahdi Akef, downplayed the conflict and pointed out that he himself had masterminded the creation of the Wasat (author's interview with Akef).

contested parliamentary elections of 2011, it gained 3.7 percent of the vote, which sounds modest, but is a not so insignificant success given the elitist nature of the movement and strong competition within the Islamist establishment.

Militant Islamist Groups

Apart from moderate groups, underground Islamist groups—the most prominent of which were Jihad, Jama'a Islamiya, and Takfir wa al-Hijra— comprised loosely organized, more or less cohesive bonds of single-action groups founded during the 1970s. The Jama'a Islamiya had its roots in Islamist student groups, whereas Jihad was formed as a radical splinter group of the Muslim Brotherhood. A common denominator among these groups was that their ideological doctrine was based on the thinking of Islamic philosophers like Sayyid Qutb and Ibn Taimiya, a fourteenth-century philosopher. It was centered around the claim to establish an Islamic state based on the shari'a and jihad. These groups have employed militant means of action with the aim of overthrowing the Egyptian regime. Despite marked differences concerning ideas, aims, and especially organizational structures, these groups were united in the aim to combat the "near enemy," that is, the political incumbents in their home country. This was the main difference between these groups and Usama bin Laden's internationally operating al-Qa'eda organization. This inward-looking strategy was justified by ideological and practical reasons: ideologically, the Egyptian state and society was described as *jahiliya* ("state of ignorance" in the pre-Islamic period); practically, the groups found it the more promising strategy to "liberate" home turf first before successfully combating the "far enemy," that is, the Jewish state and the West.

Their militant agenda (both in terms of political ideology and the employed means of political activism) constituted the main difference to popular-centrist Islamist movements, like the Muslim Brotherhood and the Wasat Party; thus, we shall refer to the militant Islamist movements as the main form of resistance to the Egyptian regime rather than a form of institutionalized political opposition whose relations with the regime were based on a minimum degree of mutual acceptance.

In the early years of Islamist radicalization, Anwar Sadat encouraged the emergence of Islamist movements in an attempt to counterbalance leftist groups that upheld the memory of his predecessor, Gamal Abdel Nasser. This genie escaped its bottle in October 1981 when a Jihadi group carried out the assassination of Sadat. During the following decade, Jihad and Jama'a Islamiya challenged the state violently and called bluntly for the overthrow of the Mubarak government (see Ansari 1984a; Hafez 2003; Hafez and Wiktorowicz 2004). Consequently, the 1990s were a decade of violent confrontation between the regime and these radical opponents. The Egyptian regime under Mubarak gave up its two-sided strategy of accommodation and containment to stem the militant Islamists, and the country witnessed its own "war on terror" resulting in about 1,300 casualties on both sides by 1997. The Egyptian regime won this conflict by destroying the combat capacities of the militants and executing or incarcerating their leaders and activists (see Gerges 2000). One main reason for the militant groups' defeat in the armed struggle with the regime is the fact that they had lost credibility and support among the Egyptian populace even though they had, like the Muslim Brotherhood, engaged in social services (see Ismail 2000; Toth 2003).

In 1997, the Jama'a Islamiya launched a cease-fire initiative and denounced violence. Its new political visions were outlined in four booklets written by veteran leaders and prominent activists of the movement: *Silsila Tashih al-Mafahim* (The Revised Concept's Series) published by Maktaba al-Turath al-Salami, Cairo 2002 (see Rashwan et al. 2007, 313–70). These documents came as a little earthquake to the Egyptian radical Islamists for two reasons. First, the Jama'a leadership was quite outspoken in admitting that the strategy of militant resistance had failed and was unjustified. Second, the "revision" entailed two dimensions: the renunciation of militant means of activism; and a substantial programmatic overhaul, at the center of which was the relationship to the Egyptian regime, the Jama'a's positioning in the political institutions of the country, and it's perception of the rules of political procedures.

Another aspect raised attention with both Islamists and observers (see Rashwan et al. 2007, 316): the fact that the booklets were written by two authors, Ali al-Sharif and Usama Hafez, but also authorized by the historical leaders of the Jama'a Islamiya—Karam Zohdi, Nageh Ibrahim, Hamdi Abdel Rahman, Issam Eddin Derbalah, Fouad al-Dawabili, and Asim Abdel Maguid. This shows two aspects: on the one hand, the Jama'a Islamiya communicated to the public (out of their cells in the notorious Aqrab prison) that it had been able to retain its organization despite military defeat and the incarceration or exiling of their entire leadership. On the other hand, the fact that the leaders spoke with one voice lend authority to the group's denouncement of violence. It was therefore interpreted as a credible move, even though the issue has remained hotly debated among radical Islamists, both in Egypt and abroad, for the years to come.

The fact that the most important militant Islamist movement, whose organizational structure survived the harsh conditions of Egyptian prisons, had taken this stance was interpreted as the starting point of a genuine renunciation of violence on the side of the militant Islamists. As Diaa Rashwan et al. found, "the Gama'a's revisionist thought . . . does not renounce the idea that there is an enemy lying in wait. However, the Gama'a's revisionism does replace its domestic enemy in Egypt with the idea of an abstract enemy—represented by backwardness and poverty" (Rashwan et al. 2007, 325). In essence, this revisionist thought revealed the group's readiness to trade in its raison d'être as a resistance movement for becoming part of the political opposition of the country.

It took some years for the Mubarak regime to accept the Jama'a's new stance. A first sign of the authorities' readiness to at least listen to the new tones was to permit the journalist Makram Mohammed Ahmad to visit and interview several Jama'a leaders in custody. Ahmad himself, a leftist journalist from the state-owned *Musawwar* newspaper and later chairman of the press syndicate, had been a target of the Islamists (he published his findings in Ahmad 2003). It is very likely that the authorities' more lenient stance toward the radical Islamists was preceded by intensive discussions between the incarcerated members of radical groups and the security services (author's interview with Kamal Habib). From 2003 onward, the regime started to release members of the militant groups, including Karam Zohdy, one of the Jama'a Islamiya's most prominent leaders.

A somewhat different picture pertains to Jihad, which was far less cohesive an organization than the Jama'a. Jihad remained internally divided despite several attempts of its early leaders Mohammed Farag and Ayman al-Zawahiri to unite the small splinter groups under the roof of a single organization (see Rashwan et al. 2007, 74-75). There had even been attempts at a unification of Jama'a and Jihadi groups in the 1980s, but their failure only revealed the organizational and programmatic differences between the two movements (Rashwan et al. 2007, 62–64). As a consequence of statist armed containment, the Egyptian Jihad has entirely disintegrated and ceased to exist as a clearly identifiable organizational entity. The movement was left in tatters ever since its former leader Ayman al-Zawahiri left Egypt for Afghanistan and rose to the second man in the al-Qa'eda organization of Usama Bin Laden.

Whereas many of the Jihadi leaders, who have continued to serve prison sentences, declared their agreement with the Jama'a Islamiya's denouncement of militant activism, some exiled leaders of Jihad have long preferred the resumption of violence. In Egypt, however, most of the movement's members decided to participate in institutionalized politics throughout the 2000s. In representing the new ideas, the journalist Kamal Habib, a member of the historical leadership and an intellectual pioneer of Jihad during the 1980s, encouraged the transformation into a legal movement. His new stance was indicated by his claim that the Egyptian state was never the main target of Jihad, coming only third behind the United States and Israel (author's interview with Kamal Habib).

In the decade prior to the fall of Hosni Mubarak, the former militant groups were neither willing (Jama'a Islamiya) nor capable (Jihad) to uphold resistance on violent terms. This means, most important, that anti-regime resistance from Islamist groups was absent in Egypt despite the persistence of the Jama'a Islamiya's organizational capacities.[10] Whereas Jihad was internally divided, Jama'a Islamiya was, according to Diaa Rashwan, on a path "from an Islamic religious group to a social and political

---

10. This assessment was approved by representatives of the groups, such as Kamal Habib (Jihad) and Gamal Sultan, who was associated with the Jama'a Islamiya (author's interviews with Kamal Habib and Gamal Sultan). For an "inside view" on the historical development of the militant groups since the assassination of Anwar Sadat, see Al-Zayat (2005).

group with an Islamic ideology" (Rashwan 2000, 48). This would mean, in consequence, adopting an approach similar to the Muslim Brotherhood in the early 1970s. Two party projects also hint in this direction: Hizb al-Shari'a (Shari'a Party) and Hizb al-Islah (Reform Party) were both initiatives of former Jama'a and Jihad members (see Lübben and Fawzi 2000; Rashwan 2000). Among the initiators were those members of the militant groups who have spent limited prison terms and who were released by the Egyptian authorities. The parties comprised initiatives of those individuals and did not represent either the Jama'a Islamiya or Jihad. Rather, one could find among both initiatives members of each militant group. Mamdouh Ismail, for instance, was a lawyer and member of the defense team of the militants; he was himself associated with the Jama'a Islamiya and appeared on the political scene as the initiator of the Hizb al-Shari'a (Rashwan 2000, 37). Gamal Sultan, a journalist and member of Jama'a Islamiya, and Kamal Habib, a chief ideologue of the Jihad in the 1980s, were the masterminds behind the creation of Hizb al-Islah (author's interviews with Gamal Sultan and Kamal Habib).

Although the regime has made it very clear that it would not legally recognize them, these party initiatives represented a clear signal for the readiness of the militant Islamists to abstain from violence and integrate into the political system. In the late Mubarak years, engagement for these party initiatives lost momentum and the party initiators themselves expressed pessimism about the prospect of political participation (author's interview with Gamal Sultan). Indeed, many prominent figures of the militant groups—for example the lawyer Muntassir al-Zayat—joined these party projects at the time of their very announcement but stepped back from a protracted engagement when they realized that the projects were immature in terms of ideological footing and legal materialization (author's interview with Muntassir al-Zayat). With the fall of Mubarak, however, came a fundamental change in the opportunity structure for the radical Islamist movement. Whereas the former militant groups, namely, Jama'a Islamiya and Jihad, have struggled to adapt to the transition period, a new Salafi movement emerged, representing a moderate (in terms of political action), but at the same time radical form of political Islam (in terms of the aims to transform society).

Political Islam between Contestation and Regime Support

The political Islamist groups have constituted an anti-systemic opposition toward the Mubarak regime. This "opposition of principle" is not based on the movements' ideological background, mainly because the incumbency itself did not represent a clearly secular social and political order. The anti-systemic nature of this opposition originates from two different qualities: in the case of the militant groups, the term "opposition" does not fully apply because their armed struggle with the regime's security forces qualifies them as a force of resistance, rather than opposition—lacking a minimum degree of mutual acceptance between the groups and the regime incumbents (Albrecht 2010b, 3). In the case of the Muslim Brotherhood, militancy did not characterize relations with the Mubarak regime. The MB was an opposition of principal with regard to their capacities to offer a counterhegemonic political force, threatening the monopoly over decision-making procedures claimed by Nasser's epigones. It was their popular and organizational strength, their problem-solving capacities, and their drive toward politicization that made the Muslim Brotherhood a threat—that is, their *potential* to challenge the regime incumbents rather than the actual challenge. In the Mubarak era, the Muslim Brotherhood was, through its financial and organizational autonomy, vulnerable to repression, but not to co-optation. Geoffrey Pridham's claim, discussed earlier, receives empirical evidence (1995, 54): not the lack of legitimacy was threatening to an authoritarian regime, but rather the organization of counterhegemony.

Smaller groups from the ambit of political Islam, such as the Wasat Party and the SLP, did not qualify as an anti-systemic opposition so long as they distinguished themselves clearly from the MB and the militant groups. The SLP's protracted party status and its operations in the 1980s and 1990s (the most troubling times for relations between Islamists and the regime) support the assumption that the incumbents did not have any principle reservations with the Islamist ideological background of an opposition group. Organizational weakness and limited popular outreach qualified the SLP for toleration despite the party's religious credentials. Neither was the Wasat would-be party an anti-systemic platform. Whereas its leaders attempted to distinguish themselves from the MB, the authorities have remained suspicious of the group for its founding history as an MB offspring and denied it legal party status.

The Egyptian experience can also help to understand the phenomenon of anti-system opposition in a more general perspective. In democracies, a political group will qualify as an anti-systemic opposition when it calls into question one or several defining traits of the polity—and when the group agitates proactively to alter not only government, but also the polity itself. This is usually accompanied by a clear vision—of a communist, fascist, egalitarian, etc. nature—to reconstruct the state. The anti-systemic opposition in the Egyptian case was different in several ways. Whereas the militant Islamists had a clear goal to bring down the regime, their visions to erect an alternative political system, based on an "Islamic state," have remained vague and erroneous. The Muslim Brotherhood, in turn, remained similarly vague and conciliatory in their political discourse (pronouncing that "the Islam is the solution"), but they had a better idea of the state and society to be erected—and they started to incubate this vision in the post-Mubarak political reality. What distinguishes the Muslim Brotherhood from most anti-systemic oppositions in democracies is that it refrained from directly challenging the incumbency.

Concerning the *codes of contestation*, there were marked differences between the moderate Islamists, represented by the MB, and the largely secular opposition parties. There was an inverse relation between programmatic incentives and policy substance: whereas the Muslim Brotherhood remained unclear in its ideological promises, it had developed a strong approach toward proactive engagement in society and politics. Quite to the contrary, political parties of different ideological colors have worked to develop and communicate their ideas about the country's political future, with strong references to the value systems of the ideologies concerned: nationalism, egalitarianism, liberalism, and socialism. Yet they have avoided substantiating their pledges and preparing to implement their promises in policymaking.

Quite interestingly, the Muslim Brotherhood has seldom worked to apply one of the entrapment strategies at the proposal of oppositions to antagonize authoritarian incumbents. The Muslim Brotherhood did not often call on the courts, and therefore did not engage in legal entrapment of the regime. MB members were also somewhat reluctant to proactively participate in a democracy discourse to disavow the regime, primarily because the MB itself had an ambiguous position toward liberal democracy. The MB refused co-optation and largely refrained from targeting the institutional infrastructure of the state. Despite the growing influence of a younger generation, the movement has operated primarily as a social group. Mosques, Islamist voluntary associations, and private clubs have comprised the natural habitat of the MB, rather than parliament, government, and syndicates. Those latter institutions came as a welcome vehicle for younger cadres to rise in importance within the organization, but the raison d'être of the MB itself did not ultimately depend on its success in these institutions. The legal political parties needed parliament to exist; the human rights organizations could not operate without a relatively independent court system. The Muslim Brotherhood has adapted to the existence of this institutional framework, but it did not need all these opportunities in order to persist.

It is out of a position of strength—based on its roots in society—that the Muslim Brotherhood could persist without challenging the regime up front on its institutional framework. The Mubarakist political order therefore witnessed a strong, autonomous social forces existing over time parallel to a strong liberal-authoritarian regime. In fact, the latter had also positive incentives to allow the Muslim Brotherhood the space it needed to operate in society and politics—despite the perceived latent danger originating from the organization. At certain points in time, the existence of the Islamist groups came as welcome excuse for the incumbency to execute repressive policies. Anti-Islamist action was, at least secretly, widely approved in the international arena after the terrorist attacks of September 11, 2001. But the coercive containment of Islamists was also approved by parts of the Egyptian population reminiscent of the disastrous experience in Algeria's civil war in the 1990s or the daunting experience of the "Islamic Republic" in Iran.

Most important, the existence of the Muslim Brotherhood has served the regime in its attempt to channel and moderate conservative dissent in society. Allowing the Muslim Brotherhood and smaller moderate Islamist groups some space for political activism has prevented a large-scale radicalization of the larger Islamist movement. It has also created a role model of political participation, despite obvious limitations, for the formerly militant groups. Defeated in military combat during the 1990s, the MB's protracted activities throughout the same period showed the Jama'a Islamiya a future scenario beyond their failed armed struggle. The persistence and tacit toleration of the popular moderate movement of the Muslim Brotherhood constituted a major incentive for the Jama'a Islamiya and Jihad to actively reconsider their own strategy of militant resistance. The attempts of several members of these militant groups to form political parties in the Mubarak period underlines the value of the moderation hypothesis; and so does the smooth integration of the Salafi movement, hitherto entirely apolitical in nature, into the political process after the fall of Mubarak.

5

Political Institutions between Contestation and Control

Whereas the previous empirical chapters have focused on the *agents* of contestation, this section adopts a structuralist perspective and examines the institutionalized *channels* governing contentious relations between the regime and its various forms of oppositions. They have been established from above with the aim of controlling society but emerged into channels of political participation. Focusing on the electoral regime and parliaments, civil society organizations, the judiciary, and the religious institution of *al-Azhar*, this chapter reflects on the functions of such institutions between co-optation and control, on the one hand, and contentious political participation performed by the opposition, on the other hand.

Formal political institutions in Egypt have been crafted in an authoritarian framework. Elections, parliaments, the judiciary, and professional organizations under Mubarak did not perform the same functions as in democracies; they have rather been "imitative institutions" in that they have formally mirrored democratic processes and endorsed authoritarian functions (see Albrecht and Schlumberger 2004, 380–82). The "natural" aim of authoritarian incumbents' institution building endeavors is not democratic competition, but rather the co-optation of important groups and individuals and the control of society at large. According to Jennifer Gandhi and Adam Przeworski, an authoritarian logic of institution building brings about those channels of state-society relations, "which can be controlled, where demands can be revealed without appearing as acts of resistance, where compromises can be hammered out without undue public scrutiny, and where the resulting agreements can be dressed in a legalistic form and publicized as such" (Gandhi and Przeworski 2006, 14).

Under authoritarianism, institutions are not crafted with the aim of accepting a threat to incumbents' power maintenance or as a harbor for rebellious groups. If this happens, something went wrong from the incumbents' perspective. The authorities will then quickly repress the relevant contentious actor and change the institutional arrangement. On the flip side, co-optation means also inclusion and, for that matter, political participation; the former is not possible without accepting the latter. Authoritarian institution building always implies that actors participate in the respective institutions—and it therefore perpetuates the idiosyncratic nature of liberalized authoritarianism. Some of these societal agents will, first, strive to preserve some degree of autonomy from statist control, and, second, formulate dissent toward government policies. Whereas open systemic rebellion and the quest to overthrow an authoritarian regime is foreclosed—and any attempt into this direction (or even the threat of it) will most likely trigger the removal of the opponent from that very institution—such realms can be used by opposition forces: for regime-entrapment strategies discussed earlier; to secure relative gains; to challenge singular regime policies and representatives to a degree that may, at times, even lead to the revocation of the respective policy or the expulsion of singular regime members; and eventually for the weakening of an authoritarian regime that will then have to reinvent itself by force or accept its breakdown.

In this chapter, I will explore the dual virtue of Egyptian political institutions between contestation and control. In the focus are parliaments and elections, professional syndicates and labor unions, the judiciary, and the religious institution of al-Azhar. Several questions guide the inquiry: what is the reason for the inception of institutions? What is their impact on government-opposition relations? How and to what extent do opponents challenge incumbents in the respective institutions? How does contentious politics affect the political institutions where contestation happens?

Parliament and Elections

In most polities, parliaments and elections are central to government-opposition relations. This holds true for democracies as much as for authoritarian regimes (among the emerging body of literature on authoritarian institutions, see Way 2005; Schedler 2006; Gandhi and Przeworski 2006; Lai and Slater 2006). In Egypt, elections and parliaments have been an important tool of authoritarian control of society, but they have also become the core institutions for the struggle between incumbents and opponents since the early 1980s. This holds certainly true for the post-Mubarak transition period that saw the Muslim Brotherhood and other Islamist forces capitalize on their strong popular support and win an outright majority in Egypt's first competitive parliamentary elections from November 2011 to January 2012. But it also holds true for authoritarian politics under Mubarak, in which parliament and elections were engineered to arrange uncompetitive government-opposition relations.

The Egyptian parliament consists of two chambers: the *Majlis al-Sha'ab* (People's Council, lower house) and the *Majlis al-Shura* (Consultative Council, upper house). The members of each chamber were elected for a period of five years; the Majlis al-Sha'ab in a central vote and the Majlis al-Shura in three electoral rounds within one term during each of which roughly one-third was elected. According to the 1971 constitution, the Majlis al-Sha'ab was by far the more influential chamber compared to the Majlis al-Shura, and this power arrangement between the two chambers has remained intact in the new constitution endorsed in a popular referendum in December 2012. Whereas Robert Springborg described the Shura Council quite depreciatingly as a "retirement haven for burned-out top-level bureaucrats, ministers, and politicians" (Springborg 1989, 137), it has been an important arena for co-optation.

When the nineteenth-century building of the Shura Council burned down to ruins in a devastating blaze on August 21, 2008, some cynics claimed that the closure of parliament would not have any major effect on Egyptian politics. However, since the early 1980s, the importance of these two parliamentary bodies was accepted by the incumbents as well as the opposition forces. Political struggles were mostly about representation in parliament; and this did not change in the immediate post-Mubarak transition period: despite the protracted uncertainty on the institutional powers of parliament (with the new constitution written several months after the elections), political actors, new and old, engaged in heavy competition about parliamentary seats and thereby outlined the dominant battle lines in the post-Mubarak period, between Islamists and secularists.

The strong engagement of opposition actors in parliamentary politics is not surprising in the case of the political parties because their fate is closely associated with these institutions. The Muslim Brotherhood has also, in the course of its development from a social movement to a more politicized actor, shown increasing interest in participation in elections. This is more in need of an explanation than with the political parties. First, the hindrances for the MB have been much greater than for other opposition forces. Second, most of the Brotherhood's leadership saw its core mission in social activism. Third, the Brotherhood possessed a property that the opposition parties did not have at their disposal: popular mass appeal. Yet, the participation in elections, the results of which were engineered by an authoritarian regime, did not produce any outcome that would mirror that mass appeal.

Neither did the Brotherhood's participation necessarily increase its popularity because elections and the parliament were considerably discredited among the wider Egyptian public. Jennifer Gandhi and Adam Przeworski argued that elections under authoritarianism usually remain a tool to indicate primarily the might of authoritarian incumbents: "Elections are intended to show that the dictatorship can make the dog perform tricks, that it can intimidate a substantial part of the population, so that any opposition is futile. Under dictatorship, everyone knows that their rulers are not selected through elections" (2006, 21). Why, then, should the Muslim Brotherhood—and other opposition forces— participate in elections and, as a consequence, offer legitimacy to these institutions?

Opposition actors perceive elections as a good opportunity to hurt the regime and challenge singular policies at relatively little costs and risks. In a nutshell, elections and parliaments constitute an important component of the regime's outside-oriented legitimation strategy, at the core of which is the attempt to portray the picture of a relatively liberal authoritarian regime that is on its way toward democracy. Sheila Carapico has uncovered the "election trick" quite precisely: "Incumbent national leaders invite foreign monitors only when it is in their interest to do so," and, "under these circumstances, electoral festivities are choreographed by and for visiting dignitaries" (1998, 20). On the other hand, this legitimation strategy involves restricting repressive countermeasures toward oppositional activism in the electoral and parliamentary arena. As a consequence, electoral participation is a good opportunity for *regime entrapment* by the opposition.

The participation of opponents in the electoral arena has indeed been a delicate issue for the Egyptian incumbency under Mubarak. Challenges within parliaments and elections had more serious political implications than in other authoritarian regimes in the MENA region. The Egyptian regime was more vulnerable than, for instance, the traditional monarchies because it suffered from a structural legitimacy deficit. The monarchs in Jordan, Morocco, and Saudi Arabia, along with the emirs in the small Gulf states, could rest on traditional personalized legitimacy. An inherently embedded, automatic right to rule, including the hereditary shift of power within the ruling family, was not easily available for the republican presidents in Egypt. The unsuccessful attempt to shift power from father to son under Mubarak, which certainly contributed to the January 25 uprising, is a telling example for the Egyptian regime's failure to mimic such traditional authority in engineering political succession.

Whereas traditional legitimacy of a monarch, closely bound to the national idea of the state itself, is not at stake for authoritarian presidents, their stress on public support would be based to a greater degree on the perception of their personal qualities and individual efficacy, that is, on what they do rather than on who they are. As a consequence, and quite in line with the logic of the core working mechanisms of a liberalized authoritarian regime, strategies of co-optation and control remained of central importance for the Egyptian incumbency; and, in comparison, the institutional pillars established to this aim have been of greater importance than in the monarchies. Even a quick comparison of Egypt with Morocco and Jordan reveals that the Egyptian NDP as a mass party was central to the regime's quest for societal co-optation and control, whereas the Moroccan and Jordanian regimes lacked such an authoritarian organization. The reason is that the Moroccan and Jordanian kings do not necessarily need a ruling party to secure their power maintenance.

The Egyptian regime did need such a body. From this perspective, electoral politics, despite the parliament's obvious lack of leverage in political decision making, became an important playing field for intra-elitist negotiations and power struggles, obvious in the fierce internal battles within the NDP prior to the 2000, 2005, and 2010 elections. Hence, the competitive nature of elections in the late Mubarak years did not primarily characterize the struggle between incumbents and oppositions, but rather the internal dissent within the ruling party (see Collombier 2007; Köhler 2008).

This had palpable implications for the institutional arrangements in which such state organizations operate: parliaments and elections. The Egyptian regime needed a strong ruling party and therefore had to restrict the degree of competition to which the NDP was exposed (on ruling parties in authoritarian regimes, see Brownlee 2007). In comparison, the Jordanian, Moroccan, and Saudi kings could observe, relatively unworried, the struggles within their respective parliamentary bodies. Among parliaments, Albrecht and Wegner therefore distinguished between more "competitive" (monarchies) and "hegemonic" (republics) arenas for regime-opposition relations (Albrecht and Wegner 2006, 128). Baaklini, Denoeux, and Springborg identified three characteristics of contentious relations between regime and opposition in Egypt. "The first is that access to parliament is the principal point of contention between government and opposition. The second is that the centrality of parliament varies inversely with the degree to which the executive has consolidated power. The final characteristic is that presidential legitimacy is largely a function of the representation of the opposition within the legislature: the fewer opposition MPs in parliament, the lower the level of presidential legitimacy" (Baaklini, Denoeux, and Springborg 1999, 229).

In the political context of the Mubarak regime, it was rational for opponents to engage in formal activism in electoral politics. While the number of seats distributed to the opposition was limited, the opposition had something to win at relatively little cost because the regime had an interest in keeping the image of multiparty politics alive. This explains the great effort that opposition groups have invested in the attempt to be legally recognized as political parties, and of individual politicians to strive for a seat in parliament. Such a strong motivation and dedication can be observed throughout the entire opposition landscape: the established political parties; the "frozen" parties that have struggled for their reintegration in formal politics; the Muslim Brotherhood; and even the Kifaya movement, which has considered trading in its credentials as a street protest movement for parliamentary representation.

On the flip side, elections under Mubarak were always subject to "electoral engineering" (Pripstein Posusney 1998; Norris 2004). The regime has changed the rules of the electoral game and what Ellen Lust-Okar has called the "structures of contestation" (Lust-Okar 2005) in frequent intervals, most important, by adapting the legal rules of the electoral process each time during the run-up of electoral rounds. Moreover, the degree of coercion toward opponents has changed from one parliamentary rally to the next. Both the formal rules of elections and the degree at which coercion was used depended on the general situation in which elections took place (including the national and the international political environment) as well as on the political challenger. Whereas formal rules and regulations were meaningful—and therefore subject to regular changes—their application very much depended on the performance and the threat potential of different opposition actors.

The Egyptian regime has shown its readiness and capability to employ the whole range of possible "manipulative skills" to control outcomes in elections (Case 2006). Yet, there were remarkable differences in the degree to which different measures of contention have been employed. In the Mubarak era, seven rounds of parliamentary elections took place during liberal and illiberal phases. Very roughly, one can distinguish between three phases: (1) a protracted phase of electoral institution building under a liberal framework (1984–1987), (2) illiberal elections (1990–2000), and (3) an authoritarian failure (2005–2010).[1]

The parliamentary elections of 1984 and 1987 took place in a relatively liberal political environment, at least for opposition parties. The regime's strategy of confinement concentrated on the intimidation of the media and individual opposition figures (see Springborg 1989, 191–97). Hence, the opportunity structure for opposition groups was relatively promising. Two reasons were responsible for this development. First, the mid-1980s proved to be a honeymoon period for the opposition, with Hosni Mubarak still consolidating his grip on power. Second, the party system and parliamentary life were still in the making. The two elections of 1984 and 1987 were the first elections during which the authoritarian post-1952 regime was pit against a formally independent political opposition: the new ruling party NDP against some infant opposition parties (the Tagammu, the Liberal Party, and the SLP), along with the reestablished New Wafd Party and an informal participation of the Muslim Brotherhood that was not granted legal party status.

Both elections should thus be seen as test cases for the regime that needed to learn how to deal with an emerging opposition, and the opposition that had to find its place in the Egyptian political system. A good indicator can be seen in the changes of electoral laws and amendments in the run-up to the elections. Never again in the Mubarak period have these changes been as significant as in these early years of electoral

---

1. The first multiparty elections in modern Egyptian history took place in 1978, shortly after the issuance of Law No. 40 of 1977. At the time, the political environment became decidedly illiberal after Sadat had signed the Camp David peace accord with Israel and faced fierce opposition from society and the political elite. While, at first sight, more than one party participated, the elections were entirely orchestrated and the running "opposition" parties (Liberal Party, SLP, Tagammu) were still perceived as platforms and, thus, an integral part of the regime. In the end, the NDP won 347 seats, the SLP 29, and independent candidates 10 seats (see Baaklini, Denoeux, and Springborg 1999, 226–28).

politics (see Kassem 1999, 94–101).[2] Containment policies in the 1984 elections were directed toward the New Wafd Party that was expected to become the leading opposition force. Yet, the regime realized that the established party-list system and the electoral threshold of 8 percent of the votes encouraged intraparty cohesion and interparty alliances among the opposition. The opposition parties learned the lesson of Nicolas van de Walle that there is a "clear correlation between cohesion and electoral victory" (Van de Walle 2006, 78). Irrespective of the shallow prospect of ousting authoritarian incumbents, the only promising way for opposition parties to succeed in authoritarian elections is to forge cohesive coalitions. Indeed, the opposition scored some successes at the polls. The numbers of opposition representatives rose remarkably during the 1980s: from thirty-three in 1979 to sixty-four in 1984 and finally to one hundred members in parliament after the 1987 elections (see Alam 2006, 140).

The most important modifications after the 1987 elections pertained to the change from a party-list system to an individual-candidacy system, which has become the core mechanism of electoral politics ever since and caused the "individualization" of Egyptian politics in general, and of the organizational fragmentation of political parties in particular. More-over, the 1990 parliamentary elections marked a decisive shift toward a more illiberal electoral framework. The incumbency was obviously not very enthusiastic about sustaining the opportunities for the opposition that it had made available in the 1980s. With the 1990 parliamentary elections, observers witnessed the starting point of a decade of political deliberalization, embracing higher degrees of repression not only toward the Islamist challenge but also political opposition at large (see Kienle 1998; Brownlee 2002).

As a consequence of a more illiberal electoral framework, all opposition parties and the Muslim Brotherhood, but with the Tagammu Party

---

2. Moreover, all electoral rounds in the 1990s were legally contested by the opposition; and the amendments regulating the elections have been judged unconstitutional by the Supreme Constitutional Court. This explains why the regular parliamentary sessions of five years have not been completed.

as a prominent exception, boycotted the 1990 elections. They witnessed a sharp drop of opposition representation in parliament from one hundred (1987) to a mere seven seats. Whereas the smaller opposition parties resumed participation in the 1995 and 2000 elections, regime-opposition relations continued to be under the impetus of the struggle between the incumbents and the Islamist current. The opposition parties suffered from political deliberalization and were able to take only twelve (1995), sixteen (2000), and fourteen seats (2005), respectively (see Kassem 1999, 101–21; Kienle 2001, 51–62).[3]

In retrospect, the 2000 parliamentary elections proved to be another turning point in electoral politics (see Abdel-Latif 2001; Makram-Ebeid 2001; Ouda, al-Borai, and Se'ada 2001; Kassem 2004, 63–81). This is not because the opposition was able to secure a substantially higher stake in the vote. From a total of 444 seats, the New Wafd Party received 7, Tagammu 6, the Nasserists 2 (plus 5 independent Nasserists), and the Liberal Party 1. Unaffiliated independents won 14 seats. Still subject to a high degree of violence, vote rigging, and repression preceding the polls, three aspects are worth special attention. First, the Supreme Constitutional Court decided that the elections were to be placed under the supervision of the judiciary. Whereas this decision was not fully implemented, it was an important signal to the judiciary as the institution designed to theoretically perform this task. Empowered by the court ruling—and embarrassed by the authorities' neglect of it—the independent courts, at the helm of which were the Supreme Constitutional Court and the Court of Cassation, emerged into a prominent arena of contestation to the regime in the following decade.

Second, during the 2000 election, struggles within the NDP intensified, and so did intra-elite competition in the electoral process.

---

3. It should be noted here that it is misleading to take representation numbers in parliament as a viable indicator to assess the general strength or weakness of opposition parties. While we may contend, with a fair degree of certainty, that the importance of political parties has declined during the 1990s with respect to their organizational capacities and public support, their performance in elections does not primarily depend on their own strength or weakness, but on the degree of openness of the elections.

Contestation did not increase between the incumbents and opposition, but rather within the NDP. Yet, the very fact that there was something at stake in elections boosted the overall significance of the electoral process. Third, even though the Muslim Brotherhood experienced, in the second half of the 1990s, the most repressive period since the Nasser era, the movement was able to secure seventeen seats in the 2000 parliament.

These aspects became even more prominent in the following period of political liberalization, culminating in the 2005 parliamentary elections that witnessed a stunning success of the Muslim Brotherhood, an increasing intra-regime competition among NDP cadres, and a struggle between the regime and the judiciary (see Meital 2006; Shehata and Stacher 2006; Hassabo 2006; Albrecht 2007; Fürtig 2007). The year 2005 saw a liberal window of opportunity for the opposition, which affected the electoral process considerably. It all started with a political earthquake in April 2005 when the regime announced that it would amend the constitution for the first time since 1980. The amendments were subjected to a popular referendum on May 25, 2005. According to government sources, 82.9 percent voted in favor of the amendments. Official voter turnout was high at 53.6 percent, a figure heavily disputed by the opposition.

At the center of the changes stood article 76 governing presidential elections. According to past regulations, a single candidate had been chosen by a two-thirds majority vote in parliament, with the ballot being reduced to a mere yes-or-no referendum. The amended article stipulated that, in the 2005 presidential election, every member of a legal party's board could run for president. For the next presidential elections, candidates from political parties securing 5 percent in both chambers of parliament would be eligible.

Although the authorities' concessions still contained fundamental restrictions that foreclosed any real competition for the power to rule, they fuelled rising hopes among the opposition to challenge the regime at its very core: the presidency. Consequently, several opposition figures announced their intention to run in the presidential elections. In addition to some independent opposition figures (Saad Eddin Ibrahim, Muhammad Farid Hassanein, and Nawal Saadawi), some parties quickly filed their own candidates as well. In the end, Ayman Nour (Ghad Party) and

Noman Gomaa (at the time, a member of the New Wafd Party) were the most prominent contestants from the opposition forces. Needless to say, the presidential election of September 7, 2005, was not an open race. The official result was designed to see Mubarak (88.5 percent of the votes) lead Ayman Nour (7.6 percent) and Noman Gomaa (2.9 percent); official voter turnout was 23 percent (Hassabo 2006, 49).

Nevertheless, there was enthusiasm among the opposition about the fact that the incumbents met some of their most prominent demands. With the experience of greater openness in the presidential elections, the opposition parties went one step further in their preparation for the parliamentary elections, which took place in a three-round rally between November and December 2005. Whereas the presidential elections had once again revealed substantial disagreement among the opposition parties—some parties participated and filed candidates and others (like Tagammu) defected—an attempt to unify the opposition took many observers by surprise: on October 8, 2005, the National Front for Change (NFC) saw the light of day under the leadership of the well-respected former prime minister Aziz Sidqi (who passed away on January 25, 2008); the leading figures of the main opposition parties (except the Ghad Party of Ayman Nour); prominent representatives of the "civil society business," Kifaya; and—quite remarkably—the Muslim Brotherhood. The aim of the NFC was to unite the opposition forces and coordinate a common strategy in the parliamentary elections. But these aims did not materialize, and the NFC initiative remained another short-lived adventure (see Kraetzschmar 2010). Albeit unity proved to be short-lived, it is noteworthy that opposition forces of all colors gathered at the Brotherhood's traditional *Iftar* feast at a five-star hotel in suburban Cairo.

During the course of the year 2005, it seemed that the parties had been capable of successfully challenging the boundaries established by the authorities and widening the scope of political action. The NFC decided to file a common list of candidates, though without the Muslim Brotherhood, which, in the end, chose to present its own list of candidates. The parliamentary elections in November and December 2005, however, appeared as a terrible blow to the rejuvenated hopes of the opposition parties. Their results were miserable: only around 12 to 15 successful candidates (of 222 running) were associated with the NFC (8 New Wafd, 2 Tagammu, 1 Liberal Party, some independent candidates). At the same time, the MB scored a great success at the polls that triggered a rapid shift in the regime's engineering of electoral politics and a new wave of repressive containment.

While the 2005 elections proved the strength of the Muslim Brotherhood and the weakness of the legalized opposition parties, the 2010 parliamentary elections were disastrous for both camps. In anticipation of dawning leadership change (planned to see Gamal Mubarak succeed his father) and with increasing internal rivalries within the NDP (between Gamal's younger cadres and the old elite), the regime's power brokers were compelled to abandon the liberal experiment in parliamentary elections. The engineered outcome of almost 95 percent of seats occupied by NDP members were the result of significant and openly executed electoral fraud. As the Brotherhood's *murshid al-'amm*, Mohammed Badie, said: "These were not elections with rigging; it was rather rigging with a hint of elections" (quoted in El-Ghobashy 2010).

Elections can become a viable arena of contention; they can be used by opposition parties as "showrooms" to sharpen their programmatic distinctiveness and mobilization capacities both in front of their own constituency and toward outside actors. On the other hand, elections provide the opportunity for a learning curve for an authoritarian regime: different electoral designs can be tested along with different degrees of openness concerning the inclusion of opponents in the formal political realm. Yet, incumbents cannot always avoid a misperception in authoritarian strategies of limited inclusion. In the 2005 elections, the regime obviously underestimated the capacities of the Muslim Brotherhood. In the midst of the electoral process, the authorities decided to terminate a liberal experiment and introduce a more repressive containment strategy. Elections provide a source of authoritarian learning—and failure. The Mubarak regime had a history of adaptation of the electoral process—from liberalism in the 1980s to the illiberal period in the 1990s, and back to the liberal window of opportunity in 2005. In retrospect, however, the closure of electoral politics and the reinvention of a hegemonic ruling party proved fatal for the late Mubarak regime, with an opposition fully aware that electoral politics had ceased to exist as a viable political arena in 2010. Because their own attempts to form a "parallel parliament" were ill-founded from the very beginning, the consequence was as disastrous for the opposition parties as for the regime, because the former were associated with the parliament as much as the latter. Electoral politics have been viewed as largely meaningless, farcical political exercises, which led people to the streets rather than the ballot boxes.

Labor Unions, Professional Syndicates, and "Dialogue Organizations"

In Mubarak's Egypt, participation in electoral politics was long deemed the main option of activism among the opposition forces, but it was also subject to substantial government interference. This explains why the Egyptian opposition has always searched for other opportunities to engage in political activism. Other institutions at the intersection of state and society included the lobby and interest groups of labor and professional guilds as well as a number of state committees that have been established to address distinct policy issues. Different opposition forces have staged several attempts at entering these institutions and increase their influence in them. The aims were manifold: some organizations have proved useful to increase organizational capacities and communication channels, others could be used to increase popular support, and yet another rationale was to enter into a dialogue with the regime.

The post-1952 Nasserist regime in Egypt has established a large state bureaucracy that included labor unions and professional associations. Quite naturally from an authoritarian logic, they have not been designed with the aim to orchestrate, at least not as autonomous organizations, the organization and representation of the interests of the relevant parts of society.[4] Rather, these organizations were crafted mainly for co-optation purposes. In some of these organizations, however, a dynamic emerged,

---

4. In that latter respect, Egyptian society has remained rather "unincorporated" until the time being (Moore 1974; see also Bianchi 1989).

at the center of which was the inclusion of opposition forces. As a consequence, they have shifted away from mere co-optative instruments of statist control and developed into institutionalized harbors for contentious activism. This process set in, and experienced a new dynamic, when the state lost control over some of these organizations in the 1980s.

First, it should be said that the Egyptian corporatist structure did not share the fate of other regimes in the region with respect to the labor organizations. For instance, Islamists have taken over large parts of the statist structure of labor unions in Tunisia and Algeria; and, as a consequence, these organizations have changed sides and became part and parcel of the Islamist challenge toward the state (see Alexander 2000). This did not happen in Egypt until the last years of Mubarak's reign.[5] Despite the defection of several labor groups in the course of workers protests, ever since the foundation of labor unions under Nasser, the organizations have remained under the tight control of the state and embedded in a hierarchical, unified organizational structure, at the top of which was the General Federation of Trade Unions (GFTU) (see Pripstein Posusney 1997).

Two statist organizational bodies have been in charge of labor affairs: the GFTU and the Ministry of Manpower. Contrary to other countries in the region, such as Morocco and Algeria, Egypt under Mubarak had a unified system of labor unions that was organized strictly along hierarchical top-down arrangements and did not allow for the emergence of competing unions (see Pripstein Posusney 1997, 86–91; El-Mikawy and Pripstein Posusney 2000). In the later Mubarak years, however, the workers' movement included the activism of some labor representatives who began to mobilize for independent organizations of labor representation. The most prominent example was the case of real estate tax collectors who have since 2008, under the leadership of the charismatic Kamal Abu Eita, rallied for autonomous organization (see Bishara 2012).

5. In the 1940s, the Muslim Brotherhood had been quite determined to penetrate labor organizations in its efforts of societal outreach and mobilization, but this proved difficult mainly because of the Brothers' own ideological reservations. As Joel Beinin recalled, the Brotherhood "thought of strikes and other expressions of working class struggle simply as plots of atheistic communism which must be combated" (Beinin 1988, 219).

One consequence of the co-optation of union leaders was that, according to Maye Kassem, "it is not unusual to find individuals who simultaneously represent workers and government" (Kassem 2001, 65). This was quite important for the regime, given the vast potential of labor protest in a country that belongs to the comparatively well-industrialized in the developing world, and therefore has a large labor force among its populace. Jennifer Gandhi and Wonik Kim found that, "the co-optation of labor is especially important for dictatorships when workers constitute a large segment of the population and an important input to production" (Gandhi and Kim 2005, 6). This was certainly the case in Mubarak's Egypt.

Corporatist development does not mean that the labor unions were always in line with central regime policies. As Agnieszka Paczynska observed, "corporatist labor institutions, established . . . with the goal of politically controlling unions, over time became more autonomous from the state and provided organized labor with the institutional tools to challenge the state" (Paczynska 2006, 47). Yet, opposition forces were never able to "take over" single labor unions. The latter have, in some instances, indeed successfully lobbied for autochthonous labor interests, but they have not opened up any space for oppositional activism. What is more, in times of neoliberal reforms and the advent of "crony capitalism," lobbying on behalf of labor was much more difficult than on behalf of the interests of private capital holders. The latter could rely on excellent personal connections with the political incumbency and—if at all necessary—on potent lobby associations, such as the Egyptian Businessmen's Association or the American Chamber of Commerce (see Kassem 2001, 71–76).

Whereas some members of the opposition parties (in particular the Tagammu Party) have been active in the labor union structure, the boards of the labor unions have remained under tight control of the state. The Muslim Brotherhood has occasionally attempted to increase its influence by filing candidates in the unions' board elections. These attempts, however, have been met by substantial countermeasures from the authorities that remained keen to keeping the MB out of the labor representing institutions (author's interview with Mohammed Sayyed Sa'id). After all, labor unions were organizations in which intra-elitist dissent has become

sentenced to multiple years in prison. Hence, since the 1990s, the doors of parliament remained closed for the top MB cadres, and the importance of the syndicates even rose as alternative organizations for political activism and organization.

Carry Wickham summarized that, by entering the syndicates, "Muslim Brother activists gained an opportunity to hone their leadership skills, broaden their base of support, and present an alternative model of political life" (Wickham 1997, 131). The syndicates' board elections, in which the MB scored their first remarkable successes in the formal political arena, were conducted in a comparatively open, just, and liberal fashion and developed into islands of democratic practice. Robert Springborg said: "Professional Syndicates . . . provide through their elections a good indication of the balance of power between government and the secular and religious oppositions" (Springborg 1989, 188).

To create an alternative model of political life was certainly not in the minds of Egypt's rulers; they must have been on high alert concerning the takeover of the syndicates by the Muslim Brotherhood. As of the early 1990s, the Islamists had occupied the majority in the boards of the engineers', the doctors', the pharmacists', and the lawyers' syndicates (Kienle 2001, 85). Their performance in these organizations was perceived, from the very beginning, as effective and professional, not only among their own followers but also among others concerned with the relevant professional field and among political commentators (see Wickham 1997; Fahmy 1998). The political incumbency reacted to these developments shortly after the Islamists had taken over the majority in the board of the Bar Association in September 1992. This had come as a minor political earthquake because the lawyers' syndicate had always been a stronghold of liberal and national tendencies. Moreover, the effect that this might have on the judicial system was seen as particularly critical.

Consequently, the regime endorsed, among other restrictive countermeasures, Law No. 100 of 1993, which has governed syndicate board elections. The new formal rules complicated such board elections considerably by the requirement that 50 percent of all syndicate members had to participate in order to render election results valid. As a consequence, future board elections often ended in a legal limbo because the necessary margin could not be obtained and the syndicates were put under external judicial supervision (see Kienle 2001, 85; Fahmy 2002, 107).

Through these measures the authorities did not succeed in foreclosing oppositional activism within the syndicates and bring them back under statist control. The doctors' syndicate remained firmly in the hands of the Muslim Brotherhood and provided a platform for important figures of its younger leading cadres such as Essam al-Irian, Abdel Mun'eim Abul Futuh, and the Alexandria-based Gamal Heshmat. Within this syndicate, the MB has regularly organized meetings and activities. The engineer's syndicate was another stronghold of the Brotherhood, leading to the virtual freezing of the syndicate's activities since 1995 on the grounds of the restrictive Law No. 100. The trick here was the protracted impediment, by the law, of holding board elections that would have almost certainly witnessed a sweeping victory of the Islamists.

In the press syndicate, many independent liberal, leftist, and nationalist intellectuals have found a platform where they could exchange political views and communicate with each other in lack of an alternative political platform. This syndicate was particularly politicized because many journalists were among the most active opposition figures. Examples include the Nasserist and Karama founder Hamdeen Sabahi (one of the most outspoken opposition members of parliament between 1995 and 2005, and presidential candidate in 2012); his Karama party fellow, Abdel Halim Qandil (editor in chief of the movement's mouthpiece al-Karama, established in September 2005); Rif'at Sa'id (Tagammu party chairman); Magdi Husayn (chairman of the SLP); Mohamed Abdel 'Alim (another member of the 2000–2005 parliament); the leftist-nationalist journalists Mustafa Bakri (editor in chief of the weekly al-Usbou, as an MP affiliated with the military establishment post-Mubarak); and Ibrahim Eissa (editor in chief of al-Dustour, received a one-year prison sentence for attacking President Mubarak in July 2006). A journalist associated with the Muslim Brotherhood was Mohamed Abdel Quddous. The syndicate's chairman was Galal Arif of the Nasserist Party's al-Arabi newspaper.

The syndicate fell somewhat out of regime control when its longtime chairman Ibrahim Nafie, then editor in chief of the statist al-Ahram newspaper and known to be Mubarak's man in the national press, failed to

be re-elected. In 2005, Nafie fell into disgrace and faced charges of corruption for the alleged misappropriation of public funds. Journalists were
united, for instance, in their appeal for a new press law in summer 2006.
Yet they were unable to prevent the return of a more restrictive stance of
the authorities toward critical voices in the press after the 2005 parliamentary elections.

Another organizational body to represent a professional guild was
the Bar Association. This syndicate for lawyers and judicial personnel
became an organization divided between roughly equal factions of secular and Islamist opposition forces. Before the January 25 uprising, ten out
of twenty-four board members were affiliated with the Muslim Brotherhood. One of the more prominent MB representatives was Ahmed Saif
al-Islam al-Banna, son of the movement's founder, Hassan al-Banna, and
member of the Brotherhood's *maktab al-irshad*. Gamal Tageddin was the
MB's speaker in the Bar Association, and Muntasser al-Zayat was an independent Islamist with good connections to the former militant groups of
Jama'a Islamiya. Tal'at Sadat, nephew of late Anwar Sadat, represented
the Liberal Party (he passed away in November 2011). The former New
Wafd Party chairman Noman Gomaa has also been active in the Bar
Association. The chairman of the Bar Association (since 2001), Sameh
Ashour, was a Nasserist who suspended his party membership in order
to appear as a candidate of compromise between the different political
currents. He scored a sweeping victory at the syndicate's board elections
in February 2005. Similar to the press syndicate, the association was of
particular importance for the communication between the different
political camps. The Bar Association, together with the adjacent court
building and the nearby Press Syndicate, marked what one could call
the "protest corner" in downtown Cairo where the geographical point
of origin for Kifaya demonstrations and many other protest activities was
located, before Tahrir Square became the iconic symbol of the January
25, 2011, uprising.

In sum, the professional syndicates remained an important arena of
contention between the regime, on the one hand, and various forms of
oppositions, including the Muslim Brotherhood, on the other hand. The

political relevance of these organizations rose when opposition actors perceived their opportunities to vanish in other areas of contention, in particular elections and parliament. This was the case at the outset of the 1990s. The regime incumbents have been reluctant to intervene too forcefully into the syndicates' affairs; they made sure, by various legal and informal means, that Islamist outreach was contained at the level reached in the early 1990s. In the end (and this may well explain the relatively moderate stance of the regime), the effectiveness of activism in the syndicates was somewhat restricted to an expansion of organizational skills as well as to communication and cooperation among opposition forces; the degree of challenge in politics proper was limited.

This also holds true for another kind of institution regulating state-opposition relations: the "dialogue organizations." I denote with this term a number of committees and organizations that have been invented by the regime with the aim of providing a forum for discussions on thriving current affairs and issues of contestation. Such issues include foreign policy and economic policy issues as much as the discourse about political reforms, more freedom, and democracy.

Starting in the early 1990s, there have been several waves of national dialogue (*al-hiwar al-watani*) initiatives. This was a common phenomenon throughout the MENA region. It was often employed by the regimes as a first conciliatory step designed to ease popular discontent in times of political or economic crisis. A national dialogue of sorts was generally preferred over concessions in the realm of formal institutions of political participation, for example, elections or constitutional amendments.[6] National dialogue initiatives have been initiated with the aim of communication between the Egyptian incumbents, on the one hand, and the secular opposition forces, on the other hand. Islamists, both the radicals and the

---

6. A good case of comparison is Saudi Arabia, where in 2000, followed by subsequent sessions in 2003 and 2004, then Crown Prince (since 2005 King) Abdallah initiated a "national dialogue" in order to present a forum for Islamist and secular opposition (see Kapiszewski 2006, 467–68).

moderate mainstream political Islam, have usually been excluded, even though the regime did not have any principal objections toward Islamist discourses and ideas. Rather, it was the strength and degree of autonomy of the Islamist opposition (in particular the Muslim Brotherhood) and, in turn, the weakness of political parties and the civil society business that qualified the latter for co-optation and the former for exclusion.

According to Salwa Ismail, the politics of national dialogue have always been part and parcel of the "maneuvers and efforts carried out by the holders of power to maintain the existing structure" (Ismail 1995, 37). From the regime's perspective, two often intertwined reasons account for the establishment of dialogue organizations: first, they could serve as security valves in times of political crisis, to placate challengers; and second, as an option to feed carrots to opposition demands. Political dialogue initiatives have often paralleled coercive measures toward parts of the opposition, usually Islamists. The motivation was to balance illiberal and exclusionary policies with other channels of inclusion; playing one opposition camp against the other was the name of this game. The establishment of such national dialogue institutions began in the early 1990s when the regime started to engage in a fierce military battle with militant Islamists (see Ismail 1995, 39).

The last decade has witnessed a new dynamic in "dialogue politics." In early 2005, the regime called on the (legal) political parties to participate in a national dialogue (see Rey 2005, 42–45). With Kifaya demonstrations having broken out in the preceding months, the regime initiated a liberal experiment. The new initiative of dialogue talks initiated a process of political liberalization that led to amendments of the Egyptian constitution, the first multiparty presidential elections, and an open first round in the parliamentary elections. Again, a quite familiar rationale applied: invited to the national dialogue were the legalized political parties that were on the defensive in front of a stronger (Muslim Brotherhood) and more visible (Kifaya) opposition forces. Representatives of the latter two movements were not included in these talks.

Already in April 2003, the authorities had announced the establishment of the National Council on Human Rights (NCHR) as a committee in which members of the tolerated human rights groups were invited to participate.[7] It was, according to Law 93 of 2003, officially designed to become an advisory committee fostering human rights affairs and fairness in the political and legal processes, but it did not have any legislative power. Its twenty-five members were appointed by the president, but it has reported to the parliament's upper chamber, the Shura Council (see Stacher 2005). The NCHR came effectively into being only in February 2004. Since 2005, it has issued annual reports in which human rights violations, police torture, and the effects of the emergency law were on top of the agenda.

At first sight, the establishment of the NCHR seemed to prove the regime's dedication to listen to the demands of politically relevant civil society organizations and political opposition working in NGOs. "Human rights," "civil liberties," and "more democracy" have been the terms of the day; and the regime has learned quickly how to intone this narrative without offering any reason to believe that demands were to be materialized. Rather, the establishment of the NCHR followed the logic of observing and controlling those groups, individuals, and NGOs that figured prominently in such public discussions. The timing of the installation of the NCHR is particularly intriguing. Whereas discussions about the establishment of such a forum have spread among the political establishment in Cairo since around 2000, it was presumably not coincidental that the plans materialized shortly after the US-led military invasion of Iraq in 2003. In the latter's immediate aftermath, the Egyptian regime came under pressure from opposition forces that have organized demonstrations and demanded an official condemnation of the war, which, however, the regime remained reluctant to issue because of its strategic partnership with the United States.

The new organization provided an institutionalized channel for human rights groups to put these issues on the agenda and engage in

---

7. Throughout the Middle East, there was a whole wave of human rights institutions since the early 1990s; such bodies were formed in seven other countries: Morocco (1990), Tunisia (1991), Algeria (1992), Palestinian Territories (1993), Yemen (1997), Jordan (2000), and Qatar (2003) (see Cardenas and Flibbert 2005).

discussions with the power holders. The NCHR served as an important institutionalized scene of cooperation between the tolerated opposition and an increasingly prominent faction of the political elite that has initiated, under the leadership of the president's son Gamal Mubarak, a reform discourse that voiced state-sanctioned democracy talk. Whereas democracy was never at stake, it served the purpose of granting Gamal Mubarak and his new guard some space to establish themselves in the political arena. Gamal Mubarak has risen in the ranks of the political incumbency ever since he entered the NDP as head of the influential Policies Secretariat. Observers of Egyptian politics have since speculated that Gamal Mubarak would be built up as the coming president. Moreover, an ostensible split within the political elite was identified, pitting an "old guard" of close, longtime political advisors of the incumbent president and the new guard of young, dynamic, business-oriented "Gamalists" (see Hassabo 2006; Brownlee 2007, 134–37; Collombier 2007).

NCHR members who belonged to the regime's reform faction included former UN Secretary-General Boutros Ghali, Hossam Badrawi, the NDP-parliamentarian Mustafa al-Fiqqi, and the journalist Osamal al-Ghazali Harb. Some people from the realm of the regime-loyal and tolerated opposition included the Wafd Party's Mounir Fakhry Abdel Nour; the Nasserist (and head of the press syndicate) Galal Arif; the head of the Egyptian Organization for Human Rights, Hafez Abu Saada; and another human rights activist, Bahey Eddin Hassan (Stacher 2005, 3). The lawyer and moderate Islamist intellectual Ahmad Kamal Abul Magd served as the organization's secretary-general and deputy chairman.

Other human rights groups and oppositional NGOs have distanced themselves from both the NCHR and those activists who decided to participate in it. Critics have pointed out that the committee had been established solely for window dressing; and those human rights activists who have participated in it, would serve that very purpose. Indeed, government officials have repeatedly referred to the NCHR when the regime was criticized for human rights violations. It comes as an ironic twist that, in May 2007, Egypt was awarded a seat in the UN Human Rights Council, established in March 2006 out of the former UN Human Rights

Commission, which also triggered criticism from Egyptian and international human rights organizations.

Whereas the NCHR, and to a lesser extent the National Council for
Women (NCW), headed by Suzanne Mubarak, was the most prominent
among the dialogue institutions under Mubarak, it was not the only one.
Other committees have been less visible because they have focused on
less catchy debates. They included the Foreign National Defense Committee, the Industry and Energy Committee, the Human Resources
Development Committee, the Higher Press Council, the Political Parties
Committee (PPC), and the Legislative and Constitutional Affairs Committee (LCAC). As mentioned above, the PPC was in charge of the legalization of political parties. The LCAC rose to prominence in the course of
the preparation of the constitutional amendments in May 2005, and again
in March 2007. In contrast to the NCHR, these two committees (like most
other committees reporting to the Shura Council) were in the hands of
NDP members or other individuals closely affiliated with the incumbency
because the issues at stake were much more vital and sensitive for the
regime than the token discussions within the NCHR. An organ similar to
the regime-dominated Shura committees came into being in July 2005:
the Presidential Election Commission was established in order to prepare
and supervise the 2005 presidential elections. The ten-member council
consisted of judges from the higher courts along with a number of regime-
affiliated people.

The Shura Council is an important body in Egypt's political structure.
While often referred to as a rather purportless second chamber of parliament with insignificant formal powers, it remained—as the state institution with which most of these committees were affiliated—an important
arena of co-optation and control, but also a channel of participation for
those who have been included in the committees.

The Judiciary

The Egyptian judiciary has become, since the late 1980s, of paramount
importance as a realm where contentious politics and opposition to the

regime could be crafted and voiced. Eberhard Kienle said that "the judiciary—with the obvious exception of special and military tribunals—
remains the most active and effective countervailing power in relation to
the regime. Though ultimately part of the state, the courts have, to vary-
ing degrees, escaped regime control" (Kienle 2004, 77).

Egypt looks back at a history of a comparatively well-established judiciary system that has its roots in the Ottoman legal system of the early
nineteenth century and European influence since the second half of that
century (see Brown 1997, 23–60). Accordingly, Egyptian laws and the
judicial system were heavily influenced by both Islamic and liberal European, particularly French, principles.[8] After 1952, Gamal Abdel Nasser
brought the judges under his control and embedded the legal system in
the new authoritarian-populist state structure. With the 1971 constitution, the judges regained a measure of space because it "guaranteed in
principle the independence of the judiciary, the irremovability of judges
and the non-interference of the executive in trials" (Kienle 2001, 42).

The judiciary, however, never became an institution autonomous
from state control; rather, it was part of the latter. Particularly the Ministry of Justice has exercised control over the judiciary. Moreover, when
Mubarak came to power in 1981 and as a response to his predecessor's
assassination, the incumbency invented a parallel system of jurisdiction by
applying a "state of emergency" to establish State Security Courts and Military Courts.[9] These latter courts became instrumental for the legal prosecution of politically sensitive cases. For instance, the legal prosecution
of Islamists and other opposition figures during the 1990s was enforced
through these state security courts and military courts, whose importance for the power holders rose in the course of the 1990s parallel to an

8. Scholars connected to the Cairo-based Centre d'Études et de Documentation
Économiques, Juridiques et Sociales (CEDEJ) have put much effort in the study of Egyptian "legal pluralism" (see, in detail, Dupret, Berger, and al-Zwaini 1999; Dupret 2000).

9. The emergency law was applied in Egypt until the January 25, 2011, revolution (see Singerman 2002). During 2007, discussions within the NDP—in particular
among the "reform-oriented" people around Gamal Mubarak—have intensified about
the replacement of the emergency law through an "antiterrorist law."

increasing self-consciousness of the civil courts. These special courts have been usually employed in politically sensitive cases. A well-remembered example is the case of Saad Eddin Ibrahim, the human rights activist and director of the Ibn Khaldoun Center, who was convicted and sentenced to seven years in prison by a state security court in 2002.

The emergency law was not immediately abolished after the January 25 uprising, despite the authorities' announcement to do so. In January 2012, military leader Mohammed Hussain Tantawi announced the partial lifting of the law as soon as an improvement of the country's security situation would allow for that move. Yet, Egyptian and international human rights groups claimed that military courts have been used extensively to charge protesters and political activists. Estimates put the number of prisoners under military jurisdiction at twelve thousand, which would far exceed the numbers in the Mubarak era. The most widely publicized cases were those of the Coptic blogger Michael Nabil, who was handed down a three years prison sentence in April 2011 on charges of "insulting the military," and the blogger-cum-activist Alaa Abdel Fatah, who defied the legitimacy of the military courts after he had been interrogated on his participation in the bloody "Maspero demonstrations" of October 9, 2011. The protracted and extensive usage of the special court system after the fall of Mubarak underlines its importance.

In sum, the subsequent regimes of Nasser, Sadat, and Mubarak made careful attempts to integrate the judicial system into their state-building endeavors. At the same time, the incumbents established measures to make sure that courts could be used as another tool to control society. As Robert Springborg aptly put it, "Egypt has rule *by* law but not rule *of* law. Far from being lawless, the state is careful to cloak its actions in both constitutional and legal legitimacy" (Springborg 2003, 186). The development of the Egyptian legal system in the second half of the twentieth century was part of a modernization process initiated by Anwar Sadat and sustained by Hosni Mubarak. Interestingly (and that was certainly not in the minds of the incumbency), the importance in politics and society of the "independent" judiciary (in contrast to the "emergency-law" judiciary) increased in response to the establishment of other formal political institutions: laws and regulations, the constitution of the state, political procedures in elections and parliaments. This, in combination with the fact that the Egyptian legal system, along with al-Azhar, was already present before the 1952 revolution, may well explain why exactly these two institutions—since then part of the Nasser regime and discretely embedded in authoritarian control mechanisms—have encapsulated a higher degree of dissent *within* the authoritarian realm than other institutions established as "autochthonous" pillars of the 1952 regime, such as the labor unions, the ruling party, and the electoral-parliamentary realm.

Given the substantial formal and informal constraints on the freedom of the courts, it is striking to witness that numerous court rulings opposed regime policies and regulations. Especially the three highest courts—the Court of Cassation (CC), the Supreme Administrative Court (SAC), and the Supreme Constitutional Court (SCC)—have regularly stretched the limits imposed on legal rights and freedoms. According to Nasser Amin, director at the Center for the Independence of the Judiciary and the Legal Profession (CIJLP), the CC and the SAC were the most independent legal units during the last decade of Mubarak's rule, whereas the lower courts were much more subject to regime control. The SCC lost some credibility after the appointment of Fathi Naguib in August 2001. A former assistant to the Minister of Justice, Naguib was the first-ever chief justice appointed from outside of the court (author's interview with Nasser Amin).[10]

According to other observers, however, the Supreme Constitutional Court was the "guardian of public liberties" (Bernard-Maugiron 1999). Numerous decisions of the SCC since the 1980s called electoral laws and legislative procedures unconstitutional, whereas other court rulings have repeatedly denounced human rights violations.[11] Obviously, many judges (particularly at the superior level of the judiciary pyramid and in the SCC) felt obliged to the constitution as well as a "spirit of

10. Naguib passed away in 2003.

11. Since 1995, there has been a significant increase in the number of cases in which the SCC judged laws and regulations unconstitutional (see Moustafa 2003, 884).

independence" (Kienle (2001, 45). This was one of the more intriguing facets of the Mubarakist political order when we keep in mind
that the superior judges have been appointed by the president. Nasser
Amin's assessment of the Egyptian judicial system is telling: "We have
independent judges but no independent judiciary" (author's interview
with Nasser Amin). This is not to say that the judges have constituted a
power center in its own right. Neither could these independent judges
be perceived as part of the political opposition in the country. Rather, as
Nathan Brown and Hesham Nasr explained, "only a small minority of
judges might truly be considered sympathetic to the political opposition,
with the vast majority anxious to preserve a non-partisan reputation"
(Brown and Nasr 2005, 4). As a state institution that possessed a distinct
measure of independence, however, the judiciary was often used by the
opposition as a *means* and a "judicial support structure" (Moustafa 2003,
895) to confront the regime.

Why did the Mubarak regime accept this situation? First, since the
2000 parliamentary elections, judicial supervision has become a major
asset in the regime's attempt to create political legitimacy. Second, the
development of the Egyptian judiciary was quite in line with the logic of
a state institution's "channeling dimension," in serving as an institutionalized "Geiger counter" in order to feel the people's pulse and detect the
degree of societal dissent. Martin Shapiro said that "a 'right' of appeal is
a mechanism providing an independent flow of information to the top on
the field performance of administrative subordinates" (Shapiro 1981, 49;
see also Moustafa 2007, 27). Third, it is true that the judges of the superior
courts have struggled to enforce the text and spirit of the Egyptian constitution. But the constitution itself was ultimately designed to strengthen
executive powers. Moreover, with the overwhelming NDP majority in
parliament, the regime was able to alter the constitution whenever it was
deemed necessary.

These were the positive incentives for the Egyptian incumbents to
accept a relatively independent judiciary. At the same time, the authorities
have retained mechanisms undermining the efficacy of the judiciary as to
its assumed role to control and check executive power. In this regard, the
independent judiciary often came as a toothless tiger because other state

institutions (ministries, security forces) did not hesitate to ignore court rulings whenever results were judged unacceptable by the power holders. An example is the case of the Socialist Labor Party: according to its deputy secretary Magdi Qorqor, the party received eleven rulings from the courts, between May 2000 and November 2001, that called to lift the ban on the party and its mouthpiece *al-Sha'ab*. However, the verdicts have not been implemented by the authorities (author's interview with Magdi Qorqor).

After all, the judiciary system has remained a double-edged sword for the Egyptian incumbents, who had to accept that "courts inevitably serve as dual-use institutions, simultaneously facilitating some state functions while paradoxically opening new avenues for activists to challenge regime policy" (Moustafa 2007, 20). Anti-authoritarian reflexes among parts of the judiciary became particularly apparent in the course of the year 2005, which saw a "revolution of the judges," that is, the revolt of a majority of judges organized in the Judges Club in Cairo and supported particularly by the judges of the Court of Cassation. The Judges Club was founded in 1939 with the aim of representing the interests of Egyptian judges. In the late Mubarak years, it has represented around eight thousand judges and served as the only independent body within the judicial system quite similar to the professional syndicates.

Spearheaded by the CC, higher judges have repeatedly demanded a free hand in the supervision of elections as well as independence from the Ministry of Justice. This initiative received a new dynamic after the government's announcement to amend the 1971 constitution in May 2005. With an enhanced attention to legal affairs and presidential and parliamentary elections on the horizon, the role of the judiciary in political affairs became increasingly important. The judges thought that the time was right to twist the regime's arm on long-held postulations, and their calls for "dual independence"—*for* the supervision of elections and *from* government control—became louder (see El-Ghobashy 2006). The amendments to article 76 of the constitution stipulated electoral supervision by two government-appointed bodies rather than the judiciary: the Supreme Judicial Council (SJC), a body at the intersection of state and judiciary that was created in 1984 to balance interests between the judges and the Ministry of Justice, and the Presidential Election Commission

(PEC).[12] Both committees were discredited in the eyes of the rebellious judges, organized in the Judges Club, for their alleged readiness to serve the interests of the political power holders. Contradicting the Judges Club's majority, the SJC announced that it would be ready to supervise elections without any preconditions.

In a move that fuelled the confrontation further, the threat of a majority of judges in the Judges Club, on May 13, 2005, to boycott the supervision of the forthcoming elections was indeed taken seriously by the regime because, since the 2000 parliamentary elections, judicial supervision had become a major asset in the regime's reform narrative. In response to the boycott threat, the authorities tried to split the judges' ranks, for instance by offering financial rewards to regime-loyal judges (see Brown and Nasr 2005). But some judges resisted all threats and enticements, deepening the rift between the pro-regime and the rebellious judges. Most prominent among these rebellious judges were the Cairo Judges Club's president Zakaria Abdel Aziz and his deputy Hesham Geneina, the Judges Club representative in Alexandria Mahmoud al-Khudayri, the Alexandria-based Mahmoud Makki, the deputy chief justice of the Court of Cassation Hesham Bastawisi, and judge Hossam al-Ghiryani.[13] On the regime's side were the judges of the Courts of Appeal, the chair of the Supreme Judicial Council Fathi Khalifa, and the former president of the SCC Mamdouh Mar'ei (see El-Ghobashy 2006, 23–24). In the course of a limited cabinet reshuffle endorsed in August 2006, Mar'ei replaced Mahmoud Abu al-Leil

12. The PEC came under criticism again prior to the presidential elections of 2012. Empowered by a constitutional amendment making its decisions binding (without right of legal appeal), the ten-member PEC singlehandedly barred ten candidates from the electoral race, among whom were very serious candidates, such as Omar Suleiman (Mubarak's intelligence chief and last vice president), Khairat al-Shater (official MB candidate), and Hazem Abu Ismail (a Salafi candidate with strong social support), one month ahead of the polls on May 23, 2012. In another criticized move, the PEC approved Mubarak's last prime minister and former army general, Ahmed Shafiq.

13. Hesham Bastawisi was a presidential candidate for the leftist Tagammu Party in 2012.

as the Minister of Justice and held his post as one of the few Mubarak-era ministers in the Egyptian cabinet post–January 25, 2011.

The standoff between the incumbents and the "revolutionary judges" of the Judges Club did not come to an end after the 2005 elections. They even escalated after April 2006 and led to the prosecution of two of the most outspoken rebellious judges, Mahmoud Makki and Hesham Bastawisi, both deputy chairmen of the Court of Cassation.[14] Other measures to stem the Judges Club included the suspension of the allocation of funds to the club in October 2006. Since January 2008, divisions among pro-government judges and reformist judges intensified further with the government-backed Ismail al-Basyuni taking the club's chairmanship. This led to the division of the chamber's board in two roughly equally strong camps. Since early 2007, critical discussions have intensified about the regime's alleged plan to amend article 88 of the constitution, which has governed the supervision of elections. Judges in the Judges Club raised their concerns that the regime may attempt to restrict the role of independent judges in the supervision process further. Indeed, in March 2007, the incumbency endorsed the amendment of thirty-four articles of the constitution, triggering a wave of criticism from opposition forces and the rebellious judges.

Despite the contest between rebellious judges and the authorities, it would be simplistic and misleading to equal critical judges with the political opposition. On several occasions, independent courts and judges have ruled against opposition figures or groups. This indicates that the main driving force for the critical judges' activism was professional work ethics rather than a certain political position. By most rebellious judges, the confrontation with the incumbency was not perceived as a goal in itself, but rather the consequence of professional spirit. In the same month when Makki and Bastawisi faced charges of tarnishing the image of the

14. Makki and Bastawisi coauthored a widely circulated article in 2006, in which they heavily criticized the Mubarak regime for its authoritarian nature and control over the judiciary; see Mahmud Mekki and Hisham Bastawisi, "When Judges Are Beaten," *The Guardian*, May 9, 2006 (www.guardian.co.uk/commentisfree/2006/may/10/comment .egypt).

judiciary, their Court of Cassation rejected an appeal of al-Ghad party leader Ayman Nour to abolish his five-year prison sentence handed down in December 2005. Then, in October 2006, the Court of Cassation ruled that the parliamentary elections of late 2005 had been subject to electoral fraud in several constituencies, decrying the authorities' practice to engineer electoral outcomes.

These rulings support the assessment that there existed pockets within the Egyptian legal system that were not necessarily part and parcel of the opposition landscape, but nonetheless unique in that they constituted formally institutionalized, independent bodies that would adhere to the rule of law. Multiple rulings of the Court of Cassation, but also of the SCC and the SAC, stand out as examples of the application of the rule of law. But the independent courts and judges were not necessarily an easily exploitable tool for the political opposition to challenge the incumbents.

Al-Azhar

There is a last institution that is at the intersection of state and society, government and opposition, and co-optation and participation: al-Azhar. It is in the center of the struggles about the interpretation of Islam. In times of a protracted Islamicization of society at large, the significance of al-Azhar in the political system, as well as in contentious politics between the incumbency and the oppositional Islamists in particular, should not be underestimated. Al-Azhar is the oldest and most prestigious institution of (Sunni) Islamic teaching and jurisdiction. Owing to its reputation among Muslims worldwide, al-Azhar was co-opted by the state as soon as Gamal Abdel Nasser took over power. This was to control an influential institution and to draw on traditional-religious legitimacy despite the regime's modern, revolutionary, and nationalist discourse (see Hudson 1977, 237; Ansari 1984a). Most important, the regime has reserved the prerogative to choose the Grand Imam of al-Azhar, creating a personal dependence of the helm of the institution to the president of the republic.[15] Moreover,

---

15. The shaykh of al-Azhar was appointed by the prime minister.

al-Azhar's budget, which has increased dramatically since the early 1960s, was controlled by the state (see Moustafa 2000, 6; Brown 2011).

Nasser's move transformed the traditional *ulema* of al-Azhar, which henceforth began to deal with modern aspects of politics and society. Yet, the inclusion of al-Azhar into the state has had repercussions on that very state, especially since the 1970s (see Zeghal 1999). Owing to al-Azhar's inclusion in the state apparatus, it would be a profound misunderstanding to assume that the political regime had an entirely secular character. Rather, the incumbency has established a religious complex comprising al-Azhar, the bureau of the Grand Mufti, which has come under state control much earlier,[16] and several state ministries endowed with religious affairs. Pockets of Islamist thinking within the state included, for instance, the ministries of Religious Endowments (Awqaf), Education, and Interior, respectively, apart from al-Azhar. This religious complex came as a state pillar offering support for the regime much like other institutions, for example, the ruling party NDP, the bureaucratic apparatus, or the security services.

Religion has come to play an ever-increasing role in the legitimacy creating endeavors of the Mubarak regime (see Bernard-Maugiron and Dupret 1999; Jolen 2003). This was reflected in public discourses as well as in the fact that the Islamic law, shari'a, was made the principal source of jurisdiction in the Egyptian constitution of 1971. Apart from al-Azhar, the Ministry of Awqaf was a particularly important organization for the regime because it has performed, by way of the institutionalized control of thousands of religious endowments, an eminent role in countering the Muslim Brotherhood's attempts at social outreach through such charity endowments (see Moustafa 2000; Pioppi 2007).

As Steven Barraclough maintained, Al-Azhar's importance for politics and society rose when the government, "in its long struggle with Islamist

---

16. The mufti was appointed by the president. The institution of the Grand Mufti was "nationalized" already in 1895 (Jolen 2003, 114) and came under even greater regime control than the more ambiguous institution of al-Azhar.

groups, and in particular with the Muslim Brotherhood, repeatedly called upon the services of al-Azhar to issue statements justifying campaigns against Islamists, and supporting the introduction of legislation that might otherwise have aroused religious opposition" (Barraclough 1998, 237). In support of this observation, Judith Jolen detected a correlation between the launching of media campaigns by al-Azhar and incidents of Islamist violence (Jolen 2003, 120). Some examples are well-remembered, such as the violent attacks on liberal intellectuals like Naguib Mahfuz and Faraj Fuda, the apostasy cases of Nasr Hamid Abu Zayd and Hassan Hanafi, or the removal of books from shelves and articles from newspapers. All these attacks on secular intellectuals were either directly initiated or quietly, and sometimes openly, approved by al-Azhar. One instance illuminates clearly how al-Azhar has contributed to the imprint of public morality by orthodox religious discourses: the extremist group that claimed responsibility for the murder of Faraj Fuda in 1992 referred to an al-Azhar judgment calling Fuda an apostate (see Barraclough 1998, 241; Ismail 1999).

Al-Azhar has actively fuelled Islamist discourses. Since the early 1980s, al-Azhar has been directly involved in the censorship of the media and figured as one of the leading forces of the Islamicization of Egyptian society. The Islamic Research Center of al-Azhar had censorship responsibilities limited to "Islamic issues" only; however, the Center's recommendations were hardly ever left unimplemented. More often than not, al-Azhar has determined what would constitute "Islamic issues" and what not (Barraclough 1998, 242).

Al-Azhar came as a double-edged sword for the regime. On the one hand, it was one of the most important "legitimacy creating institutions" of the regime (Fawzy and Lübben 2000). The late Grand Imam of al-Azhar, Shaykh Mohammed Sayyed Tantawi, has repeatedly issued *fatwas* (religious verdicts) that supported government policies.[17] For instance,

17. Tantawi, a former grand mufti of Egypt, was chosen as head of al-Azhar by Mubarak in March 1996 (Moustafa 2000, 16). He was considered to be a staunch "Mubarakist" and passed away on March 10, 2010.

numerous fatwas have discredited the thinking and actions of moderate and militant Islamist opposition groups. Another incident exemplifies the great influence that the political incumbency exerts on al-Azhar: in the wake of pushing through the constitutional amendments in early 2007, an al-Azhar fatwa was issued saying that voting would be "a duty before God."

Al-Azhar's role as a largely regime-supporting institution notwithstanding, it was often at odds not only with a liberal morality proposed by the West, but also with the secular parts of the incumbency. This conflict had two dimensions: ideology and competency. The main statist task of al-Azhar was censorship, which was, however, also executed under the auspices of the Ministry of Information. Second, a subliminal conflict about competencies existed between al-Azhar and the Ministry of Culture. The Egyptian judicial system was another arena in which al-Azhar exerted significant influence, potentially at odds with a regular court system striving for independence. By monitoring the application of the shari'a as the main source of legislation in the Egyptian constitution, al-Azhar has exerted (at least indirectly and much to the dislike of the judicial system) great impact on specific court rulings. Despite its institutionalized affiliation with the regime, al-Azhar has avoided being identified too closely as one of its pillars because this has, over time, tarnished the institution's image in the Egyptian public. It is in this context that, during the 1990s, "*al-Azhar* increasingly opposed government policy on a number of sensitive issues" (Moustafa 2000, 13).

What did this mean for the religious political opposition? On the one hand, al-Azhar was the most prestigious contender in the struggle for the representation and interpretation of Islamic values. On the other hand, al-Azhar could turn into a natural ally when advocating programmatic ideals against secular ideological currents. There is reason to believe that the relations between the Muslim Brotherhood and al-Azhar have historically been (and probably still are) closer than one would expect from a relationship between the pillar of an authoritarian regime and the regime's most determined contender. Barbara Zollner (2007, 424) speculated that al-Azhar was actively involved—and with the consent of the Nasser regime—in the moderation and programmatic reinterpretation of the

Muslim Brotherhood during the 1960s by influencing the book *du'at la qudat* (preachers not judges). The book was authored by the organization's leadership in prison and is widely seen as an internal move of the MB to distance itself from its radical ideologue, Sayyid Qutb. In turn, Nathan Brown maintained that the "Brotherhood has advocated for a stronger public role for al-Azhar; it has its supporters within the institution; and it has denounced attempts by leading political officials to make it toe on official line" (Brown 2011, 6).

One example shows that the Islamist opposition could attempt to make use of al-Azhar even though it was a statist institution: in June 1998, the Front of the Ulema of al-Azhar, a bastion of radical Islamist thinking, was dissolved by the newly appointed Shaykh Muhammad Sayyid Tantawi after candidates close to the Muslim Brotherhood had allegedly won a majority in the Front's board (Kienle 2001, 113). The education system provided a potential playground for a possible entrapment strategy by which an opposition could, on occasions, turn a state-controlled institution—in this particular case al-Azhar—into an ally in order to challenge other state institutions, individuals, or policies. For instance, in June 2003, then Minister of Education Husayn Bahaa Eddin was criticized by MB parliamentarians for the alleged recognition of the U.S. administration's call to reform school curricula. It is an example of the Muslim Brotherhood to effectively place criticism and at the same time hide behind al-Azhar, which had a similarly defensive approach toward the "Westernization" of school curricula. The risks that Muslim Brothers faced in proposing such a contentious position, yet in line with al Azhar's views, were substantially lower than with other policy issues. This may well explain why, in the late Mubarak years, discussions on the education system have turned into a constant critical debate, often fuelled by the MB (author's personal communication with Florian Kohstall and Ivesa Lübben).

On March 10, 2003, a statement of al-Azhar's Islamic Research Academy revealed the whole malaise for the regime: in criticizing the US-led military campaign against Saddam Husayn, the statement employed the term "jihad," thereby indicating a call of militant resistance against

Western engagement in the region. This was clearly in disaccord with the regime's policy of avoiding confrontation with its most important ally, the United States. Whereas the shaykh of al-Azhar, Mohamed Sayyed Tantawi, did not sign the religious verdict, it reflected the ambiguous position of the institution in politics: *institutionally* part of the regime, but fueling the *discourse* of the regime's most ardent challenger—the Islamist movement.

6

The Transformation
of Contentious Politics

Egypt after Mubarak

Egypt's political system under Mubarak stands out among liberalized authoritarian regimes in that it inhabited a large, colorful, and heterogeneous landscape of political opposition. Since the late 1970s, a multiparty system has emerged that has become increasingly fragmented over the thirty-five years of its existence; the 1990s saw the rise of private voluntary associations, part of which politicized in a realm of outspoken human rights NGOs. The strongest opposition force in the country was composed of a politicizing Islamist current, consisting of the Muslim Brotherhood and a number of breakaway factions, both moderate and radical. The movement has grown ever since Anwar Sadat released the Islamists from the Nasserist prisons. These forms of organizations correspond with distinct modes of political opposition: party politics embraced regime-loyal opposition, tolerated opposition was represented by the mainstream of human rights groups and smaller protest movements, and the Islamist current conforms to an anti-systemic opposition of sorts.

Emerging contestation in state-society relations signaled distinct types of opposition agents and an institutional infrastructure governing the relations between regime incumbents and their opponents. The authoritarian nature of the polity prevented these relations from becoming truly competitive. Both opposition forces and this institutional infrastructure have been ambivalent as to the functions they perform in the political system as well as to the aims, strategies, and discourses performed by political actors. The opposition has made use of the ambiguities of a liberalized authoritarian regime by applying a number of entrapment strategies; at the same time, they have supported through their very existence, and various strategic decisions and behavior, the political system. In turn, the Egyptian regime under Mubarak consisted of ambiguous political institutions. Created with the aim of controlling society and securing the incumbents' hold on power, these institutions have turned into arenas where oppositions could challenge policies, legal outlines, and incumbent personnel.

This has led to the protracted coexistence of a strong authoritarian regime and a strong societal opposition (El-Ghobashy 2011). Both regime incumbents and opposition groups have refrained from calling into question the existence of one another, injecting a significant dose of stability to the political system. On the other hand, this contentious system was highly dynamic in many respects. First, the degree of constraints and opportunities for opposition actors has changed considerably, more often than not in short intervals. The dynamic reciprocity of political liberalization and deliberalization explains changes in the *performance* of different opposition actors; the degree of the challenge performed by an opposition; the strength (or weakness) of an opposition actor; and the strength (or weakness) of the incumbency, or part of the incumbency, subject to an opposition's challenge.

Liberalized authoritarian regimes grant a significant measure of political rights and freedoms to society, at least to a much higher degree than in hegemonic and repressive systems of authoritarian rule. However, rights and freedoms are granted in an unjust, exclusive, and discriminating way, to the benefit of some and the disadvantage of other social groups. Such regimes employ coercion as a last resort in the struggle for power maintenance, that is, when coercion is perceived as *necessary* rather than *possible*. In Egypt, the 1990s can be seen as a decade of indiscriminate political deliberalization. In turn, the empirical parts of this study have shown that the year 2005 marked a short, but remarkably open, window of opportunity for all opposition actors that was, however, quickly closed again when these new opportunities have been used by the opposition to fundamentally challenge incumbents: by the Kifaya movement and, in particular, by the Muslim Brotherhood in the 2005 parliamentary elections.

Opportunities and constraints were different for individual opposition actors. I have discussed the Muslim Brotherhood, political parties, human rights organizations, and the Kifaya movement as examples. The Muslim Brotherhood benefited from the Sadat regime's support in the second half of the 1970s. The subsequent generally more liberal phase of state-society relationships in the 1980s witnessed the rise of opposition parties, which came at the expense of the Brotherhood, which was not granted legal party status. Therefore, the organization as a whole did not benefit as much as one might have expected in that phase of limited liberalization; rather, it was a specific strata within the organization—the then younger generation of politicized activists (today referred to as the *gil al-saba'inat*)—that was enabled to train their political skills within those institutions that opened up in the context of political liberalization: parliaments and professional syndicates.

In retrospect, in the 1990s—widely judged as the most illiberal phase in modern Egyptian history—the statist control of society had quite different effects on opposition groups. The activities of the opposition parties and their performance in elections stagnated between 1990s and 2000, but the 1990s were the founding years for civil society associations in the field of human rights. Political deliberalization targeted primarily the Islamist current; but the effects were also ambivalent: within the Muslim Brotherhood, for instance, those strata that were on the sunny side of political liberalization during the 1980s were hit hardest by the persecution through security forces and the incarceration of the *gil al-saba'inat* in the second half of the 1990s. On the other hand, the older leadership generation within the Brotherhood was able, in this period, to hold its position in front of a new dynamic generation. This explains, at least in part, why the Brotherhood's leadership has remained firmly in the hands of the older generation, politically socialized in Nasser's prisons.

Turning to the year of 2005, the major beneficiary of the liberal opening were the political parties (as the natural targets of liberalization measures in the realm of electoral politics) and a new form of political opposition, the Kifaya protest movement. The Muslim Brotherhood started to free-ride on political liberalization and cashed in on its mass constituency in electoral politics. When it was obvious for the authorities that the Islamists would celebrate a significant success on the ballot boxes, the political opening was quickly reversed, leaving behind the identified target of liberalization measures, the political parties, as the main casualties. Finally, political deliberalization in the post-2005 period culminated in the sham elections of 2010, which left the Mubarak authority ultimately discredited and helped to bring about the January 2011 uprising.

Three general lessons can be learned from the Egyptian experience. First, politics of liberalization and deliberalization did not target all opposition forces indiscriminately; and the impact of statist measures on opposition actors was different. Second, the specific timing of deliberalization measures and the way in which they were performed have not only had an impact on a singular opposition actor as a distinct organization, but also on the internal dynamics within the concerned group: the relationship among different factions, strata, and generations. Third, the liberalized autocracy argument has its merits in explaining the strength and weakness of an opposition actor at a certain point in time. In turn, the forms and capacities of opposition actors can become a useful *indicator* of the degree of inclusiveness of an authoritarian polity. From this perspective, studies of opposition are an integral part of studies on the working mechanisms of authoritarianism.

A main caveat as to the generalizability of the findings in this book is that an opposition and the institutional infrastructure, as it was found to operate in Egypt, might not be detected as such in other authoritarian regimes. First, and foremost, closed-hegemonic examples of autocracies—such as in China, the military regimes in Latin America of the 1960s and 1970s, the traditional monarchies in the Gulf states, or some ethnic autocracies in sub-Sahara Africa—present forms of nondemocratic rule quite distinct from liberalized authoritarianism. But also among liberalized authoritarian regimes, we will find significant differences in the institutional infrastructure.

In relatively liberal monarchies, such as in Jordan, Morocco, and Kuwait, a ruling party is lacking, which certainly has an impact on the dynamics of regime-opposition relations. Other cases would see liberalized authoritarian regimes to be erected in ethnically divided societies

(Kenya could be a valuable case of comparison); this has consequences for the formation and internal fabrics of opposition groups, as well as for the relations between the opposition and the incumbency. Yet, other examples of liberalized authoritarian regimes would contradict some of the core findings for the Egyptian case. Not all autocracies would be characterized by the almost complete absence of the rule of law (Putin's Russia could be a case in point where laws and the constitution are more meaningful than in Egypt); and not all liberalized autocracies would be as void of ideological substance as was the case in Mubarak's Egypt (the Islamic Republic of Iran, Mexico under the Partido Revolucionario Institucional, are examples of liberalized autocracies with a valuable programmatic substance).

Varieties among liberalized authoritarian regimes notwithstanding—and, hence, despite the theoretical limitations of the empirical material discussed here—the core findings of this book have the potential to reveal significant insights for the study of liberalized authoritarianism at large: on the persistence of opposition as both an indicator and a necessary precondition for the existence of liberalized authoritarianism; on the idiosyncratic nature and interplay of political opposition and the incumbency in such a polity; on the functions that opposition agents play, and the entrapment strategies that they endorse; and on the, sometimes protracted, presence of political contestation beyond the struggle about the power to rule.

Struggles about Public Space

It is this finding—contestation between incumbents and opposition without political power at stake—that leads me back to questioning the Egyptian opposition on their rationale for engaging in political activism. Opposition activists had a deep understanding of the framework within which they have operated and about the limits in place for their hopes, aims, and demands. They were not so naïve as to believe that democratization was an aim that would realistically be materialized, even though they have upheld such claims in their discourses; rather, speaking openly to the inquirer, some of them admitted to judging political scientists who posed such questions as naïve—prior to the January 2011 uprising, of course.

In retrospect, the fall of Mubarak presented an ironic twist to the opposition forces in Egypt: that it happened was beyond their imagination even though they had made it a constant narrative in their political discourse. If they did not believe that their dreams and demands could materialize, why did opposition activists engage at all? And what did they really want? When analyzing political opposition under authoritarianism, one should ask about the rationale for engaging in political activism outside of the possibility of regime change (even if that happens).

One crucial development of the Egyptian regime was that the discourses within its elite coalition have depoliticized considerably since the years of the populist experiment under Gamal Abdel Nasser. Politics within the NDP, among the members in parliament, and in the official media was narrowed down to the approval of decisions that have not been thoroughly discussed, let alone made, within these very circles, but rather on a superior level among the ruling personnel around the Egyptian president. Whereas activism on the side of the regime entailed a political dimension simply through the proximity to the power center of the polity, such activism was usually void of any ideological substance. Ideological credentials have been employed from above, in a rather eclectic fashion, possibly to legitimize singular policy decisions.

"Real" politics—in terms of a competitive contest between ideas and programs—was *outsourced* from a political regime, which remained preoccupied with political survival. As a consequence, those who wanted to engage in politics proper—for whatever personal motivation—would have found themselves, sooner or later, within the realm of the opposition. Activism within this realm served the ambitions of those who believed in the struggle of different opinions and ideas. For them, it was possible to gain a certain standing in public life that was foreclosed to the NDP herd of "political sheep" nodding through decisions made by the power brokers, more often than not against personal convictions.

The flip side for an opposition figure was the tangible likelihood to becoming the target of statist repression in its "harder" or "softer" form. One indicator supports the claim that the various opposition actors have perceived this opportunity of political—in the sense of politicized—activism attractive: despite the restrictive settings and seemingly feeble opportunities, the opposition in Egypt has seldom opted to boycott participation, with the 1990 parliamentary elections as a notable exception. This is noteworthy because it is counterintuitive to the findings of large-n studies, which have revealed that around one-third of authoritarian elections are boycotted by opposition actors (Lindberg 2006).

An unspoken understanding has existed in Egyptian politics according to which the incumbency was accepted to develop and oversee the rules of this activism. Those rules have been subject to constant changes, but the regime has granted space perceived as sufficient by the opposition for enduring activism—until the parliamentary elections of 2010. Such public space was the subject of political liberalization and deliberalization described in this book. The term "political space" refers to the physical body of regulations—both of formal and informal nature—as much as to the discourses in which opposition forces have engaged. Discourses pertain to the subjects, themes, and ideological backgrounds as much as to the degree to which criticism and opposition has been voiced. Whereas the different opposition forces in Egyptian politics were able to develop and frame political discourses, the channels through which these discourses have been communicated, as much as the degree to which they could be employed in order to criticize incumbents, have remained under the discretion of the incumbents.

The physical realm of public space denotes the forms of organization employed by opposition forces: party activism, civil society, street protest activism. This has remained largely under the control of the Egyptian incumbency, but some exceptions are noteworthy: Islamist activism in the professional syndicates from the mid-1980s onward, the MB's thrilling success in the first round of the 2005 parliamentary elections, and the defection of workers from the corporate body of the state economy show that the regime lost control over oppositional activism, triggering more repressive responses and the contraction of the space for activism previously granted.

This space for political activism outside of the regime remained highly contested: among the *forms* of the organization of political opposition (legalized parties, human rights NGOs, street protest movements, mass-based movements), but also among different *strata* and *generations* within any of these organizational forms of opposition (for a similar argument, see Ismail 1995; Langohr 2004). Not only were these modes of opposition in constant flux, but also the institutions governing incumbency-opposition and opposition-opposition relations. One major finding of this perspective is that the opposition groups in Egypt have struggled with one another at least as much as they struggle with the authoritarian incumbents: pitting parties against human rights groups, engagement in formal political institutions against street protest, Islamists against secularists and leftists, moderates against radicals, and young against old.

This study has exclusively focused on political opposition working within an authoritarian political setting. Again, major political change was beyond imagination for most opposition actors, and democracy was a battle cry in political contestation rather than a viable future scenario for which it was worth fighting. Nevertheless, it was an important component of the political discourse, not the least because it has endowed the opposition with some options for entrapment tactics. Geoffrey Pridham said, with a look at democratic transition, that "the image of the campaign of democracy as a struggle of the society against the state is a useful fiction during the first period of transition, as a unifying slogan of the forces opposed to the current authoritarian regime. But societies are divided in many ways, and the very essence of democracy is the competition among political forces with conflicting interests. This situation creates a dilemma: to bring about democracy, anti-authoritarian forces must unite against authoritarianism, but to be victorious under democracy, they must compete with each other" (Pridham 1995, 66).

Suddenly, democracy turned from a useful fiction to a viable future scenario. With the fall of Mubarak, on February 11, 2011, regime change has happened—despite the opposition. And Pridham's notion could be used as a test for an opposition, trained in their struggle about public space, which would now have to rage not against, but rather without the regime. At least the initial phase of political transition post-Mubarak saw a new version of the struggle about public space: between those who would claim revolutionary legitimacy, and who have continued to engage in street politics, and others who would be primarily engaged in the building of political institutions and in intra-institutional contestation, such as in parliament, committees, and backroom negotiations.

Raging Without the Machine

It is unclear, as of the time of the completion this book, whether Egypt experienced a full breakdown of its authoritarian order or whether Mubarak's fall on February 11, 2011 indicated a critical timing of change and reshuffle of authoritarian leadership (see Albrecht 2012). The transition to consolidated democracy cannot be ruled out entirely, but it is unlikely. Whereas its end result remains obscure, the process of political transformation is an intriguing case of political change under authoritarianism. In the eighteen days between January 25 and February 11, Egypt witnessed a meltdown of political institutions and policing capacities. But the regime's core institution—the military apparatus—survived and took over power in the immediate post-Mubarak period to establish a junta regime in transition (Albrecht and Bishara 2011; International Crisis Group 2012).

The January 25 uprising and Mubarak's fall were not the result of political engagement by the political opposition analyzed in this book. Several of the "loyal opposition" parties had criticized the calls of youth groups to participate in demonstrations, defying street politics as a viable means to initiate change; rather, the parties—including a popular initiative to support Mohammed El-Baradei—were engaged to establish a "counter parliament" as a consequence of the 2010 parliamentary elections. The leadership of the Muslim Brotherhood had also initially discouraged its members to participate but was ignored by its own youth groups, who have contributed to the organization of the events. Neither were the demonstrations organized by the established circle of human rights activists and the individuals who had been engaged in Kifaya's leadership.

The uprising, initiated by the calls of "Facebook groups," started as planned riots to protest a new state holiday (Police Day) on January 25. Another catalyst was the Tunisian revolution, which had led to the ousting of president Ben Ali only a few weeks earlier. Mona El-Ghobashy argued that the uprising "did not happen because Egyptians willed it into being. It happened because there was a sudden change in the balance of resources between rulers and ruled" (El-Ghobashy 2011, 3). Even many protesters on the first few days of the uprising admitted that they would have accepted some limited concessions. The success of the January 25 uprising, evidenced by its continuation beyond the stage of politically motivated riots and the fall of Mubarak, was conditional on the failure of repressive containment strategies, mainly the regime's anti-riot force—the Central Security Forces (CSF)—which disappeared on the early evening of January 28 after four days of fierce street battles.

Apart from the meltdown of the regime's coercive and policing capacities, another major consequence of the January 25 uprising was the implosion of the ruling party NDP, evidenced in the torching and complete destruction of its headquarter in downtown Cairo. Those politicians who had engineered the day-to-day political affairs of the country—such as the NDP's secretary-general Safwat al-Sharif, the interior minister Habib al-Adli, the president's chief of staff Zakariya Azmi, the Gamal-Mubarak henchman Ahmed Ezz, and even Gamal Mubarak himself—disappeared from the public scene. Only hours after the CSF's coercive capacities had broken down, some prominent NDP members were identified at Cairo's international airport and prevented from leaving the country. These attempted escapes, in conjunction with the desperate attempt of some NDP bigwigs to actively reconquer Tahrir Square on what came to be known as the "Battle of the Camel" on February 2, indicate that those former members of the political incumbency were no longer in a position to influence decision making, henceforth monopolized by the military junta.

By the first competitive presidential elections in May and June 2012, Egypt's political landscape had fundamentally changed, with the meltdown of authoritarian regime capacities; younger strata of society gaining confidence and leverage in politics; protracted street politics on and beyond iconic Tahrir Square; competitive and fair parliamentary elections with the Islamists, the former regime's arch enemy, winning a majority of seats; an inclusive process of constitutional reforms; and competitive presidential elections in mid-2012. Egypt's authoritarian regime is certainly in a process of transition, and so is the political opposition established under the Mubarak era. The Muslim Brotherhood formed a political party, the Freedom and Justice Party (FJP); the Salafi movement has emerged as a new significant player in politics; political parties have mushroomed, sidelining the established loyal opposition parties; and new freedoms and competitive electoral processes pose new standards and requirements to the political opposition socialized in an authoritarian framework.

But the ancien régime has not completely vanished; and neither did the fabrics and mechanisms regulating the work of opposition forces. With the SCAF in a dominant position, the engineering of the transition process has been somewhat path-dependent. Path-dependency also applies to the political agents in the transition process, most of whom had only learned how to play authoritarian politics, rather than democracy or the transition to democracy. This holds true for both regime and opposition. One intriguing facet of the post-Mubarak transition period is that the lines between these two poles—regime and opposition—have further evaporated. Whereas this was an immediate consequence of the meltdown of the regime, it also reflects on one of the core findings of this analysis: the fact that the lines between the authoritarian regime and its equally authoritarian opponents had always been blurred.

During Mubarak, this phenomenon was indicated by the parties' loyalty to the power center, the Brotherhood's self-limitation, and the individual intellectuals' unwillingness to join forces to confront the incumbency. After Mubarak, the establishment of organizations and the drawing of new battle lines demand a longer time period; and, as of the time of finalizing this book, it remained impossible to guess who would represent the regime and who the opposition. But the actions and decisions of some individual figures, regarded as representatives of the opposition, imply that the distinction between regime—now represented by the army officers in the SCAF—and opposition might have always been somewhat artificial—at least for the individuals concerned. It is striking that Tal'at Sadat—the nephew of the former president Anwar Sadat—accepted the SCAF's call to serve as the NDP's last chairman, despite the fact that he was the former head of the Liberal Party and served a one-year prison sentence in 2006 for his critique of the military. Mustafa Bakri, a journalist, former editor of the *Dustour* newspaper, and vocal opposition member representing the secular-nationalist camp rose to one of the most powerful members of parliament as the unofficial representative of the military's interests. And Mounir Fakhry Abdel Nour, the secretary-general of the New Wafd Party, accepted the invitation to serve in the military-appointed cabinet in February 2011.

Apart from the lack of distinction between regime incumbency and opposition, a number of other facets of transitional politics indicate a path-dependent development of the former opposition. Fragmentation among political players has continued, with the formation, prior to parliamentary elections in the winter of 2011/12, of around seventy new political parties or would-be parties and roughly two hundred youth groups. This has replicated some of the ills of the opposition establishment in the ancien régime. Personal rivalries among individuals prevent the formation of groups and coalitions strong enough to generate political leverage. Some of these new groups and parties looked like "political fiefdoms" quite similar to the internal fabrics of political organizations during the Mubarak era. Another problem inherited from the past was the organizations' programmatic diffusion. In part because of the short time frame for the establishment of organizations, the political messages of most of the new groups have pronounced broad ideals to which everybody could subscribe, such as "democracy," "human rights," "people's empowerment," "social justice," and "national unity." But most groups did not offer any clear concepts and concrete outlines on social, economic, and political reforms.

Transition to Uncertainty

Most problematic among the path-dependent facets of the transition process is the lack of the rule of law. Whereas uncertainty about the application of the law and formal procedures was an essential trait of the Mubarak regime, the lack of certainty is a natural component of any transition process. Hence, the very existence of uncertainty is not surprising, given the lack of policing capacities, the breakdown or dissolution of political institutions (ruling party, constitution, parliament), and the protracted unclear power relations among political institutions including the SCAF;

the elected president Mohammed Morsi and his cabinet; the parliament dominated by Islamists; the judiciary called on for political litigation on a regular basis; and several committees established to communicate and negotiate among the political forces.

What was peculiar about the immediate post-Mubarak transition process is the attempt of the dominant political force—the SCAF—to uphold the picture of an orderly and lawful transition, consisting of a constitutional declaration allotting significant powers to the SCAF (issued on March 30, 2011, and serving as an interim constitution); new laws regulating the institution-building process (such as party formation, elections, etc.) but also restricting contentious political participation (such as a new anti-strike law, issued on March 23, 2011); and a political discourse pronouncing the meaning of the law (as in the official reasoning for the prosecution of Egyptian and international NGOs in early 2012).

Quite like under Mubarak, the political reality defies the image of the rule of law. The implementation of the anti-strike law has remained erratic; the NGO saga was solved, on alleged US pressure, by the sudden emigration of the defendants (on March 1, 2012); hardly any human rights violations before and during the Egyptian revolution have been brought to justice; and, owing to unclear regulations, several bodies have been engaged in a battle of litigation (for instance, involving conflicting sentences and judgments of the Presidential Elections Committee and several Administrative Court decisions prior to the presidential elections in 2012).

The former opposition, henceforth proactive political forces in a fluid transition environment, therefore operates under similar conditions as under Mubarak—the main differences being that, first, the larger regime structure has disappeared, and, second, not only the rules of the political game are subject to a fair dose of uncertainty, but also the outcome of contestation. On March 19, 2011, a limited number of constitutional amendments were put to a popular referendum, the outcome of which was uncertain despite the clear result of 77 percent in favor of the changes. Similarly, the parliamentary elections between November 28, 2011, and January 11, 2012, saw a clear majority of Islamists taking roughly 70 percent of the seats (composed of Muslim Brothers and Salafi candidates); other than the Mubarakist election regime, which saw results engineered to secure a majority for the ruling party, the outcome was uncertain, qualifying the elections as the first democratic process in the country's modern history.

It is worth recalling Adam Przeworski's dictum that democracies comprise a high degree of uncertainty with respect to the outcome of political processes, while relying on significant certainty concerning policymaking rules and procedures. By contrast, authoritarian regimes embrace high uncertainty concerning rules and procedures but certainty about outcomes of processes (Przeworski 1991, 10–14). Hybrid regimes, in turn, witness uncertainty in both political procedures and the outcome of contestation. In this light, Egypt's transition process mirrors a "hybrid regime" of sorts, that is, a political entity involving uncertainty in procedures and their outcome, and including characteristics of both democracy and authoritarianism.

This is not to engage into the debate, prominent in political science, whether transition phenomena would qualify as hybrid regimes at all.[1] I also refrain from discussing the methodological question whether hybrid regimes would constitute a regime type in its own right situated on a continuum between democracy and authoritarianism, or subtypes—annotated by a set of defining adjectives—of an established typology, featuring, for instance, democracy (illiberal democracy) versus authoritarianism (competitive authoritarianism).

What matters here is the situation within which political agents in Egypt started to operate after the fall of Mubarak, irrespective of the time

1. Leonardo Morlina, among other scholars, argued that "some sort of stabilization or duration, at least . . . for a decade, of those ambiguous uncertain institutional set-ups" would be required for a case to qualify as a "hybrid regime" (Morlina 2009, 282). His approach, however, remains somewhat fuzzy and arbitrary, disqualifying the typological classification of a significant number of political entities beyond democracy and authoritarianism. For more discussion of "hybrid regimes," the "gray zone" between democracy and authoritarianism, and the concept of "diminished subtypes," consult Diamond (2002); Levitsky and Way (2002); Rüb (2002); Ottaway (2003); Merkel (2004); Schedler (2006); Howard and Roessler (2006); Wigell (2008); Morlino (2009).

span of a political transition and its result: democracy, authoritarianism, or a consolidated hybrid regime in the "gray zone" between those two poles. Given that the country experienced a path-dependent transition process, the ambiguities and idiosyncrasies of institutions and agents discussed in this book will continue to inspire the transition process. A protracted phase of uncertainty is likely to characterize the country's immediate future because several conditions for democratic consolidation seem to be missing, whereas popular political engagement precludes the quick return to a Mubarak-type authoritarian order.

Glossary

Bibliography

Index

Glossary

'adala: justice
amn al-dawla: state security
amn al-markazi: central security
awqaf: religious endowments
da'wa: religious call
duf'a: university graduate class
fatwa: religious edict
gil al-saba'inat: generation of the seventies
gil al-wasat: middle generation
hiwar al-watani: national dialogue
hizb: party
hurriya: freedom
infitah: open-door policy
islah: reform
jahiliya: state of ignorance
jihad: holy war
kutla: bloc
majlis: council
maktab al-irshad: guidance bureau
manabir, pl. of *minbar*: platform
murshid al-'amm: supreme guide
rabta: association
sha'ab: people
sharika madania: nonprofit company
shari'a: Islamic law
shilla: peer group
shura: consultation
tanzim: organization

ulema: Islamic clergy
umma: Muslim community
wasatiya: centrist movement
zakat: religious alms

Bibliography

Abd al-Al, Tariq. 2004. *Hurriya al-Tanzim wa al-Ahzab al-Siyasiya fi Masr* [The Freedom of Organization and the Political Parties in Egypt]. Cairo: Hisham Mubarak Law Center.

Abd al-Hafiz, Ahmad. 2005. *Silsila al-Ahzab al-Siyasiya: Al-Hizb al-Dimuqrati al-Arabi al-Nasseri* [The Political Parties Series: The Arab Democratic Nasserist Party]. Cairo: Al-Ahram Center for Political and Strategic Studies.

Abd el-Wahab, Ayman el-Sayed. 2000. "The Law on Non-Governmental Associations towards the Stimulation of Civil Society in Egypt." *Strategic Papers* 89/2000. Cairo: ACPSS.

Abd al-Wahab, Essam. 2005. "Al-Tagriba al-Hizbiya al-Masriya min Nasser ila Sadat" [The Egyptian Party Experience from Nasser to Sadat]. *Magalla al-Dimuqratiya* [Democracy Review] 17: 149–58.

Abdel-Latif, Omayma. 2001. "Egyptian Electoral Politics: New Rules, Old Game." *Review of African Political Economy* 28, no. 88: 273–79.

Abdel Rahman, Maha. 2002. "The Politics of 'Uncivil' Society in Egypt." *Review of African Political Economy* 29, no. 91: 21–36.

Abdelrahman, Maha. 2004. *Civil Society Exposed: The Politics of NGOs in Egypt*. Cairo: American University in Cairo Press.

Abed-Kotob, Sana. 1995. "The Accomodationists Speak: Goals and Strategies of the Muslim Brotherhood of Egypt." *International Journal of Middle East Studies* 27: 321–40.

Aclimandos, Tewfik. 2006. "Les Frères: De la clandestinité au *Tamkin*." In Kohstall, *L'Égypte dans l'année 2005*, 83–107.

———. 2002. *Officiers et Frères Musulmans*. Cairo: CEDEJ.

Ahmad, Makram Muhammad. 2003. *Mu'amara 'am Muraga'a? Hawar ma'a Qadat al-Tatarruf fi Sign al-Aqrab* [Conspiracy or Revisionism? Conversation with the Leadership of Extremism in al-Aqrab Prison]. Cairo: Dar al-Shourouq.

Al-Ahram Hebdo, several issues, 2003–2006.

Al-Ahram Weekly, several issues, 2003–2011.

Alam, Do'a Husayn. 2006. "Ahzab al-Mu'aradh fi Inhisar al-Daur fi Waqt al-Istihqaqat" [The Opposition Parties' Limited Role in the Moment of Truth]. *Magalla al-Dimuqratiya* [Democracy Review] 21: 135–46.

Al-Awadi, Hesham. 2005. "Mubarak and the Islamists: Why Did the 'Honeymoon' End?" *Middle East Journal* 59, no. 1: 62–80.

———. 2004. *In Pursuit of Legitimacy: The Muslim Brothers and Mubarak, 1982–2000*. London: Tauris Academic Studies.

Albrecht, Holger. 2012. "Authoritarian Transformation or Transition from Authoritarianism? Insights on Regime Change in Egypt." In Korany and El-Mahdi, *Arab Spring*, 251–70.

———, ed. 2010a. *Contentious Politics in the Middle East: Political Opposition under Authoritarianism*. Gainesville: University Press of Florida.

———. 2010b. "Introduction: Contentious Politics, Political Opposition, and Authoritarianism," In Albrecht, *Contentious Politics in the Middle East*, 1–14.

———. 2010c. "Political Opposition and Arab Authoritarianism: Some Conceptual Remarks," In Albrecht, *Contentious Politics in the Middle East*, 17–33.

———. 2008. "The Nature of Political Participation." In *Political Participation in the Middle East and North Africa*, edited by Ellen Lust-Okar and Saloua Zerhouni, 15–32. Boulder, CO: Lynne Rienner.

———. 2007. "Authoritarian Opposition and the Politics of Challenge in Egypt." In Schlumberger, *Debating Arab Authoritarianism*, 59–74.

———. 2005. "How Can Opposition Support Authoritarianism? Lessons from Egypt." *Democratization* 12, no. 3: 378–97.

Albrecht, Holger, and Dina Bishara. 2011. "Back on Horseback: The Military and Political Transformation in Egypt." *Middle East Law and Governance* 3: 13–23.

Albrecht, Holger, and Florian Kohstall. 2010. "Ägyptens letzte Wahl." *Informationsprojekt Naher und Mittlerer Osten* 16, no. 64: 39–43.

Albrecht, Holger, Peter Pawelka, and Oliver Schlumberger. 1997. "Wirtschaftliche Liberalisierung und Regimewandel in Ägypten." *WeltTrends* 16: 43–63.

Albrecht, Holger, and Oliver Schlumberger. 2004. "'Waiting for Godot': Regime Change without Democratization in the Middle East." *International Political Science Review* 25, no. 4: 371–92.

Albrecht, Holger, and Eva Wegner. 2006. "Autocrats and Islamists: Contenders and Containment in Egypt and Morocco." *Journal of North African Studies* 11, no. 2: 123–41.

Alexander, Christopher. 2000. "Opportunities, Organizations, and Ideas: Islamists and Workers in Tunisia and Algeria." *International Journal of Middle East Studies* 32: 465–90.

Al-Korachi, Aliaa, and Chaimaa Abdel-Hamid. 2005. "Ils font la pluie et le beau temps." *Al-Ahram Hebdo* 578 (October 5–11, 2005): 5.

Allain, Jean. 2003. *The Perpetual State of Emergency in Egypt.* Lecture held at the American University in Cairo, February 25.

Al-Sayyid, Mustafa K. 2009. "Kefaya at a Turning Point." In *Political and Social Protest in Egypt,* edited by Nicholas Hopkins, 45–59. Cairo Papers in Social Science 29. Cairo: American University in Cairo Press.

Al-Zayat, Montasser. 2005. "Al-Gamaʻat al-Islamiya—Ruʼiya min al-Dakhil" [The Islamic Groups—A View from Inside]. Published in an articles series in *Al-Hayat,* January 10–14, 2005.

Anderson, Lisa. 1987a. "Lawless Government and Illegal Opposition: Reflections on the Middle East." *Journal of International Affairs* 40, no. 2: 219–32.

Ansari, Hamied N. 1984a. "Sectarian Conflict in Egypt and the Political Expediency of Religion." *Middle East Journal* 38, no. 3: 397–418.

———. 1984b. "The Islamic Militants in Egyptian Politics." *International Journal of Middle East Studies* 16: 123–44.

Aspinall, Edward. 2005. *Opposing Suharto: Compromise, Resistance, and Regime Change in Indonesia.* Stanford: Stanford University Press.

Assaad, Ragui. 2002. "The Transformation of the Egyptian Labor Market: 1988–1998." In *The Egyptian Labor Market in an Era of Reform,* edited by Ragui Assaad, 3–64. Cairo: The American University in Cairo Press.

Auda, Gehad. 2004. *Gamal Mubarak: Tajdid al-Liberaliya al-Wataniya* [Gamal Mubarak: The Renewal of National Liberalism]. Cairo: Dar al-Hurriya.

Baaklini, Abdo, Guilain Denoeux, and Robert Springborg, eds. 1999. *Legislative Politics in the Arab World: The Resurgence of Democratic Institutions.* Boulder, CO: Lynne Rienner.

Baker, Raymond W. 2003. *Islam without Fear: Egypt and the New Islamists.* Cambridge: Harvard University Press.

———. 1978. *Egypt's Uncertain Revolution under Nasser and Sadat.* Cambridge: Harvard University Press.

Barker, Rodney, ed. 1971. *Studies in Opposition*. Basingstoke: Macmillan.

Barraclough, Steven. 1998. "Al-Azhar: Between the Government and the Islamists." *Middle East Journal* 52, no. 2: 236–49.

Bayat, Asef. 2002. "Activism and Social Development in the Middle East." *International Journal of Middle East Studies* 34: 1–28.

Beinin, Joel. 2006. "Egyptian Textile Workers in the Transition to a Neo-Liberal Order." *Historical Perspectives* 1, no. 3: 16–18.

———. 1988. "Islam, Marxism, and the Shubra al-Khayma Textile Workers: Muslim Brothers and Communists in the Egyptian Trade Union Movement." In *Islam, Politics, and Social Movements*, edited by Edmund Burke III and Ira M. Lapidus, 207–27. London: I. B. Tauris.

Beinin, Joel, and Hossam el-Hamalawy. 2007. "Egyptian Textile Workers Confront the New Economic Order." *Middle East Report Online*, March 25, http://www.merip.org/mero/mero032507.

Beinin, Joel, and Zachary Lockman. 1988. *Workers on the Nile: Nationalism, Communism, Islam, and the Egyptian Working Class, 1882–1954*. London: I. B. Tauris.

Bellin, Eva. 2004. "The Robustness of Authoritarianism in the Middle East: Exceptionalism in Comparative Perspective." *Comparative Politics* 36, no. 2: 139–57.

Bermeo, Nancy. 1997. "Myths of Moderation: Confrontation and Conflict during Democratic Transition." *Comparative Politics* 29, no. 3: 305–22.

Bernard-Maugiron, Nathalie. 1999. "La Haute Cour constitutionelle, gardienne des libertés publiques." In *Le prince et son juge: Droit et politique dans l'Égypte contemporaine*, edited by CEDEJ (Égypte/Monde Arabe no. 2), 17–53. Cairo: CEDEJ.

Bernard-Maugiron, Nathalie, and Benoit Dupret. 1999. "'Les principes de la Sharia sont la source principale de la législation': La Haute Cour constitutionelle et la référence à la loi islamique." In Bernard-Maugiron, *Prince et son juge*, 107–25.

Bianchi, Robert. 1989. *Unruly Corporatism: Associational Life in Twentieth-Century Egypt*. Oxford: Oxford University Press.

———. 1985. "Businessmen's Association in Egypt and Turkey." *Annals of the American Academy of Political and Social Science* 482: 147–59.

Bishara, Dina. 2012. "The Power of Workers in Egypt's 2011 Uprising." In Korany and El-Mahdi, *Arab Spring*, 83–103.

Blaydes, Lisa. 2011. *Elections and Distributive Politics in Mubarak's Egypt*. Cambridge: Cambridge University Press.

Blaydes, Lisa, and James Lo. 2012. "One Man, One Vote, One Time?: A Model of Democratization in the Middle East." *Journal of Theoretical Politics* 24, 1: 110–46.

Blondel, Jean. 1997. "Political Opposition in the Contemporary World." *Government and Opposition* 32, no. 4: 462–86.

Brooker, Paul. 2000. *Non-Democratic Regimes: Theory, Government, and Politics.* New York: St. Martin's Press.

Brouwer, Imco. 2000. *US Civil-Society Assistance to the Arab World: The Cases of Egypt and Palestine.* EUI Working Paper, No. 2000/5. Florence: Robert Schuman Center, EUI.

Browers, Michaelle. 2009. *Political Ideology in the Arab World: Accommodation and Transformation.* Cambridge: Cambridge University Press.

Brown, Nathan. 2012. *When Victory Is Not an Option: Islamist Movements in Arab Politics.* Ithaca: Cornell University Press.

———. 2011. "Post-Revolutionary Al-Azhar." The Carnegie Papers, September, carnegieendowment.org/files/al_azhar.pdf.

———. 1997. *The Rule of Law in the Arab World: Courts in Egypt and the Gulf.* Cambridge: Cambridge University Press.

Brown, Nathan, and Hesham Nasr. 2005. *Egypt's Judges Step Forward: The Judicial Election Boycott and Egyptian Reform.* Washington, DC: Carnegie Endowment for International Peace.

Brown, Nathan, and Kirsten Stilt. 2011. "A Haphazard Constitutional Compromise." Carnegie Endowment for International Peace, Commentary, April 11, http://www.carnegieendowment.org/2011/04/11/haphazard-constitutional -compromise/2ql.

Brownlee, Jason. 2007. *Authoritarianism in an Age of Democratization.* Cambridge: Cambridge University Press.

———. 2005. "Political Crisis and Restabilization: Iraq, Libya, Syria, and Tunisia." In *Authoritarianism in the Middle East: Regimes and Resistance,* edited by Marsha Pripstein Posusney and Michele Penner Angrist, 43–62. Boulder, CO: Lynne Rienner.

———. 2002. "The Decline of Pluralism in Mubarak's Egypt." *Journal of Democracy* 13, no. 4: 6–14.

Brumberg, Daniel. 2005. "Liberalization versus Democracy." *In Uncharted Journey: Promoting Democracy in the Middle East,* edited by Thomas Carothers and Marina Ottaway, 15–35. Washington, DC: Carnegie Endowment for International Peace.

———. 2002. "The Trap of Liberalized Autocracy." *Journal of Democracy* 13, no. 4: 56–67.

Bueno de Mesquita, Bruce, and George W. Downs. 2005. "Development and Democracy." *Foreign Affairs* 84, no. 5: 77–86.

Butterworth, Charles E., and I. William Zartman, eds. 2001. *Between the State and Islam.* Cambridge: Cambridge University Press.

Cairo Times, several issues, 2003–2004.

Cappocia, Giovanni. 2002. "Anti-System Parties: A Conceptual Reassessment." *Journal of Theoretical Politics* 14, no. 1: 9–35.

Carapico, Sheila. 2002. "Foreign Aid for Promoting Democracy in the Arab World." *Middle East Journal* 56, no. 3: 379–95.

———. 2000. "NGOs, INGOs, GO-NGOs, and DO-NGOs: Making Sense of Non-Governmental Institutions." *Middle East Report* 30, no. 1: 12–15.

———. 1998. "Mission: Democracy." *Middle East Report* 28, no. 209: 17–20.

Cardenas, Sonia, and Andrew Flibbert. 2005. "National Human Rights Institutions in the Middle East." *Middle East Journal* 59, no. 3: 411–36.

Carey, Sabine. 2006. "The Dynamic Relationship between Protest and Repression." *Political Research Quarterly* 59, no. 1: 1–11.

Case, William. 2006. "Manipulative Skills: How Do Rulers Control the Electoral Arena?" In Schedler, *Electoral Authoritarianism*, 95–112.

Cavatorta, Francesco, and Azzam Elananza. 2010. "'Show Me the Money!' Opposition, Western Funding, and Civil Society in Jordan and Lebanon." In Albrecht, *Contentious Politics in the Middle East*, 75-93.

Collombier, Virginie. 2007. "The Internal Stakes of the 2005 Elections: The Struggle for Influence in Egypt's National Democratic Party." *Middle East Journal* 61, no. 1: 95–111.

Dahl, Robert. 1975. "Governments and Political Oppositions." In *Handbook of Political Science*, vol. 3, *Macropolitical Theory*, edited by Fred I. Greenstein and Nelson Polsby, 115–74. Reading, UK: Addison Wesley.

———, ed. 1973. *Regimes and Oppositions*. New Haven: Yale University Press.

———. 1971. *Polyarchy: Participation and Opposition*. New Haven: Yale University Press.

———, ed. 1966. *Political Oppositions in Western Democracies*. New Haven: Yale University Press.

Dawisha, Adeed, and I. William Zartman, eds. 1988. *Beyond Coercion: The Durability of the Arab State*. London: Croom Helm.

Diamond, Larry. 2002. "Thinking about Hybrid Regimes." *Journal of Democracy* 13, no. 2: 21–35.

Dodge, Toby. 2002. "Bringing the Bourgeoisie Back In: Globalization and the Birth of Liberal Authoritarianism in the Middle East." In *Globalization and the Middle East–Islam, Economy, Society, and Politics*, edited by Toby Dodge and Richard Higgott, 169–87. London: Royal Institute for International Affairs.

Dupret, Baudouin. 2000. *Au nom de quel droit*. Cairo: CEDEJ.

Dupret, Baudouin, Maurits Berger, and Laila al-Zwaini, eds. 1999. *Legal Pluralism in the Arab World*. The Hague: Kluwer.

Egyptian Organization for Human Rights (EOHR), several reports, 2003–2005.

El-Ghobashy, Mona. 2011. "The Praxis of the Egyptian Revolution." *Middle East Report* 258: 2–13.

———. 2010. "The Liquidation of Egypt's Illiberal Experiment." *Middle East Research and Information Project*, December 19, http://www.merip.org/mero /mero122910.

———. 2008. "Constitutionalist Contention in Contemporary Egypt." *American Behavioral Scientist* 51: 1590–1610.

———. 2006. "Egypt's Paradoxical Elections." *Middle East Report* 238: 20–29.

———. 2005. "The Metamorphosis of the Egyptian Muslim Brotherhood." *International Journal of Middle East Studies* 37, no. 3: 373–95.

El-Ghonemy, Riad, ed. 2003. *Egypt in the Twenty-first Century: Challenges for Development*. London: Routledge.

El-Khawaga, Dina. 2002. "La génération *seventies* en Égypte: La société civile comme répertoire d'action alternative." In *Résistances et protestations dans les sociétés musulmanes*, edited by Mounia Bennani-Chraibi and Olivier Fillieule, 271–91. Paris: Presse de Sciences-Po.

El-Mahdi, Rabab. 2009. "Enough! Egypt's Quest for Democracy." *Comparative Political Studies* 42: 1011–39.

El Mahdy, Alia. 2002. "The Labor Absorption Capacity of the Informal Sector in Egypt." In *The Egyptian Labor Market in an Era of Reform*, edited by Ragui Assaad, 99–130. Cairo: The American University in Cairo Press.

El-Megharbel, Nihal. 2008. "The Impact of Recent Macro and Labor Market Policies on Job Creation in Egypt." In Kheir El-Din, *Egyptian Economy*, 179–200.

El-Mikawy, Noha, and Marsha Pripstein Posusney. 2000. "Labor Representation in the Age of Globalization: Trends and Issues in Non-Oil-Based Arab

Countries." Paper presented at the 3rd Mediterranean Forum, Cairo, Egypt, March 5–8.

El Shafei, Omar. 1995. *Workers, Trade Unions, and the State in Egypt*. Cairo Papers in Social Science 18. Cairo: The American University in Cairo Press.

Elyachar, Julia. 2003. "Mappings of Power: The State, NGOs, and International Organizations in the Informal Economy of Cairo." *Comparative Studies of Society and History* 45, no. 3: 571–605.

Fahmy, Ninette. 2002. *The Politics of Egypt: State-Society Relations*. London: Routledge.

———. 1998. "The Performance of the Muslim Brotherhood in the Egyptian Syndicates: An Alternative Formula for Reform?" *Middle East Journal* 52, no. 4: 551–62.

Farah, Nadia. 2009. *Egypt's Political Economy*. Cairo: American University in Cairo Press.

Fawzy, Essam, and Ivesa Lübben. 2000. "Zensur und Inquisition in Ägypten— Das Dilemma des ägyptischen Legitimationsdiskurses." *Informationsprojekt Naher und Mittlerer Osten* 23/24: 54–59.

Ferrié, Jean-Noel. 2006. "La parlementarisation de l'islam politique: La dynamique des modérés." In *Le Kiosque: L'Égypte à la veille de changement*, edited by Jean-Noel Ferrié [www.ceri-sciencespo.com/cerifr/kiosque.htm]. Paris: CERI.

Franklin, James C. 2002. "Political Party Opposition to Noncompetitive Regimes: A Cross-National Analysis." *Political Research Quarterly* 55, no. 3: 521–46.

Fürtig, Henner. 2007. "Transformation to Persist: Political Reform in Egypt since 9/11." In *The Arab Authoritarian Regime between Reform and Persistence*, edited by Henner Fürtig, 26–56. Newcastle: Cambridge Scholars.

Gandhi, Jennifer, and Adam Przeworski. 2007. "Authoritarian Institutions and the Survival of Autocrats." *Comparative Political Studies* 40, 11: 1279–1301.

———. 2006. "Cooperation, Cooptation, and Rebellion under Dictatorships." *Economics & Politics* 18, no. 1: 1–26.

Gandhi, Jennifer, and Wonik Kim. 2005. "Cooptation and Coercion of Workers under Dictatorship." *Journal of Politics* 72, 3: 646–58.

Gates, Scott, et al. 2006. "Institutional Inconsistency and Political Instability: Polity Duration, 1800–2000." *American Journal of Political Science* 50, no. 4: 893–908.

Gerges, Fawaz. 2000. "The End of the Islamist Insurgency in Egypt: Costs and Prospects." *Middle East Journal* 54, no. 4: 592–612.

Ghadbian, Najib. 1997. *Democratization and the Islamist Challenge in the Arab World.* Boulder, CO: Westview Press.

Ghalioun, Burhan. 2004. "The Persistence of Arab Authoritarianism." *Journal of Democracy* 15, no. 4: 126–46.

Grodsky, Brian. 2007. "Resource Dependency and Political Opportunity: Explaining the Transformation from Excluded Political Opposition Parties to Human Rights Organizations in Post-Communist Uzbekistan." *Government and Opposition* 42, no. 1: 96–120.

Gunther, Richard, and Larry Diamond. 2003. "Species of Political Parties: A New Typology." *Party Politics* 9, no. 2: 167–99.

Hafez, Muhammad. 2003. *Why Muslims Rebel: Repression and Resistance in the Islamic World.* Boulder, CO: Lynne Rienner.

Hafez, Muhammad, and Quintan Wiktorowicz. 2004. "Violence as Contention in the Egyptian Islamic Movement." In *Islamic Activism: A Social Movement Theory Approach,* edited by Quintan Wiktorowicz, 61–88. Bloomington: Indiana University Press.

Hagberg, Sten. 2002. "'Enough Is Enough': An Ethnography of the Struggle against Impunity in Burkina Faso." *Journal of Modern African Studies* 40, no. 2: 217–46.

Hassabo, Chaymaa. 2006. "Moubarak 'sans cravat,' un Moubarak 'démocratique'?" In Kohstall, *L'Égypte dans l'année 2005*, 29–54.

———. 2005. "Gamal Moubarak au centre du pouvoir: Une succession achevée?" In Kohstall, *L'Égypte dans l'année 2004*, 9–24.

Hatina, Meir. 2005. "The 'Other Islam': The Egyptian Wasat Party." *Critique: Critical Middle Eastern Studies* 14, no. 2: 171–84.

Hinnebusch, Raymond A. 1985. *Egyptian Politics under Sadat: The Post-Populist Development of an Authoritarian-Modernizing State.* Cambridge: Cambridge University Press.

———. 1984. "The Reemergence of the Wafd Party: Glimpses of the Liberal Opposition in Egypt." *International Journal of Middle East Studies* 16: 99–121.

Hisham Mubarak Law Center (HMLC), several reports, 2003–2006.

Howard, Marc Morjé, and Philip G. Roessler. 2006. "Liberalizing Electoral Outcomes in Competitive Authoritarian Regimes." *American Journal of Political Science* 50, no. 2: 365–81.

Hudson, Michael. 1977. *Arab Politics: The Search for Legitimacy.* New Haven: Yale University Press.

Human Rights Watch. 2005. "Egypt: Mass Arrests and Torture in Sinai." *Human Rights Watch Report* 17, no. 3, http://www.hrw.org/sites/default/files/reports /egypt0205.pdf.

Huntington, Samuel P. 1991. *The Third Wave Democratization in the Late Twentieth Century.* Norman: University of Oklahoma Press.

Hussein, Aziza. 2003. "NGOs and the Development Challenges of the Twenty-first Century." In El-Ghonemy, *Egypt in the Twenty-first Century,* 199–217.

Hussein, Marwa. 2005. "La rumeur gronde." *Al-Ahram Hebdo* 578, no. 5: 14.

International Crisis Group. 2012. *Lost in Transition: The World According to Egypt's SCAF.* Middle East/North Africa Report No. 121, April 24. Brussels: International Crisis Group.

International Crisis Group. 2007. *Egypt's Sinai Question.* Middle East/North Africa Report No. 61, January 20. Brussels: International Crisis Group.

International Crisis Group. 2005. *Reforming Egypt: In Search of a Strategy.* Middle East/North Africa Report No. 46, October 4. Brussels: International Crisis Group.

Ionescu, Ghita, and Isabel de Madariaga. 1971. *Die Opposition: Ihre politische Funktion in Vergangenheit und Gegenwart.* Munich: Beck.

Ismail, Salwa. 2000. "The Popular Movement Dimension of Contemporary Militant Islamism: Socio-Spatial Determinants in the Cairo Urban Setting." *Comparative Studies in History and Society* 42, no. 2: 363–93.

———. 1999. "Religious 'Orthodoxy' as Public Morality: The State, Islamism, and Cultural Politics in Egypt." *Critique* 14: 25–47.

———. 1995. "State-Society Relations in Egypt: Restructuring the Political." *Arab Studies Quarterly* 17, no. 3: 37–52.

Jolen, Judith. 2003. "The Quest for Legitimacy: The Role of Islam in the State's Political Discourse in Egypt and Jordan (1979–1996)." PhD diss., University of Nijmegen.

Jouvenel, Bertrand de. 1966. "The Means of Contestation." *Government and Opposition* 1, no. 1: 155–74.

Kapiszewski, Andrzej. 2006. "Saudi Arabia: Steps Toward Democratization or Reconfiguration of Authoritarianism?" *Journal of Asian and African Studies* 41, nos. 5/6: 459–82.

Karawan, Ibrahim A. 2001. "Political Parties between State Power and Islamist Opposition." In Butterworth and Zartman, *Between the State and Islam,* 158–83.

Karumidze, Zurab, and James V. Wertsch. 2005. *"Enough!": The Rose Revolution in the Republic of Georgia, 2003*. New York: Nova Science.

Kassem, Maye. 2006. *Egypt: Politics in the New Millennium*. UNISCI Discussion Paper, no. 12, October.

———. 2004. *Egyptian Politics: The Dynamics of Authoritarian Rule*. Boulder, CO: Lynne Rienner.

———. 2001. "Information and Production of Knowledge or Lobbying?: Businessmen's Association, Federation of Labor Unions, and the Ministry of Manpower." In *Institutional Reform and Economic Reform in Egypt*, edited by Noha El-Mikawy and Heba Handoussa, 61–78. Cairo: American University in Cairo Press.

———. 1999. *In the Guise of Democracy: Governance in Contemporary Egypt*. Reading, UK: Garnet.

Kheir El-Din, Hanaa, ed. 2008. *The Egyptian Economy: Current Challenges and Future Prospects*. Cairo: The American University in Cairo Press.

Kheir El-Din, Hanaa, and Heba El-Laithy. 2008. "An Assessment of Growth, Distribution, and Poverty in Egypt: 1990/91–2004/05." In Kheir El-Din, *Egyptian Economy*, 13–52.

Kienle, Eberhard. 2007. "Democracy Promotion and the Renewal of Authoritarian Rule." In Schlumberger, *Debating Arab Authoritarianism*, 231–49.

———. 2004. "Transformation without Democratization? Egypt's Political Future." *Internationale Politik und Gesellschaft* 4: 70–86.

———. 2001. *A Grand Delusion: Democracy and Economic Reform in Egypt*. London: I. B. Tauris.

———. 1998. "More Than a Response to Islamism: The Political Deliberalization of Egypt in the 1990s." *Middle East Journal* 52, no. 2: 219–35.

Kirchheimer, Otto. 1966. "Germany: The Vanishing Opposition." In Dahl, *Political Oppositions in Western Democracies*, 237–59.

Klaus, Enrique. 2004. "Un nouveau Guide Supreme, une nouvelle ère? Eléments d'analyse de l'actualité médiatique des Frères Musulmans." In *L'Égypte dans l'année: Chronique politique*, ed. Florian Kohstall, 47–56. Cairo: CEDEJ.

Köhler, Kevin. 2008. "Electoral Politics under Neopatrimonialism in Egypt: Formal Institutions and Informal Mechanisms of Rule." *Democratization* 15, no. 5: 974–90.

Kohstall, Florian, ed. 2006. *L'Égypte dans l'année 2005*. Cairo: CEDEJ.

———, ed. 2005. *L'Égypte dans l'année 2004*. Cairo: CEDEJ.

Korany, Bahgat. 1998. "Restricted Democratization from Above: Egypt." In *Political Liberalization and Democratization in the Arab World*, vol. 2, *Comparative Experiences*, edited by Bahgat Korany, Rex Brynen, and Paul Noble, 39–69. Boulder, CO: Lynne Rienner.

Korany, Bahgat, and Rabab El-Mahdi, eds. 2012. *Arab Spring in Egypt: Revolution and Beyond*. Cairo: American University in Cairo Press.

Koszinowski, Thomas. 1999. "Die Ohnmacht der ägyptischen Parteienopposition: Strukturbedingt oder hausgemacht?" In *wuquf 12: Politische Opposition in Nordafrika*, edited by Sigrid Faath and Hanspeter Mattes, 99–123. Hamburg: edition wuquf.

Kraetzschmar, Hendrik 2010. "Opposition Coordination in Electoral Autocracies: The UNFC in Egypt's 2005 Parliamentary Elections." In Albrecht, *Contentious Politics in the Middle East*, 94–114.

Kramer, Karen. 2006. "Arab Political Pacts: An Unlikely Scenario." *Journal of Democracy* 17, no. 4: 160–65.

Lai, Brian, and Dan Slater. 2006. "Institutions of the Offensive: Domestic Sources of Dispute Initiation in Authoritarian Regimes, 1950–1992." *American Journal of Political Science* 50, no. 1: 113–26.

Land Center for Human Rights (LCHR), several reports, 2003–2006.

Langohr, Vicky. 2004. "Too Much Civil Society, Too Little Politics: Egypt and Liberalizing Arab Regimes." *Comparative Politics* 36, no. 2: 181–204.

Lawson, Stephanie. 1993. "Conceptual Issues in the Comparative Study of Regime Change and Democratization." *Comparative Politics* 25, no. 2: 183–205.

Lesch, Ann. 2012. "Concentrated Power Breeds Corruption, Repression, and Resistance." in Korany and El-Mahdi, *Arab Spring*, 17–42.

Levitsky, Steven, and Lucan A. Way. 2002. "The Rise of Competitive Authoritarianism." *Journal of Democracy* 13, no. 2: 51–65.

Lia, Brynjar. 1998. *The Society of the Muslim Brothers in Egypt: The Rise of an Islamic Mass Movement*. Reading, UK: Ithaca Press.

Lindberg, Staffan I. 2006. "Tragic Protest: Why Do Opposition Parties Boycott Elections?" In Schedler, *Electoral Authoritarianism*, 149–63.

Linz, Juan J. 1973. "Opposition to and Under an Authoritarian Regime: The Case of Spain." In Dahl, *Regimes and Oppositions*, 171–259.

Linz, Juan J., and Alfred Stepan. 1996. *Problems of Democratic Transition and Consolidation*, Part 1, *Theoretical Overview*. Baltimore: Johns Hopkins University Press.

Lübben, Ivesa. 2008. "Die ägyptische Muslimbruderschaft—Auf dem Weg zur politischen Partei?" In *Politischer Islam im Vorderen Orient: Zwischen Sozialbewegung, Opposition, und Widerstand*, edited by Holger Albrecht and Kevin Köhler, 75–97. Baden-Baden: Nomos.

———. 2007. "Das Erwachen der ägyptischen Arbeiterbewegung." *Informationsprojekt Naher und Mittlerer Osten* 13, no. 49: 51–55.

Lübben, Ivesa, and Issam Fawzi. 2000. "Ein neuer islamischer Parteienpluralismus in Ägypten?—Hizb al-Wasat, Hizb al-Shari'a und Hizb al-Islah als Fallbeispiele." *Orient* 41, no. 2: 229–81.

Luciani, Giacomo. 1994. "The Oil Rent, the Fiscal Crisis of the State, and Democratization." In *Democracy without Democrats? The Renewal of Politics in the Muslim World*, edited by Ghassan Salamé, 130–52. London: I. B. Tauris.

Luhmann, Niklas. 1989. "Theorie der politischen Opposition." *Zeitschrift für Politik* 36, no. 1: 13–26.

Lust-Okar, Ellen. 2005. *Structuring Conflict in the Arab World: Incumbents, Opponents, and Institutions.* Cambridge: Cambridge University Press.

———. 2004. "Divided They Rule: The Management and Manipulation of Political Opposition." *Comparative Politics* 36, no. 2: 159–79.

———. 2001. "The Decline of Jordanian Political Parties: Myth or Reality?" *International Journal of Middle East Studies* 33: 545–69.

Lust-Okar, Ellen, and Amaney Ahmad Jamal. 2002. "Rulers and Rules: Reassessing the Influence of Regime Type on Electoral Law Formation." *Comparative Political Studies* 35, no. 3: 337–66.

Lyall, Jason M. 2006. "Pocket Protests: Rhetorical Coercion and the Micropolitics of Collective Action in Semiauthoritarian Regimes." *World Politics* 58, no. 3: 378–412.

Makram-Ebeid, Mona. 2001. "Egypt's 2000 Parliamentary Elections." *Middle East Policy* 8, no. 2: 32–44.

———. 1989a. "Political Opposition in Egypt: Democratic Myth or Reality?" *Middle East Journal* 43, no. 3: 423–36.

———. 1989b. "The Role of the Official Opposition." In *Egypt under Mubarak*, edited by Charles Tripp and Roger Owen, 21–49. London: Routledge.

McLennan, Barbara. 1973. "Cross-National Comparison of Political Opposition and Conflict." In *Political Opposition and Dissent*, edited by Barbara McLennan, 381–93. New York: Dunellen.

Meital, Yoram. 2006. "The Struggle over Political Order in Egypt: The 2005 Elections." *Middle East Journal* 60, no. 2: 257–79.

Merkel, Wolfgang. 2004. "Embedded and Defective Democracies." *Democratization* 11, no. 5: 33–58.

Mitchell, Richard. 1969. *The Society of the Muslim Brothers*. London: Oxford University Press.

Moore, Clement H. 1974. "Authoritarian Politics in Unincorporated Society: The Case of Nasser's Egypt." *Comparative Politics* 6, no. 2: 193–218.

Moore, Pete W., and Bassel F. Salloukh. 2007. "Struggles under Authoritarianism: Regimes, States, and Professional Associations in the Arab World." *International Journal of Middle East Studies* 39, no. 1: 53–76.

Morlino, Leonardo. 2009. "Are There Hybrid Regimes? Or Are They Just an Optical Illusion?" *European Political Science Review* 1, no. 2: 273–96.

Moustafa, Tamir. 2007. *The Struggle for Constitutional Power: Law, Politics, and Economic Development in Egypt*. Cambridge: Cambridge University Press.

———. 2003. "Law versus the State: The Judicialization of Politics in Egypt." *Law and Social Inquiry* 28, no. 4: 883–930.

———. 2000. "Conflict and Cooperation between the State and Religious Institutions in Contemporary Egypt." *International Journal of Middle East Studies* 32: 3–22.

Munson, Ziad. 2001. "Islamic Mobilization: Social Movement Theory and the Egyptian Muslim Brotherhood." *The Sociological Quarterly* 42, no. 4: 487–510.

Norris, Pippa. 2004. *Electoral Engineering: Voting Rules and Political Behavior*. Cambridge: Cambridge University Press.

Ottaway, Marina. 2003. *Democracy Challenged: the Rise of Semiauthoritarianism*. Washington, DC: Carnegie Endowment for International Peace.

Ouda, Jihad, Negad al-Borai, and Hafez Abu Se'ada. 2001. *A Door onto the Desert*. Cairo: United Group.

Owen, Roger. 2000. *State, Power, and Politics in the Making of the Modern Middle East*. 2nd ed. London: Routledge.

Paczynska, Agnieszka. 2010. "The Discreet Appeal of Authoritarianism: Political Bargains and Stability of Liberal Authoritarian Regimes in the Middle East." In Albrecht, *Contentious Politics in the Middle East*, 34–51.

———. 2006. "Globalization, Structural Adjustment, and Pressure to Conform: Contesting Labor Law Reform in Egypt." *New Political Science* 28, no. 1: 45–64.

Pawelka, Peter. 1985. *Herrschaft und Entwicklung im Nahen Osten: Ägypten*. Heidelberg: C. F. Müller.

Pioppi, Daniela. 2007. "Privatization of Social Services as a Regime Strategy: The Revival of Islamic Endowments (Awqaf) in Egypt." In Schlumberger, *Debating Arab Authoritarianism*, 129–42.

Piro, Timothy. 2001. "Liberal Professionals in the Contemporary Arab World." In Butterworth and Zartman, *Between the State and Islam*, 184–206.

Potter, Allen. 1966. "Great Britain: Opposition with a Capital 'O.'" In Dahl, *Political Oppositions in Western Democracies*, 3–33.

Pridham, Geoffrey. 1995. *Transitions to Democracy: Comparative Perspectives from Southern Europe, Latin America, and Eastern Europe*. Aldershot: Dartmouth.

Pripstein Posusney, Marsha. 1998. "Behind the Ballot Box: Electoral Engineering in the Arab World." *Middle East Report* 28, no. 4: 12–16.

———. 1997. *Labor and the State in Egypt*. New York: Columbia University Press.

———. 1993. "Irrational Workers: The Moral Economy of Labor Protest in Egypt." *World Politics* 46, no. 1: 83–120.

Przeworski, Adam. 1993. "Democracy as a Contingent Outcome of Conflicts." In *Constitutionalism and Democracy*, edited by Jon Elster and Rune Slagstad, 59–80. Cambridge: Cambridge University Press.

———. 1991. *Democracy and the Market*. Cambridge: Cambridge University Press.

———. 1986. "Some Problems in the Study of Transition to Democracy." In *Transitions from Authoritarian Rule: Comparative Perspectives*, edited by Guillermo O'Donnell, Philippe Schmitter, and Laurence Whitehead, 47–63. Baltimore: Johns Hopkins University Press.

Rashwan, Diaa. 2000. *Transformations among the Islamic Groups in Egypt*. Strategic Papers, No. 92. Cairo: ACPSS.

Rashwan, Diaa, et al. 2007. *The Spectrum of Islamist Movements*. Berlin: Hans Schiler.

Rey, Benjamin. 2005. "Entre nouvelles formes de mobilisations et gestion étatique: L'opposition égyptienne en 2004." In Kohstall, *L'Égypte dans l'année 2004*, 25–45.

Robertson, Graeme. 2011. *The Politics of Protest in Hybrid Regimes: Managing Dissent in Post-Communist Russia*. Cambridge: Cambridge University Press.

Rüb, Friedbert. 2002. "Hybride Regime—Politikwissenschaftliches Chamäleon oder neuer Regimetypus? Begriffliche und konzeptionelle Überlegungen zum neuen Pessimismus in der Transitologie." In *Zwischen Demokratie und*

Diktatur: Zur Konzeption und Empirie demokratischer Grauzonen, edited by Petra Bendel, Aurel Croissant, and Friedbert Rüb, 93–118. Opladen: Leske+Budrich.

Rutherford, Bruce. 2008. *Egypt after Mubarak: Liberalism, Islam, and Democracy in the Arab World.* Princeton: Princeton University Press.

———. 2006. "What Do Egypt's Islamists Want?: Moderate Islam and the Rise of Islamic Constitutionalism." *Middle East Journal* 60, no. 4: 707–31.

Sadiki, Larbi. 2000. "Popular Uprising and Arab Democratization." *International Journal of Middle East Studies* 32: 71–95.

Sartori, Giovanni. 1966. "Opposition and Control: Problems and Prospects." *Government and Opposition* 1, no. 1: 149–54.

Schedler, Andreas, ed. 2006. *Electoral Authoritarianism: The Dynamics of Unfree Competition.* Boulder, CO: Lynne Rienner.

———. 1996. "Anti-Political Establishment Parties." *Party Politics* 2, no. 3: 291–312.

Schlumberger, Oliver. 2007. *Debating Arab Authoritarianism: Dynamics and Durability in Nondemocratic Regimes.* Stanford: Stanford University Press.

Schwedler, Jillian. 2006. *Faith in Moderation: Islamist Parties in Jordan and Yemen.* Cambridge: Cambridge University Press.

Scott, James C. 1990. *Domination and the Arts of Resistance: Hidden Transcripts.* New Haven: Yale University Press.

Shapiro, Martin. 1981. *Courts: A Comparative and Political Analysis.* Chicago: University of Chicago Press.

Shehata, Dina. 2012. "Youth Movements and the January 25 Revolution." In Korany and El-Mahdi, *Arab Spring,* 105–24.

Shehata, Samer, and Joshua Stacher. 2006. "The Brotherhood Goes to Parliament." *Middle East Report* 36, no. 3: 32–39.

Shubki, Amr. 2005. *Silsila al-Ahzab al-Siyasiya: Hizb al-Amal* [The Political Parties Series: The Labor Party]. Cairo: Al-Ahram Center for Political and Strategic Studies.

Singerman, Diane. 2002. "The Politics of Emergency Rule in Egypt." *Current History* 101, no. 651: 29–35.

———. 1997. *Avenues of Participation: Family, Politics, and Networks in Urban Quarters of Cairo.* Cairo: American University in Cairo Press.

Soliman, Samer. 2011. *The Autumn of Dictatorship: Fiscal Crisis and Political Change in Egypt under Mubarak.* Stanford: Stanford University Press.

Springborg, Robert. 2003. "An Evaluation of the Political System at the End of the Millennium." In El-Ghonemy, *Egypt in the Twenty-first Century,* 183–198.

———. 1989. *Mubarak's Egypt: Fragmentation of the Political Order.* Boulder, CO: Westview Press.

Stacher, Joshua. 2005. "Rhetorical Acrobatics and Reputations: Egypt's National Council for Human Rights." *Middle East Report* 35, no. 2: 2–7.

———. 2004. "Parties Over: The Demise of Egypt's Opposition Parties." *British Journal of Middle Eastern Studies* 31, no. 2: 215–33.

———. 2002. "Post-Islamist Rumblings in Egypt: The Emergence of the Wasat Party." *Middle East Journal* 56, no. 3: 415–32.

Stepan, Alfred. 1997. "Democratic Opposition and Democratization Theory." *Government and Opposition* 32, no. 4: 657–73.

Sullivan, Dennis. 2000. "NGO's and Development in the Arab World: The Critical Importance of a Strong Partnership between Government and Civil Society." *Civil Society* 9, no. 102: 11–16.

Tezcur, Gunes Murat. 2010. "The Moderation Theory Revisited: The Case of Islamic Political Actors." *Party Politics* 16, no. 1: 69–88.

Toth, James. 2003. "Islamism in Southern Egypt: A Case Study of a Radical Religious Movement." *International Journal of Middle East Studies* 35: 547–72.

Tucker, Robert C. 1968. "The Theory of Charismatic Leadership." *Daedalus* 97, no. 3: 731–56.

Ulfelder, Jay. 2005. "Contentious Collective Action and the Breakdown of Authoritarian Regimes." *International Political Science Review* 26, no. 3: 311–34.

Utvik, Bjorn Olav. 2005. "*Hizb al-Wasat* and the Potential for Change in Egyptian Islamism." *Critique: Critical Middle Eastern Studies* 14, no. 3: 293–306.

Vairel, Frédéric. 2006. "Quand 'Assez!' ne suffit plus: Quelques remarques sur *Kifaya* et autres mobilisations égyptiennes." In Kohstall, *L'Égypte dans l'année 2005*, 109–36.

van de Walle, Nicolas. 2006. "Tipping Games: When Do Opposition Parties Coalesce?" In Schedler, *Electoral Authoritarianism*, 77–92.

Waterbury, John. 1983. *The Egypt of Nasser and Sadat: The Political Economy of Two Regimes.* Princeton: Princeton University Press.

Way, Lucan A. 2005. "Authoritarian State Building and the Sources of Regime Competitiveness in the Fourth Wave: The Cases of Belarus, Moldova, Russia, and Ukraine." *World Politics* 57: 231–61.

Wegner, Eva. 2011. *Islamist Opposition in Authoritarian Regimes: The Party of Justice and Development in Morocco.* Syracuse: Syracuse University Press.

Wickham, Carrie R. 2004. "The Path to Moderation: Strategy and Learning in the Formation of Egypt's *Wasat* Party." *Comparative Politics* 36, no. 2: 205–28.

———. 2002. *Mobilizing Islam: Religion, Activism, and Political Change in Egypt*. New York: Columbia University Press.

———. 1997. "Islamic Mobilization and Political Change: The Islamic Trend in Egypt's Professional Syndicates." In *Political Islam*, edited by Joel Beinin and Joe Stork, 120–35. London: I. B. Tauris.

Wigell, Mikael. 2008. "Mapping 'Hybrid Regimes': Regime Types and Concepts in Comparative Politics." *Democratization* 15, no. 2: 230–50.

Wille, Marion. 1993. *Spielräume politischer Opposition in Ägypten unter Mubarak: Zum Verhältnis von Staat und Opposition in einem arabischen Land*. Münster: Lit.

Wurzel, Ulrich. 2004 "Patterns of Resistance: Economic Actors and Fiscal Policy Reform in Egypt in the 1990s." In *Networks of Privilege in the Middle East: The Politics of Economic Reform Revisited*, edited by Steven Heydemann, 101–31. New York: Palgrave Macmillan.

Yadlin, Rivka. 1989. "The Egyptian Opposition and the Boundaries of National Consensus." *Middle East Review* 21, no. 4: 18–26.

Zartman, I. William. 1988. "Opposition as Support of the State." In Dawisha and Zartman, *Beyond Coercion*, 61–87.

Zeghal, Malika. 1999. "Religion and Politics in Egypt: The Ulema of Al-Azhar, Radical Islam, and the State (1952–1994)." *International Journal of Middle East Studies* 31: 371–99.

Zollner, Barbara. 2007. "Prison Talk: The Muslim Brotherhood's Internal Struggle during Gamal Abdel Nasser's Persecution, 1954 to 1971." *International Journal of Middle East Studies* 39, no. 3: 411–33.

Index